WHY WE LIE

Also by Dorothy Rowe

Choosing Not Losing
The Courage to Live
Depression: The Way Out of Your Prison
Living With the Bomb: Can We Live Without Enemies?
Beyond Fear
The Successful Self
Breaking the Bonds
Wanting Everything
Time On Our Side: Growing in Wisdom, Not Growing Old
The Real Meaning of Money
Dorothy Rowe's Guide to Life
Friends and Enemies: Our Need to Love and Hate
*My Dearest Enemy, My Dangerous Friend: The Making and
Breaking of Sibling Bonds*
What Should I Believe?

DOROTHY ROWE

Why We Lie

To my dearest
friends at the
Forum,

Many thanks,

love

Dorothy Rowe

FOURTH ESTATE • *London*

First published in Great Britain in 2010 by
Fourth Estate
An imprint of HarperCollins*Publishers*
77–85 Fulham Palace Road
London W6 8JB
www.4thestate.co.uk

Visit our authors' blog: www.fifthestate.co.uk

1

A catalogue record for this book
is available from the British Library

ISBN 978-0-00-727885-5

Typeset in Times by Palimpsest Book Production Ltd,
Grangemouth, Stirlingshire

Printed in Great Britain by
Clays Ltd, St Ives plc

Every aspect of our national character lives in every act of character in our homes and families. If our nation keeps secrets, so too we learn to justify the secrets that *we* keep. If it isn't for national security, it's for personal security. If it's not civil defense, it's a defense of ourselves. If our leaders say one thing and do quite another, well, is it any surprise that we use the excuse of their faults to cover up our own?

Harold Lloyd Goodall Jr, *A Need to Know: The Clandestine History of a CIA Family*

Contents

Preface   ix

1   How Can We Know What Is True?   1
2   The Curious World We Live In   20
3   Do You Know What I Mean?   36
4   Why Lying Is Necessary   45
5   How We Learn to Lie   61
6   The Danger of Being Obedient   87
7   Deciding What Is True   107
8   How Important Is the Truth to You?   127
9   Fantasies Are Important   143
10   The Delights of Shared Fantasies   153
11   Special Fantasies: Beliefs and Delusions   172
12   Varieties of Lies   188
13   The Same Old Lies   208
14   Denying What Is There   220
15   Hypocrites All   238
16   Being Lied To   245
17   Lying for Your Government   265
18   Never Say You're Sorry   278
19   Some Hard Truths   293

Notes   331
Index   349

Preface

Lying has been in the news, but then it always has been. While I have been writing this book, we have had the lies of the bankers with their versions of, 'It's not my fault', the lie that is based on the lie that many people tell themselves, 'Because I am such a superior person I cannot be blamed for anything.' This lie is based on the very popular but exceedingly stupid lie, 'I can make reality do what I want it to do.' As if reality ever bent to some mere mortal's will! As I write, bankers and politicians are seeking to restore the public's confidence in them with the delusional lie, 'We can go back to where we were.' We can never go back to where we were. Paranoid right-wing Americans are busy trying to spread their lie that Obama was born in Kenya and not in Hawaii as his birth certificate shows. Meanwhile, in Australia, everyone has been transfixed by the unbelievable lies told by a Federal Court judge who was caught for speeding and did not want to pay a $A77 fine (about £39) and get 3 demerit points on his licence. By the time you are reading this you will have learnt of even more amazing lies.

None of us likes being lied to. The only time we do is when we do not want to be told a particular truth that we already know, or at least suspect. We do not like to acknowledge that we lie, and do so frequently. We try to avoid using the words 'lie' and 'lying' in relation to ourselves. The only lies we willingly admit to are those we call 'white lies'. We see these as being virtuous. We want to spare another person's feelings, but the feelings we actually want to spare are our own. We do not want to be upset

ix

when another person becomes upset, or have that person reject us for being unkind.

Lies are words or actions that are intended to deceive other people or ourselves. We use a variety of words and phrases to hide the fact that someone is lying. If we want to seem to be very knowledgeable in matters psychological, we say about someone, 'He's in denial', when in fact the person in question may be lying to himself. We can strenuously deny that certain events have happened or are happening. According to some people, the Holocaust never happened, or the climate is not changing. We can claim to hold certain views that in fact we do not hold, and defy anyone to call us hypocrites.

Why do we lie? In certain situations where your own or someone else's life is in danger, lying can be a sensible thing to do. However, this kind of situation arises very infrequently. Most of us never encounter one. Sometimes we lie almost without thinking, but sometimes we lie in response to feeling that we are in great danger, even though there is no threat to our life. We are frightened, and so we lie.

What we see as being in danger is something we value even more than our life. It is our sense of being a person. We take our sense of being a person for granted, but we refer to it often as 'I' or 'me' or 'myself'. It is our sense of being alive, our sense of existence. We might take it for granted but we know when it is under any threat. We move very quickly to protect it.

Each of us has experienced an extreme threat to our sense of being a person, yet we rarely talk about it. We might talk about the event itself, but not what we actually experienced. We might say, 'I was shattered', and our audience assume that we were using a cliché, but we were not. We might say, 'I was panicking', and our audience assume that we were exaggerating for effect. Very likely our audience were resisting hearing what we were saying because they did not want to be reminded of something terrible in their own life.

We have all had the experience of discovering that we are wrong in our assessment of our situation. It might be that you are being denied by someone the respect you feel you deserve, and you are being humiliated. It might be that the person you depend on and love has disappeared from your life, or has harmed or betrayed you. It might be that you discover that your future will not be what you planned it to be, or that your past proves not to be what you thought it was. In all of these situations, you discover that you have made a serious error of judgement. There is a huge discrepancy between what you thought your life was and what it actually is. As soon as you discover your mistake, you feel shaky, very shaky. Something inside you is falling apart. As the implications of your mistake become increasingly clear, the shakiness intensifies. Anxiety turns to fear, and fear to terror as you feel that you are shattering, crumbling, even disappearing.

Of course, you do not actually crumble and disappear, but you do change. You might now be older and wiser, or perhaps not wiser, but you do see things differently. From then on, you try to make sure that you never have such an experience again. Whatever your circumstances, consciously or unconsciously, you are watching for the slightest hint that such a situation might occur again. You develop many different skills aimed at deflecting such a possibility, or, when it does threaten to recur, to protect yourself from its impact. The simplest and easiest skill to employ is lying. However, no matter how skilled you are as a liar, it is rarely sensible to lie.

This is not a book about the morality of lying. I am not concerned with comparing the vice of lying with the virtue of telling the truth, nor with examining what God or Allah said about lying. Nor do I want to discuss lying in the abstract, as many moralists do. I am concerned with why we lie, and the consequences of our lies. We are very foolish indeed if we lie and fail to think about what the consequences will be.

While many thousands of people are struggling with the

consequences of the terrible lies told by George Bush, Dick Cheney and Tony Blair, Bush is being paid handsomely to give lectures to his supporters, Cheney is on the talk-show circuit, warning of the terrorist threat that is even greater now, something, he says, that Obama fails to recognize. Like Bush, Blair is enjoying some very lucrative directorships and lecturing engagements. He has established his Faith Foundation, and been appointed Envoy to the Middle East to establish peace and reconciliation there. This appointment is the equivalent of the appointment of Sir Fred Goodwin, who played a major part in setting in train the economic crisis in Britain, to be in charge of a new body to regulate British banks. However, his experiences of the last few years have changed Blair. The journalist Decca Aitkenhead spent a day with Peter Mandelson, and, in the course of that day, they visited Blair. She wrote,

> When we arrive I'm completely taken aback at the former PM's appearance, for he resembles a bad actor playing Blair in the grip of some awful psychiatric meltdown. He really does look quite mad, with his face all over the place – a grotesque dance of eyebrows and teeth, manically gurning away, every feature in permanent motion – beside which Mandelson looks like a vision of poised sophistication. There are warm greetings, and as I'm introduced Mandelson pretends I'm there to shadow Blair, provoking another great jerky grimace.[1]

Blair, Bush and Cheney made the grave mistake of forgetting that everything we do has a whole network of consequences, most of which we never anticipated. Even when we get what we wished for, it is never quite what we wanted. The lies we tell might protect us in the short term, but, in the long term, the consequences can be disastrous. When we lie to ourselves, we multiply a thousandfold the inherent difficulties we have in trying to determine what is actually going on inside us and around us.

Good relationships are based on trust. When we lie to others, sooner or later, our lies will become apparent, and trust is destroyed.

On his twenty-third birthday in 1978, Timothy Garton Ash drove to West Berlin and some time later went to live for a while in East Berlin where he soon attracted the attention of the Stasi, the secret police. When the Berlin Wall fell in 1989 the Stasi files were opened, and those who had been spied upon could apply to see their own file. Garton Ash read his own file, and from that the files on those who had spied on him. All of those who had spied on him were ordinary Germans whom he had met, sometimes socially, sometimes in connection with his research for his doctoral thesis on Berlin under Hitler. One of the spies was code-named Michaela. She had been director of the Weimar Arts Galleries. After studying his and Michaela's files, he went to see her. During their conversation it became clear that the Stasi had tempted her with promises of trips to art galleries outside East Germany, places where few East Germans were allowed to go. She let herself be seduced, and pretended to herself that what she was doing was harmless. She must also have told herself that no one would ever know. She had not learnt from history that all tyrannies eventually come to an end. Amongst those she spied on were her daughter and her step-daughter, and the men with whom they were associated. When the Wall came down her step-daughter read her own file, and severed her ties with her step-mother. Garton Ash did not record what Michaela's daughter did when she discovered that her own mother had spied on her, but we can surmise.[2]

Relationships can be very complicated, and consequently many people limit the number and kind of people to whom they will pay attention. Some people decide that, 'Anyone who isn't family doesn't count', or, 'I don't want to have anything to do with anyone who isn't the same nationality as me.' People who decide to treat as important only those who are family, or those who share their nationality, religion, race, class live in what Gillian Tett calls 'silos', those huge, windowless cylinders that stand, often in complete isolation, perhaps full of wheat, perhaps empty, beside a single rail track in the Australian Outback.

Gillian Tett is Capital Markets Editor of the *Financial Times* and winner of the British Press Award 2008 for the business journalist of the year. She was one of the few people who predicted two years ago the collapse of the world's financial system. Five years ago when all the talk in the City was about mergers and acquisitions, and the equity markets, she became interested in collateral debt obligations (CDOs) and credit default swaps (CDSs), the products that proved to be the bad debts acquired by banks and building societies. Tett had trained as an anthropologist. In an interview, she explained how anthropologists are trained to think holistically.

> You look at how all the bits move together. And most people in the City don't do that. They are so specialized, so busy, they just look at their own little silos. And one of the reasons we got into this mess we are in is because they were so busy looking at their own little bit that they totally failed to understand how it interacted with the rest of society. Bankers like to imagine that money and the profit motive is as universal as gravity. They think it's basically a given and they think it's completely apersonal. And it's not. What they do in finance is all about culture and interaction.[3]

Everything in the world is connected to everything else. In early 2009 the car industry was in trouble. The demand for new cars had dropped to its lowest levels, as people faced their own individual financial crisis. News reports spoke of 'the American car industry', 'the Japanese car industry', and the like, as if these were discrete industries, but they were not. The car industry is a global industry. For instance, in the motor industry in 2009, Fiat provided diesel engines to Mercedes for use in commercial vehicles. GM built Fiat diesel engines under licence for use in Vauxhall, Opel and Saab cars. Peugeot Citroen provided diesel engines for Ford vehicles and used BMW petrol engines in its Citroën and Peugeot cars, while running Joint Venture programmes for shared small cars with Toyota and commercial vehicles with Fiat.[4]

In January 2009, the World Economic Forum met in closed session at Davos in Switzerland. Tim Weber, the Business Editor for the BBC website, was allowed to report what was said, but not who said it. There was general agreement that the root causes of the crisis were 'too much debt, a culture of short-term rewards for long-term risk-taking and fatally flawed mathematical models. And plain old greed.' One speaker who did allow his name to be used was Nassim Nicholas Taleb, a former derivatives trader and now writer, who said, 'Derivatives trading is all about how to make a bonus and how to screw your client.' It became clear that, 'Financial institutions took on debt worth 40 times their assets – and failed to understand how risky this was.'[5] When financial institutions became computerized, they acquired software that produced 'models' that purported to predict the outcome of certain financial activities, that is, what risk was being run by these financial activities. The model was an abstract concept called value at risk (VAR). When VAR included the kinds of crises that occur once in a lifetime, the result would suggest that the venture to be undertaken was far too risky. If once-in-a-lifetime crises were not included, the result suggested that it was fine to undertake what Paul Mason, Economics Editor of BBC *Newsnight*, called 'suicidal risk-taking'.[6] This was the kind of risk-taking that financial institutions preferred. After all, it won't happen, will it? But it did.

The unexpected often happens in private and public life. Everyone should know that from their own personal experience. Yet many people tell themselves the comforting lie, 'My actions will have limited consequences.' We learn as children that small actions can have surprisingly large and unexpected results, yet in adulthood many people pretend that they never knew this. When three windows of Sir Fred Goodwin's large home were smashed, as was the rear window of his Mercedes parked in the driveway, Sir Fred was reported to be 'shaken'. Why would people do a thing like that? Sir Fred, when head of the Royal Bank of Scotland, had plunged the bank into ruinous debt, resulting in the bank having to be propped up by £20 billion of public money. When he resigned, he could see no reason why he should not keep his £3 million tax-free lump sum as well as his £700,000 a year pension.[7] Why would that lead to people feeling so angry that they destroyed his property? When people tell themselves, 'My actions will have limited consequences', they have usually already constructed a fantasy about what those limited consequences will be. Perhaps Sir Fred had a fantasy about a very pleasant early retirement with a few lucrative directorships and the occasional attendance at some committee of the Great and the Good. Apparently, Sir Fred had no idea that some people might hate him so much they would try to harm him, nor that for the rest of his life he would be pursued by the paparazzi. In March 2009 the world's media were offering the top price for a photograph of Sir Fred relaxing. By August he was back in Edinburgh. According to Phillip Inman of the *Guardian*, writing in October 2009, 'He has turned to PR experts to rebuild his reputation, as yet to no avail.'[8]

The universal and most popular lie we tell ourselves is, 'I am superior to other people.' Many people claim this superiority because they hold certain beliefs about their religion, race, nationality, class or gender, while others claim their superiority simply because they were born into a certain family. All feel that this superiority entitles them to patronize, denigrate, ignore, cheat, or harm those whom they see as their inferiors. In clinging to this lie, they deny the similarities we all share. Our species varies very little genetically, and we have the same needs, desires and fears. We all want to be recognized for being the person that we are, to have a respected role in our society, and to enjoy good relationships with others.

All the immense problems we face today – a global financial crisis, climate change along with the pollution and despoiling of the planet – derive from the way certain people have told themselves that they are superior to the people they are harming, and therefore entitled to do what they do. When the British, Germans, French, Dutch, Spanish and Portuguese established their empires, they told themselves that they were rescuing those they colonized from their ignorance and degradation, and they were saving their souls, when the truth was that these empire builders were engaged in theft on a massive scale. Believing that merely having a religious faith is sufficient to show that you are both virtuous and superior has allowed vast numbers of people to harm others and feel no shame. Lying to ourselves is very easy, and we can always think of a lie that seems to allow us to do what we do.

Can we change?

As religious leaders have demonstrated down the centuries, exhortations to be virtuous rarely change people's ideas about how they should behave. It is always easy to deplore other people's behaviour, but we are not inclined to change our own behaviour at the behest of those who see themselves as having moral authority. Threats of punishment by the law can lead us to appear to change, but we simply keep our ideas to ourselves. Under Communist rule many people made an 'inner emigration' and lived an unpolitical life.[9] People change their ideas when they voluntarily examine their own ideas and the consequences of their ideas, and decide to change.

In the course of my work I have seen many individuals decide to change how they saw themselves and their world so that they now live a much more satisfactory life. In Germany there have been some profound changes in ideas. Many countries with pasts that many of their inhabitants want to forget or deny have tried to deal with their legacy by holding some kind of inquiry, but the Germans dealt with life under Communist rule with Germanic thoroughness. Garton Ash wrote, 'Germany has had trials and purges and truth commissions *and* has systematically opened the secret police files to each and every individual who wants to know what was done to him or her – or what he or she did to others. This is unique.'[10] In his conclusion written in 2009, Garton Ash pointed out that, since 1997, the technological revolution has put into the hands of the British and American governments, and into the hands of private security firms the means of spying on individuals that are far beyond what Nazi and Communist leaders could ever have imagined. He wrote, 'East Germans today have their privacy better protected by the state than we do in Britain. Precisely because lawmakers and judges know what it was like to live in a Stasi state, and before that a Nazi one, they have guarded these things more jealously than we, the British, who take them for granted. You value health most when you have been sick.'[11]

In 2009 when the BBC correspondent Mark Mardell was leaving his post in Europe, he wrote what he called a final essay on Europe. There he said, 'Germany is still the most important economic and political power in Europe, but with a sense of responsibility, an ability to reflect upon its past, a horror of war, that is I think unique and little short of a miracle, an outcome few historians studying the aftermath of past conflicts could even have dared to predict. It's probably the most grown-up country in the world today.'[12]

Another change in how people think began in the 1970s with what then was called self-help. People with problems such as poor housing or chronic illness lost patience with the experts who were supposed to be helping them, and got together with others suffering in the same way to solve the problem they shared.

Some of these self-help groups became movements, many of which effected the changes they sought. In her book *The Wisdom of Whores* the extraordinarily truthful epidemiologist Elizabeth Pisani, writing about AIDS, said, 'It wasn't doctors who kick-started the response to this infectious disease, it was gay men. With a flair for dramatic presentation and an inside knowledge of what makes the communications industry tick, they battered down the doors of the medical establishment, assaulted the pharmaceutical industry, took the press by storm. They gave AIDS a political face.'[13]

The Internet and the World Wide Web revolutionized how people communicate with one another. Politicians, media moguls and the police have been forced to adapt themselves, though not without complaint, to the power of disparate groups of people all around the world. Here in London the police might have changed from using force to a softly softly approach with the people in the Climate Change movement, but whether they understand and accept what the Climate Change people are doing is another matter.

Unfortunately, many of those who organize for a cause have not learned from history. Neither exhortations nor the presentations of facts will force people to change how they think. To get people to change, you have to understand how they see themselves and their world. You must never assume that you know how another person thinks and feels. The only way to discover this is to ask that person and, if he trusts you, he will tell you.

The greatest change in ideas that I have witnessed is in how parents see their children. This was not a world-wide revolution, and the majority of children are still in servitude to their parents who see them as possessions to be used as they see fit, but a significant number of parents changed their views about how children should be raised, and this changed the society in which they lived.

The revolution that led people to question the power of parents began in the 1950s when an American paediatrician, Benjamin Spock, put forward the dangerous idea that parents should not punish children three years or younger for failing to do something that was physiologically impossible for them to do, that is, have voluntary control over their bladder and bowels. Children need to learn how to do this in their own good time. Hard on the heels of Dr Spock came T-groups, consciousness-raising groups and a plethora of therapies. All these activities gave the participants permission to break the Fifth Commandment, 'Honour thy father and mother, so that your days be long in the land.' Criticize your parents and you're dead. This led these people to wonder whether, since they had suffered at the hands of their parents, they should now think hard about how they should raise their own children. Now, when I see a child doing something that would have earned me as a child a hard slap or worse from my mother, and instead the child's mother engages the child in conversation or distracts the child, I want to tell her how wonderful she is. I refrain from doing this in case I embarrass her. After all, she was simply doing what her mother had done when she was a child.

We could decide to change our ideas and thus solve the problems we are facing, both privately and publicly. However, as Elizabeth Pisani said, 'We can't solve a problem that we won't describe honestly.'[14] Are you prepared to give up lying?

Chapter One

How Can We Know What Is True?

'Why do I lie? Because I can.'

My taxi driver was presenting me with an obvious though rarely stated truth. Then he added, 'Lying keeps me out of trouble.' Truth got him into trouble. Indeed, truth was trouble. Not just inconvenient truths but the perennial question, 'How can I be sure just what is true?'

Lying is easy. All we have to do is to make up a story. It needs to be believable, but, if you tell your story with sufficient confidence and charm, many people will believe you because it suits them to believe you or they cannot be bothered to work out that you are lying and why. The truth is rarely as clear-cut and consistent as a lie. A lie is a fantasy that we can structure to suit ourselves. To find the truth we have to look at the world around us and inside ourselves, yet we are ill-equipped to see what is actually there.

We see the world, not as it is, but as we are. The world is a far less predictable and controllable place than we want it to be. Unambiguous communication with one another is impossible.

Our physiology condemns us to a lifetime of searching for the truth and then never being entirely sure that we have found it. A great many people, including people who regard themselves as being well educated, do not know this. Consequently, either they are mystified by what people do or they create some simplistic explanation that, in effect, explains nothing. If they are told that all we can do is to construct a picture of the world around us and then treat what we see as if it is real, they find

1

this very disturbing. They want certainty, yet how can we be sure that what we say is true is actually so?

From the moment we are born, we begin learning how to construct pictures of what might be around us, and then we learn how to treat these pictures *as if* they were real. To live day by day we have to be able to trust our *as if* perceptions. If we begin to doubt them, we can no longer function efficiently in the world. This happened to me when I was a child.

I had been born into a very peculiar family. It provided me with splendid training for becoming a psychologist but, at the time, living with my family was very difficult. My father's mother and sisters, all strong, intelligent women, had shown him that, charming and lovable as he was, he tended to be feckless and needed to be kept in order by a strong, good woman in the way they had kept him in order in his youth. When he returned from the First World War, he met and fell in love with a young woman who seemed to be the strong, good woman he believed he needed. In this he was wrong. He was right in that she was good. He would often say to me, 'Your mother is a good woman', but in a tone of voice that suggested that a little less application of her virtue in her judgements would not go amiss. To her, her beliefs were absolute truths, and she would never admit being wrong in any of her judgements or deeds. She was an obstinate Presbyterian who did not attend church. If asked why, she would have said that she did not approve of the minister. She would never admit the truth, which was that she was frightened of anyone who was not immediate family. She expected to be rejected, so she always got her rejection in first.

To keep herself safe she turned her home and garden into a fortress where she could control her family and anyone who dared to seek entry. She maintained her power by resorting to tantrums, sulks or an asthma attack if her decrees were ignored or challenged. Compared to my mother, Calvin and Luther were free-thinkers. No idea that was contrary to her ideas could be uttered in her

2

presence. All too often I forgot this. I would be excited by an idea or an event and out it would come. If what I said conflicted with the way my mother wanted to see the world, she would shut me up with, 'You're lying', or 'That's not true.'

Once she had spoken, discussion was at an end. I would go away and, if possible, check my sources, perhaps a book I had read or a lesson in school. Finding that I was right was very reassuring, but often the source of what I had told my mother was myself. Could I trust myself to report myself correctly? Had the event actually occurred or had I imagined it?

The issue for me was not a moral one. I was not asking myself, 'Have I deliberately and wickedly told my mother a lie?' It was not a moral issue for my mother. She did not chide or punish me for lying. She was stating absolutely and incontrovertibly that I was incapable of knowing what the truth was. She was attacking the very fundamentals of my existence. I was mistaken in what I saw, heard, thought and felt. This robbed me of any point of stability and certainty in what I was experiencing. Under the onslaught of her endless criticism, and that from my elder sister, I began to doubt that I could distinguish what I actually experienced from my dreams or from my fantasies. We are not born knowing how to distinguish what we call our perceptions of the real world from our dreams and from the stories (fantasies) we create. Toddlers struggle to learn how to do this. In adult life we occasionally wonder, 'Did that really happen or did I imagine it?' We also have those moments of confusion when we see something fairly clearly and then, on further inspection, what we thought we saw proves to be something else altogether. When we make these kinds of mistakes, we often mutter to ourselves, 'I must be going crazy.' If we are confident in ourselves, we can dismiss these mistakes as matters of no importance, but, if we doubt our ability to operate in this world, mistakes like these further diminish our self-confidence and increase our confusion.

There was no one I could talk to about what was happening to me. Sometimes my doubts became so great that I lost all confidence in the solidity of the world around me. Just putting one foot in front of the other became a matter of defying my doubts. I knew that I could easily have lost my grip on reality and plummeted into the unknown.

Now I know that what I was experiencing was not unusual. Most people have this experience at least once in their lives because few people live lives devoid of disasters. A disaster can be something that everyone would agree was a disaster, or it can be a very private matter, a loss of hope or a grave disappointment, but, whichever it is, in the chaos of the disaster, our trust in reality can fail. We can find that the world around us ceases to be real: or that which we call 'I' vanishes, leaving a hole the size of the universe inside us. If we can manage to survive this state of complete uncertainty, sooner or later our world becomes real again: our 'I' becomes safely lodged inside us again.

Two things saved me. My mother was physically lazy. She did not follow me on my excursions to the bush or the beach. She never came to my school to talk to the teachers or to attend a function there. Away from her, my confidence would revive. But it was books that developed my confidence by showing me how differently different individuals saw themselves and their world. If I did not see things the way my mother did, then that was to be expected. Literature demonstrates that each of us sees everything in our own individual way. For instance, two people look at a tree. They agree that what they are looking at is a tree. However, one person sees a beautiful, warm, friendly tree and the other an ugly, strange and possibly dangerous tree. Thus the tree itself is true for both these people but that which each person has imposed on the tree is an individual truth. There are truths which we share and truths which are our own. Shared truths make relationships and society possible: individual truths are the essence of who we are as a person.

Whenever my mother told me I was lying she was attacking

4

both my confidence in my ability to understand what was going on around me and my sense of being a person. We are not born knowing how to understand our environment and knowing who we are as a person. We spend our childhood learning this. In calling me a liar my mother was being as destructive to me as she would have been had she attempted to murder me. In my childhood I became aware of the two forms of attack. She would not only hit me but occasionally be so beside herself with rage that she would threaten to kill me and then kill herself. As I grew into a strong, solidly built child my fear of what my mother could do to me physically diminished. However, her attacks on me as a person continued until, in my mid-thirties, I left Australia and put half the world between my mother and myself. By then I had regained my confidence in the truth of my perceptions. I had no doubt about the importance of a meticulous search for truth, both our shared truths and our individual truths.

We search for truth, both shared and individual truths, in many different ways. All of our arts are concerned with the exploration of shared and individual truths. If we lack the ability to create art, we can explore shared and individual truths in the living of our life, conforming to society's expectations when it suits us to do so and at other times exploring the possibilities of our individual truths by creating alternative interpretations of our experiences. When we act on our alternative interpretations, we create different outcomes. However, there are many people who refuse to acknowledge the extraordinary and marvellous uncertainty of existence. They turn away from the wonder of being alive and construct instead something that is mundane, repetitive and deadening. Those people who are frightened by uncertainty and try to deal with their fear do this by controlling others, be they individuals like my mother or organizations like the State and the Church.

Whatever the form of government, the State has always used repression and social sanctions to produce conformity in its subjects. The recognition of individual truths has always been very limited, even in those places where people pride themselves on freedom of speech. The religions of the book, Judaism, Christianity and Islam, have always used their sacred texts as the means of enforcing conformity of thought and deed among their followers. Within each of these religions, individuals who came to believe that their individual truths were truer than the shared truths of that particular religion formed break-away groups, where the original individual truths then become shared truths which must be believed by all the members of that group. In the twentieth century, increased military efficiency and the invention of cameras, radio, film and television made possible the creation of large totalitarian states – the USSR, Communist China, North Korea – where all citizens were required to give up who they were and become what the State wanted them to be. Increasingly, computers are being used to bring together all the technologies of indoctrination and surveillance in order to ensure that all citizens live the terrible lie of denying their own individual truths. Naomi Klein, describing the vast social experiment that is taking place in the city of Shenzhen, China's first 'special economic zone', told how, 'Over the past two years, some 200,000 surveillance cameras have been installed throughout the city . . . The closed-circuit TV cameras will soon be connected to a single, nationwide network, an all-seeing system that will be capable of tracking and identifying anyone who comes within its range.' The aim is to install about two million CCTVs in Shenzhen. This is just part of a much bigger programme called 'Golden Shield'. Meanwhile, in countries that pride themselves on their freedom both government agencies and private businesses install surveillance cameras. In 1949 George Orwell saw all this and worse in his novel of what was then the future, *1984*. Orwell saw how easily we could lose our freedom and not realize that it had gone.[1]

Many people will say that surveillance is not a problem for law-abiding people. In saying this, they are assuming that the laws are just and wise because the people who make the laws are just and wise, and know what is best for their people. Heaven forfend that political leaders would ever lie to their people!

People who hold these views want certainty and security. They do not want to be told that there is nothing about which we can be absolutely certain, or that security and freedom always come in inverse proportion, but it can be difficult to predict just what these proportions will prove to be. Many a woman has married in the belief that her husband will give her the security she needs, only to find that he gives her the security of a prison. Most dictators come to power on a wave of popular acclaim, but the populace soon discover that their cheers have turned to tears.

I did not come upon an understanding of how we exist and make sense of our existence in one extraordinary revelation. Rather I stumbled towards it. By great good fortune, when I became a clinical psychologist, I was able to spend virtually unlimited time talking with troubled people about their experience of living. We talked in ordinary, everyday language about ordinary, everyday things, and about the kinds of painful, disturbing experiences which throw into doubt everything that we believed was true. Abstract concepts like traits, or personality types, or mental illnesses could not account for my clients' experiences. But, if we looked at these experiences in terms of how each person interpreted the events in their lives, everything became clear. *What determines our behaviour is not what happens to us but how we interpret what happens to us.*

My fellow psychologists did not regard what I did as proper psychology. Asking people how they saw themselves and their world was 'subjective' and 'anecdotal'. Apart from a few neuropsychologists, most of my colleagues were oblivious of the extraordinary progress there had been in the understanding of how the brain functioned. It was now clear that the traditional division of brain and mind was not just erroneous but a great impediment to our understanding of ourselves. However, in

7

ignoring all this, these psychologists were no different from other people.

The last twenty years has seen some huge advances in science. Scientists have not kept this knowledge to themselves. Many of them have written excellent books in which they not only explain their science to non-scientists but they do so in a way which excites their readers' continuing curiosity. When the science can be combined with wonderful pictures, a good script and an interesting presenter, we watch in our millions. However, when the science concerns the natural world, or geology, or geography, or astronomy what we are being told is out there, separate from us. Being told about climate change is somewhat worrying, but then we can delude ourselves it won't happen in our lifetime. But, when it comes to how our brains function or how we perceive, we cannot separate ourselves from the science. This is difficult enough when we are watching a television programme about cancer or about a nasty operation being performed, but how do we deal with what Chris Frith, Emeritus Professor of Neuropsychology at University College London, is telling us when he writes, 'Even if all our senses are intact and our brain is functioning normally, we do not have direct access to the physical world. It may feel as if we have direct access, but this is an illusion created by our brain'?[2]

Computers have been around long enough for us not to be disturbed by the idea that the brain is a kind of computer. Twenty-odd years ago neuroscientists took this metaphor seriously. Now they know that the brain is not like a computer. Unfortunately, some aspects of the brain as a computer metaphor have proved to be very popular. If you have a bad temper, it is not your fault because you were programmed early in life to be bad tempered. Those of us who have no religious beliefs are likely to be told by godly people that religious belief is 'hard-wired' into every brain, including ours. It is difficult to give up a self-serving metaphor, especially when the new metaphor, which is closer to the truth, is difficult to comprehend.

How Can We Know What Is True?

The neuroscientist Marco Iacoboni pointed out that, just as the casing of a computer is simply a container for the memory and the software of the computer, so, in the computer metaphor, 'mental operations are largely detached from the workings of the body, with the body a mere output device for commands generated by the manipulation of abstract symbols in the mind'. However, it is now clear that 'our mental processes are shaped by our bodies and by the types of perceptual and motor experiences that are the product of their movement through and interacting with the surrounding world'.[3] Our mind is shaped by the way our body interacts with the world around us. Thus our brain contains maps of, say, our hand curving around a cup and of our body balancing itself as we walk over rough ground.

When I was a psychology undergraduate in 1948, we were taught that, in our interactions with the world, first we had a sensation, then a perception, and then a response which was some kind of action. Over the following years, neuropsychologists accepted what researchers were telling them, namely that sensation and perception were one process. It was still assumed that perception and action were completely independent processes. Iacoboni is one of the neuroscientists researching the functions of what have been called mirror neurones that are located in the premotor cortex. These neurones seem to be an essential part of our ability to imitate others. What this research has shown is that perception and action are not separate functions in our brain but are 'simply two sides of the same coin, inextricably linked to each other'. Iacoboni explained, 'In the real world, neither the monkey nor the human can observe someone else picking up an apple without also invoking in the brain motor neurone plans necessary to snatch that apple themselves . . . In short, the grasping actions and the motor plans necessary to obtain and eat a piece of fruit are inherently linked to our very *understanding* of the fruit.'[4] That is, if your brain did not already contain a picture of what an apple was and how it could be eaten, you would not create motor plans

9

to snatch the fruit, unless, perhaps, you had no knowledge of good manners and were so overcome with curiosity that you planned to seize and examine this strange thing.

What I had been taught all those years ago is now called the sensory-motor model of human action, whereas now we have the ideomotor model which 'assumes that the starting point of actions are the *intentions* associated with them, and that actions should be mostly considered as means to achieve those intentions'.[5] If you want to understand another person (or yourself) you need to know not just what that person does but why he does it.

In short, our brain interprets the world, and our interpretations become our intentions in acting on the world. But, if our interpretations are only guesses about our world, how can we assess whether our actions are likely to be successful? Answer: with our Bayesian brains.

Thomas Bayes was an eighteenth-century Presbyterian minister and mathematician. He created a mathematical theorem concerning the probability of an event occurring changing as more information is accumulated. A famous example of Bayesian brains at work is that scene where people are looking up into the sky and asking, 'Is it a bird? A plane? No, it's Superman.' In this case, the Bayesian brain is working out the probability of the hypotheses of, first, a bird, then, a plane, and, with the best evidence, Superman himself, a conclusion, all without conscious effort on the part of the observers. Computers can use Bayesian methods of calculating the probabilities that arise in very complex data. As a Presbyterian, Bayes would have been pleased that his statistical method is used in computers to filter out immoral spam. My computer manages to identify all those email offers of Viagra and penis extension, but, unfortunately, it cannot distinguish these from the emails from that very august establishment The Sydney Institute in the city of that name. My Bayesian brain knows the difference, but my Bayesian computer does not.

10

We can make grave errors in deciding the probability of a particular event, but, according to Chris Frith,

> Our brains are ideal observers when it comes to making use of the evidence from our senses. For example, one problem our brain has to solve is how to combine evidence from our different senses. When we are listening to someone, our brain combines the evidence from our eyes – the sight of their lips moving – and from our ears – the sound of their voice. When we pick something up, our brain combines the evidence from our eyes – what the object looks like – and from our sense of touch – what the object feels like. When combining this evidence, our brain behaves just like the ideal Bayesian observer. Weak evidence is ignored; strong evidence is emphasized. When I am speaking to the Professor of English at a very noisy party, I will find myself staring intently at her lips, because in this situation the evidence coming through my eyes is better than the evidence coming through my ears.[6]

When I am lecturing, I make constant assessments of the probability that my audience is interested in what I am saying. When I am talking about how we operate in the world, the response from most people suggests that they have not encountered the idea that they cannot see reality directly, or that the brain calculates probabilities in making a guess about what might be going on. I find that my audiences listen with a degree of attentiveness that they do not show when I am talking about matters with which they are familiar. I found this even in an audience comprised of highly educated people who placed great value on education. These were the parents of students at a famous public school. I had been asked to talk about communication between parents and their children. To explain why communication so often failed I needed to begin by explaining how we operate as human beings.

I have given this part of my lecture many times. I usually begin

11

with something which I acquired from Ian Stewart, the Professor of Mathematics at Warwick University, but which I now pass off as my own.

Standing in front of my audience and with appropriate gestures, I say, 'As I stand here everything seems totally real. I'm here, you're over there, and beyond you are the walls, and beyond that what I can see through the windows. But actually, that isn't what is happening. I have no idea what is actually here. What is happening is that my brain has created a picture of what might be here, and then it has played a clever trick on me. It has persuaded me that, instead of the picture being inside my head and I'm all around it, I'm in the middle and the picture is all around me. The same thing is happening to you. What you're seeing is a picture inside your head, but your brain has tricked you into thinking that you're in the middle and the picture is all around you.'

I go on, 'If we could take these pictures out of our heads like a photo out of a camera and hang our pictures on the wall so that we can all walk around and look at them, we would find that no two pictures were the same.'

The next part of what I say reveals in the audience's reaction how little biology is taught in our schools, or taught in such a way that the students do not see the implications of what they have learnt. Most of my audience – even when they are medically trained – find what I say next amazing. I run through all the features of the pictures where there would be differences. In the structuring of the depth and distances in each picture there would be differences which relate to the environment in which the person had spent the first few months of his life when he was learning how to see. Babies do not just open their eyes and see. They have to learn how to see. The baby's brain has to set up connections between the reactions of the baby's retinas when light strikes them and those parts of the baby's brain which can become the visual cortex. If this learning does not take place at the precise time when it needs to take place, the baby does not learn to see, and what would have been the visual cortex is taken over by some other cortical function. Just what connections are set up in learning to see depend on the environment the baby is in. Those of us who spent our early months in rectangular rooms learned to structure depth and distance differently from those babies who were in round rooms, like kraals or yurts, or those irregularly shaped spaces that some babies, like those of refugees in Darfur, spend their first months. The paintings by Australian aboriginal artists who grew up in the Outback pay little attention to parallel lines, right angles or perspective that dominate the structure of space by those of us who were put into rectangular rooms when we were born.

I usually follow this with an account of how we have to learn how to distinguish small things close up from large things far away. If in our first year or so we spend some time in large open spaces we learn how to make fairly good guesses about an object's size and distance from us. From then on we can look down a long road and see a car in the distance coming towards us. However, few of us as small children spend much time looking down from the top of a tall building to the street below, and so, when as adults we go to the top of a tall building and look down to the street below, what we see are toy cars and not full-sized automobiles.

The next feature where there would be differences between our pictures is in colour. The world is not a colourful place. Colour is in the eye of the beholder, in the array of cones in the retina of the eye. There is no way of knowing whether what you call blue is the same as what I call blue. Some people, usually men, cannot see colour, or they confuse red with green. In my lectures I might refer briefly to the fact that there are not only huge variations in individual perceptions of colour but in the words we use when we talk about colour. The linguist Annie Mollard-Desfour is compiling *Dictionnaire des mots et expressions de couleur* (*Dictionary of Words and Expressions of Colour*).

The first volume, *Le Bleu* (*Blue*) appeared in 1998, and the fifth *Le Blanc* (*White*) in 2007 with another six to come. In an interview with Laura Spinney for *New Scientist* she said,

> There is no objective reality of colour. It's an impression, a sensation which forms in the brain based on information sent to it by the visual apparatus. To label that sensation, to transmit it to others, we revert to familiar symbols. Colour words, perhaps more than any others, reflect a society: its values, its practices, its history. In Benin in west Africa, for example, men and women have different colour vocabularies. Searching for colour words in literature, the press or slang, as I do, you are forced to confront the enormous diversity in the way different cultures, different symbolic systems, view the world.[7]

Not only do different cultures identify and name colours differently but the connotations of each colour differ markedly. For the French white means purity, cleanliness and honesty but to the Chinese it is the colour of mourning. To the French someone who is just beginning to learn a skill is blue, but to the English a novice is green. For the English a pornographic film is blue but for the French it is pink.

The biggest differences among the pictures we took out of our heads and hung on the walls would be in what each of us has noticed. No one ever walks into a room and sees everything. What we notice are those things that are significant to us. They are full of meaning. We notice the people we know, or the person we wish to avoid. We might notice an object that is strikingly different from anything we have ever seen, or something familiar but unexpectedly present. As Chris Frith wrote, 'The brain constructs a map of the world. This is essentially a map of value. The map locates the objects of high value where I am likely to be rewarded and the objects of low value where I am not likely to be rewarded.'[8] What we happen to notice is determined by our

14

past experience, and, since no two people ever have exactly the same experience, no two people ever see anything in exactly the same way.

When we look around we see a world that is appropriate to our size, a human-sized world. Mice move in a mice-sized world, and elephants in an elephant-sized world. Mice see what is important to mice, and elephants see what is important to elephants. The human-sized world we see appears to be very solid. Our body seems to be quite solid. However, we are made up of atoms, and atoms are not solid at all. There is a solid central core which is tiny. Far from the core are masses of electrons orbiting around the core. In his explanation of electricity in a booklet for non-scientists, David Bodanis explained how an atom is mainly empty space. The booklet we were holding would not slip from our hands because the electrons on the surface of our hands were shooting a powerful force field upwards, hitting the force field coming down from the electrons on the bottom of the booklet. This means that, although we think we are holding the booklet, it is actually hovering a small fraction of an inch above our skin.[9]

Presumably, if our brain were capable of seeing reality directly, this is what we would see, along with all those elementary particles with the curious names like charm, strange, tau and gluon. When physicists talk of discovering such particles, what they have actually seen is not the particle itself, but a trace that the particle has left behind. From this, the physicists conclude that a particle has whizzed by. In much the same way, when we see a straight line of gently dispersing cloud in the blue sky above us, we conclude that a plane high up in the stratosphere has flown by. We live in a human-sized world. To see particles directly we would have to be in a particle in a particle-sized world. Then the Large Hadron Collider at Cern would be unnecessary for us to establish whether the Higgs boson actually exists, but, whatever we were, we would not be human beings.

My audience listened to this first part of my lecture with the kind of fierce attention we give to a speaker when we are being told something that we did not know but which we recognize as being of great importance to us. This kind of attention is different from the polite but bored attention we give to something we already know quite well. Later in my lecture I said something about teenagers and drugs, and immediately my audience looked bored. They knew more about drugs than they had ever wanted to know. What they wanted to hear was an account of how we perceive as it related to the difficult business of being a parent.

Why didn't this group of well-educated people know how they operated as human beings?

Answer: because knowing this is both subversive and frightening, and it can challenge some of your most precious beliefs.

After my lecture I had quite a long discussion with the headmaster. I am sure he knew that what I had said was subversive. He did not charge me with this because he recognized that I had spelled out in detail the dilemma he faced in his work. He wanted his students to think for themselves, but he was expected by the parents and the school governors to foster in the students those ideas which would enable them to fit easily into a society for which the education they were receiving was a necessary qualification. He needed to encourage his students to develop their own ideas, but these ideas should not run counter to the ideas that their parents and the school governors wanted them to hold. He could have done what most parents and teachers do. They make it very clear to the children that their ideas are wrong, stupid and wicked. They have to give up their own ideas and accept those of the adults because the adults' ideas are right, intelligent and good. When children do this, they become what adults call 'good children'. As a result, many children grow up believing that, if they think anything which is different from what they have been taught to believe, there is something seriously wrong with them. They feel guilty when one of their own truths creeps into their consciousness, and they look for and follow those leaders who demand uncritical devotion. How else would people like Hitler in Germany in the twentieth century and Kim Jong Il in North Korea in the twenty-first century get such blindly obedient followers?

This was not the kind of education the headmaster wanted to give his students, but his was a high-achieving school. As he told me, the governors expected him to maintain this high standard; parents sent their children to the school in order that they do well, both at school and in their subsequent careers. Most of the children wanted to achieve, but some of the students took the need to achieve too seriously. They worked too hard and worried too much. He wanted to tell these students that such anxious effort was unnecessary, and that they should enjoy their school-days, but would the governors and the parents see this advice as being in the interests of the students?

Small children know that they see things differently from their parents. Some children manage to hang on to this knowledge and to value their own point of view, despite the authoritarian adults they encounter. Some lucky children have parents who take the child's point of view seriously. When we take another person's view seriously we are not necessarily agreeing with that person. A parent can say, 'I appreciate that you have good reasons for staying up late, but I have good reasons to want you to go to bed now. In this particular situation my reasons are going to prevail. Go to bed now.'

When we take other people's point of view seriously, we are implicitly acknowledging that our different points of view arise from the way we are as human beings. Many religious leaders talk about how important it is that we all accept people of other faiths, and there are many ecumenical gatherings of priests, rabbis, vicars, ministers and imams. In these meetings, are all these clerics saying that their different beliefs are of equal value? Or are they merely being polite to one another while secretly thinking, 'I'm the only one that is in possession of the absolute truth and the rest of you are going to burn in hell's fires'?

When the charge of being subversive is levelled at me by believers, I am always told that I am saying that all relative truths are equally valid. I immediately point out that I would not be so stupid as to say this. What I am saying is that we cannot help but have our own individual truths, but to show that our own truths are valid we have to test them by gathering evidence that this is so. This usually brings the discussion to an end, because those ideas which are claimed to be the absolute truths of a religion are usually the kind of ideas for which good evidence is hard to find.

There were no questions about religion after my lecture. Rather, parents wanted to know about their children's future. My answers were not particularly comforting. I said that no one was in a position to predict what the future of these students would be. The parents' belief that success at school led to a successful career was based on the parents' experience. They were assuming that the future would, more or less, be the same as the past. It is unlikely that the students saw the future in the same way as their parents did. Most children learn a good deal about climate change in school, so many of the students would probably know more about climate change than their parents did, and they probably did what all of us do when we hear of some likely but unpleasant outcome of climate change. We calculate what age we will be when it is predicted to occur. It is not so easy for teenagers to comfort themselves with the thought, 'I'll be dead by then.' On the BBC Radio 4 programme *Leading Edge* the scientist Richard Sellay, talking about how climate change will affect wine production in Britain, said, 'By 2080 the temperature in summer England is going to increase by 4.5 to 5 °C. So there'll be Riesling on the slopes of Snowdonia, Manchester Merlot, and Sheffield Shiraz.'[10] This sounds all very jolly, but, if this prediction is close to being correct, there will be a steady warming of the planet over the students' lifetime. However, there are so many variables involved that scientists cannot make precise predictions. Most scientists were surprised when, in the summer of 2007, the Northwest Passage became clear enough for shipping to pass through it. That the ice was melting was known, but that it would melt so quickly was not expected.

Chapter Two

The Curious World We Live In

Even as it reveals the world to us in increasing detail, science uncovers greater and greater uncertainties. This is why many people scorn science, and reject its findings, especially when these findings throw doubt on the way they see themselves and their world.

Anthropologists can only guess when our species acquired self-consciousness, but, whenever this happened, our ancestors lost the ability to accept the world around them simply as a fact of life with which they had to deal as best they could. Now they became aware of how puny they were in the vastness of the world. They could ask themselves, 'What is my place in the world?' 'How can I control what happens?' They had developed technologies for finding food and shelter, but, for this knowledge to be reliable, events such as the rising and setting of the sun had to be reliable. Now they doubted, and, in doubting, became aware of their utter helplessness in a world they neither understood nor controlled. Their lives depended on the rising of the sun, and now they could ask, 'What shall I do if the sun does not rise tomorrow?' They were learning more and more about the world, but, rather than accepting their helplessness and then working piecemeal to achieve understanding and control over parts of their world (the way science works), many people preferred the easy but delusional solution of creating a fantasy of complete power. The Incas believed that they could make the sun rise each morning by carrying out the ritual of plucking the beating heart from a human sacrifice and presenting it to their sun god. The process seemed to be effective because every morning the sun rose. They could say to themselves, as many people still do, 'I might be weak but I have access to total power through my gods.'

People create their gods in their own image. Jesus was born a Jew in Palestine but, as Christianity moved westward, Jesus acquired blond hair and blue eyes. As Howard Jacobson said, 'The last thing Jesus looks on the cross is Jewish.'[1]

Humans understand themselves through stories, and so they understood their gods through stories, including stories that explained how the world began and why it operates as it does. Gods, like parents, gave rewards and punishments. The gods punished the wicked with droughts and rewarded the good with a bountiful harvest.

Within each small society different individuals would have created a variety of gods with their stories, but such a variety would have reminded everyone that these gods and stories were fantasies. A fantasy's capacity to comfort and embolden is very limited. What was needed was an absolute truth. Very likely each person claimed that his god was the one true god, while all the others were imaginary ones. However, the mark of power is being able to force other people to abandon their ideas and to accept yours. Thus in each society the most powerful person, aided by some skilful deception masquerading as magic, could insist that his god was real and powerful, and therefore must be obeyed.

Gods have their own dogmas, and these include how the world should be understood. These dogmas need to confirm the power of the god and those who serve him, while being simple enough for everyone to comprehend. Moreover, the dogmas had to be absolute and unchanging.

Thus, in the Middle Ages, Christians explained the world in terms of the Chain of Being which stretched from the foot of God's throne to the tiniest speck of God's creations. The nodal point of the chain was man, who linked animals, birds, fish, insects, rocks and pebbles to the hierarchy of angels and so to God. Since God was perfect, everything He had made was perfect (human beings, though markedly imperfect, were deemed to be capable of perfection). The Earth was the centre of the universe, and around it, moving in perfect circles, were the planets and stars.

The idea that human beings occupy such an important position in the Chain of Being and that the Earth was the centre of the universe flattered individuals however lowly in status while maintaining the Church's power. When a few inquisitive individuals such as Copernicus and Galileo asked questions and arrived at answers that questioned the accuracy of the Church's model of the world, they were seen as radicals, iconoclasts – dangerous men who threatened the stability of society because they destroyed certainty and created doubt. In the same way Charles Darwin challenged the pride people took in themselves, and presented people with complex ideas that required people to think. The physicist and cosmologist Paul Davies said, 'Darwin struck at the root of what it is to be human. That matters so much that many Americans are still in denial about evolution, preferring to tell lies for God than embrace the truth: human nature is a product of nature, something to celebrate, not fear.'[2]

Darwin was concerned with the need of each life form to survive physically. He would have had to wait more than a century for neuroscientists to show how brains interpret the world, and how it is our interpretations that determine what we do. Out of the stream of our interpretations comes our sense of being a person. Our need to survive as a person is far more important to us than our physical survival. In certain extreme situations, many people act heroically at great risk to their life. If they survive, they are likely to explain their actions in terms of feeling that, if they had not attempted to save those at risk, they would not have been able to live with themselves for the rest of their life. When the Australian soldier Trooper Mark Donaldson put himself in great danger in a Taliban ambush to save the lives of his fellow soldiers and their badly wounded interpreter and was awarded the Victoria Cross, he explained his actions in terms of how he saw himself. He said, 'I'm a soldier. I'm trained to fight, that's what we do. It's instinct and it's natural and you don't think about it at the time. I just saw him [the interpreter] there, I went over there and got him, that was it.'[3] Many people choose to kill themselves rather than live a life where they could not be themselves. Having been severely injured in a rugby accident and left to live his life as a quadriplegic, twenty-three-year-old Dan James, who saw himself as a sportsman, persuaded his parents to take him to the Swiss clinic Dignitas where he died.[4] Evolutionary psychologists, who explain human behaviour solely in terms of physical survival, see mating as the means whereby people pass on their genes, and fail to see that we are not concerned with passing on our genes, but with seeing our children as the means by which our sense of being a person continues on after our physical death. This is one of the reasons why having children – which usually involves much expense and hard work – is very popular.

Genes do not cause specific kinds of behaviour, such as a bad temper or bipolar disorder. Denis Noble, president of the Union of Physiological Sciences, believes that systems biology is 'about recognising that every physical component is part of a system, and that everything interacts with everything else'.[5] Undeterred by this, psychiatrists diagnose 'bipolar disorder' in children as young as two and tell their parents that the disorder is caused by a gene. The possibility that the parents are having difficulty in parenting their children is ignored, though these psychiatrists insist that the family has been very thoroughly investigated. I have yet to see a greatly troubled child or adult who came from a perfectly happy, normal family. Parents do not cause their children to behave in those ways that are called mental disorders. All families have a unique pattern or system of interactions with one another and the world. Genes are part of another system, and that system interacts with the family system. Some family systems result in intense unhappiness for some or all of their members, and some do not.

In the nineteenth century, phrenologists taught that the brain was divided into a large number of characteristics such as acquisitiveness, benevolence, sublimity. A phrenologist could supposedly identify an individual's characteristics by feeling the shape of the bumps and indentations of the person's skull. Now this seems ridiculous, but in its place has come a new phrenology.

Just as physicists cannot see particles in action but only the traces they leave behind in the physicists' machines, so neuroscientists cannot see a living brain in action. They have to use machines that measure certain changes in the brain, and infer from these changes that what they have measured relates in some way to brain activity. The functional MRI scanner measures changes in oxygen levels in the brain. Neurones consume more oxygen when they are active than when they are at rest. If a part of a person's brain shows a rise in the amount of oxygen being used, it seems that that particular part of the brain is active. A researcher can say, 'There is the possibility that this part of the brain is involved in such-and-such activity.' What should not be said is, 'That part of the brain *is* engaged in such-and-such activity.' As the neurobiologist Steven Rose wrote, 'It is possible by stimulating particular brain regions to evoke sensations, memories, even emotions, but this does not mean that the particular memory or whatever is physically located in the region, merely that activity in that region may be a necessary correlate of the memory. The truth is that we don't have a comprehensive brain theory that lets us bridge the gaps between molecules, cells and systems.'[6]

The new phrenologists do not show such restraint. fMRI scans show a slice of the brain, and thus allow the new phrenologists to publish pictures of slices of the brain where they have coloured in the part of the brain where the activity was located. Such colours suggest that there is some autonomous part of the brain that relates directly to, say, risk taking, sexual arousal or lying. There are certain areas of the brain that specialize in certain types of processing, such as the visual cortex at the back of the brain and Broca's area for language in the left frontal lobe. However, the brain operates through neural networks, just as genes operate through genetic networks. fMRI scans and similar techniques are extremely useful, but they do not show the meaning that the person is creating as he carries out some activity.

Jack Gallant and his colleagues at the University of California, Berkeley, and Yukiyasu Kamitani at ATR Computational Laboratories in Kyoto, Japan, have developed techniques using brain-scanning technology to recreate simple images occurring in a person's mind's eye by decoding the brain activity of people looking at the original image and comparing this with their brain activity when they remember the image. It has been shown that the part of the brain that is active when we think about an object is similar to the part of the brain that is active when we look at the object itself. Thus these techniques might one day be able to show what particular image a person is holding in his mind's eye. Calling this 'a very significant step forward', John-Dylan Haynes, of the Max Planck Institute for Cognitive and Brain Sciences, said that this work might make it possible to 'make a videotape of a dream'. Such a video would be merely a string of images. It would not disclose what the images meant to the dreamer.[7] Whatever fMRI scans, or any other kind of brain scan show, they do not reveal what the person is actually thinking. Your thoughts are as private as they always were. When scientists claim that they can or will be able to know what a person is actually thinking, they are suffering from the delusion that afflicts many 'experts' where they think that they know more about a person than the person can ever know about himself.

We cannot be experts in all branches of science, so we rely on scientists and the media to report truthfully on important events in science. Our trust is often abused. Some scientists will lie about their results because they cannot bear to admit that their favourite hypothesis is wrong, or because they want to enjoy a moment of media fame, or because there is a financial incentive of being paid to lie by those who profit from their results. How the pharmaceutical industry suppresses results that do not favour a particular drug, or the energy industry supports biddable scientists who deny the evidence of global warming, is well documented. Many journalists lack any understanding of scientific method, and so cannot evaluate any piece of research. They do not understand that, if your subjects are people, it is relatively easy to carry out the kind of research that yields the results that you want. It is much more difficult to achieve this when your subject matter is inanimate and therefore indifferent to your desires. Frequently, when a journalist phones me for a comment on a press release about some psychological research or a news story about people, I spend some time explaining to the journalist how inadequate, even fraudulent, this particular research is, or how the journalist, in his ignorance about human behaviour, has misinterpreted some recent news. Sometimes the journalist decides that the press release has no news value, or that he has to reassess the significance of this piece of news, but sometimes the journalist, perhaps at the behest of his editor, continues his search for a psychologist who will give the comment that the journalist wants. I regret to say that I have experienced this with an editor of the *Today* programme on BBC Radio 4 who did, eventually, find the kind of psychologist he wanted. This was a psychologist who would agree with him that a parent killing his children and then himself is a rare event. Alas, it is not. In the UK, approximately one hundred children die each year at the hands of a parent or step-parent.[8] Some of these adults then go on to kill themselves. The harsh realities of life can be too difficult for some news men and women to bear, and thus we are deprived of the truth.

We would be foolish indeed to decide, as some people do, that science and the media always lie. In doing so, we would be closing our minds to those people working in science or the media who care about truth. However, we need to read reports about science very critically. Reading Ben Goldacre, in his 'Bad Science' column in the *Guardian* and *Guardian Online*, and in his book by the same name, is an excellent way of learning how to use scientific method.[9] A good question to ask of research results is, 'Who benefits from these results?' If the answer is, 'The people who funded the research', be very sceptical of the results.

The popular press makes money out of stories that pander to its readers' prejudices and vanity. In the reporting of scientific research that has to do with people, the popular press invariably reports research that purports to show all children and young people are in great danger (obesity, alcohol, drugs) and/or the current generation of children and young people are ill-disciplined, lazy, greedy, selfish, ungrateful and are growing up too quickly, unlike the generation of readers who, as children, were obedient, well-behaved, and innocent of all aspects of adult life, and, as teenagers, were well-behaved, hard-working and respectful of their elders. These stories are all versions of the 'I don't know what the youth of today are coming to' complaint.

The generation of readers are unique in a great many ways. The world they live in bears no similarity at all to the world that earlier generations lived in. History never repeats itself. Moreover, the readers' generation suffers more than all earlier generations. These stories are versions of the myth of the Golden Age.

We derive such prejudices from our vanity that tells us that we are superior to other people. We are blinded to the truth more often by our vanity than we are by the lies that other people tell us.

Physicists and cosmologists, being human, are as truthful or not in their dealings with other people, but their subject matter is very difficult to manipulate to produce results that they can turn to their advantage. If their results are wrong, sooner or later further research will show that this is so. Physicists and cosmologists are unlikely to lie to you about their research, but, if you want to see your world as controllable and predictable, they have naught for your comfort.

Did you know that on New Year's Eve, 2009, time stopped? It stopped very briefly, so that the guardians of the atomic clocks around the world could synchronize their clocks with the rotation of the planet.[10] It was not the clock running fast but the planet running slow.

Anthropologists tell us that our ancestors 30,000 years ago kept calendars. This was 25,000 years before the emergence of writing. The calendar is one of our earliest purely intellectual creations.[11] Daily time was measured by the rising and setting of the sun. Sundials, hour glasses, and water clocks were not particularly accurate, but this did not matter until the dawn of the Industrial Revolution when factory owners wanted their workers to arrive on time. The workers did not have clocks and watches because they were expensive, and remained so until well into the twentieth century. When I was a child in the 1930s a still-popular saying was, 'If you want to know the time, ask a policeman.' Now we look at our mobile phones, or we say to one another, 'Do you know what time it is?'

This is the title of a BBC4 programme presented by the physicist Brian Cox.[12] He described how time as we know it 'is an illusion'. However, it does seem that time exists as a dimension in the universe much in the way that space exists as a dimension. The question that some of the best physicists in the world are asking is, 'What is time?' There is no definite answer to this question.

Our television news programmes often end with weather forecasters predicting at what time the sun will rise and set the next day. We say that the length of the day is twenty-four hours because the Earth takes twenty-four hours to rotate on its axis, but the actual time it takes the Earth to spin on its axis changes because the Earth's speed is affected by the pull of the Moon on the Earth and by the power of the wind. World time is now determined by atomic clocks which are very accurate because they use the precise microwave signal that electrons in atoms emit when they change energy levels. However, these clocks need to be adjusted occasionally to the spin of the planet. Our time-keeping methods do not measure a time difference with some fixed point in time. They simply impose a pattern on events that has a regularity with which we can organize ourselves.

We experience time as a continuous present. The past is contained in our memory, and our future in our imagination. However, we are dependent on the light from the Sun, and that takes eight minutes to reach us. When we look up into the heavens, we see the past. When we look deeper and deeper into the heavens, we go further back into the past. Physicists have calculated that the universe began with a Big Bang about 13.7 billion years ago. The orthodox view amongst cosmologists is that time began with the universe, but unorthodox cosmologists like Neil Turack use string theory to propose that time may have begun before the Big Bang. There could be, he says, additional parallel worlds.

Different cultures have different images of space and time. When American children draw maps, they usually use a bird's-eye view in the way Google maps look down on the Earth, whereas Sherpa children in Nepal create an image of vertical distances so that they can show how much time it takes to go up and down from one place to another. Trekkers in Nepal use the same method measuring distance in time, not in linear units.[13] Seconds, minutes and hours have been accepted as units of time, although there are cultural differences in how time and dates are written. The hour after noon can be written as 1 p.m. or 13.00. The Twin Towers collapse is dated as 9/11 in the USA, 11/9 in the UK.

Seconds, minutes and hours relate to how we experience the

passing of the day, but now there are video cameras that record in units of time different from the units of time in which we see events. If a high-speed camera captures images, say, of a glass of water being thrown into Brian Cox's face, and then the images slowed right down, hidden details are revealed. The world looks very different when time is broken down into chunks as small as 10^{-43} seconds. Our eyes and our brain operate like a kind of video camera. Our eyes, like a camera, take individual still pictures, and then our brain deals with each still so quickly that we see what seems to be a continuous film. Our eyes are not fast enough to take in everything that happens within the range we are looking. We see a glass of water being thrown and what we think is the recipient's reaction, but we do not see how, under the onslaught of the water, a person's face takes on shapes and movements that, when revealed to us by the camera, seem quite strange. However, at whatever speed we are viewing the world, what we see is not just a matter of visual acuity. We see what is meaningful to us. When my son Edward and I were watching an episode of the BBC series *Spooks*, we saw one of the central characters, Ros, who was disguised as an accountant working in high finance, get into a car and drive away. We saw the car very briefly, a matter of seconds. I saw a low-slung, black convertible, and asked Edward, 'What make of car was that?' He said, 'An Aston Martin – James Bond's car.' Cars are Edward's passion.

When I was a child, time passed very slowly. I celebrated each passing year because I wanted to grow up. Now time passes at an extraordinary rate. A day passes in a blink of an eye. Why do we have to go into the future at the rate that we do? Time seems to slow down when we are bored, or in the midst of an accident or a sudden crisis, and it speeds up when we are busy. Why can't the speed with which we go into the future be moderated by events, better still, by our wishes? The apparent slowing down or speeding up of time in certain circumstances are examples of how our interpretations or constructions of the time we are experiencing are dependent on our circumstances. They are what Brian Cox called 'illusions'. According to Einstein, we cannot change the speed with which we go into the future because time is a dimension we pass along, just as we can pass along the dimension of space. We cannot move through space at the speed of light, but we move through time at the speed of light. Einstein showed that we each experience the passing of time in our own individual way. As Brian Cox said, no one has the right to claim that their time is the right time.

Einstein argued that all moments in time already exist. We are moving along time in the same way as we move along a road that has already been built. However, in the sub-atomic world of quantum mechanics, the future does not exist. Rather, it is a world of probabilities, where the future grows out of the past. Two different ways of looking at the world yield two different results.

When Brian Cox asked Neil Turack, 'Do you know what time it is?' Neil replied, 'The time today is something we have no idea about.'

A butterfly fluttering its wings and causing a huge disaster in some distant place has become a cliché to which the word 'chaos' has become attached. However, for many people, the cliché is usually taken to refer to the long line of causes resulting in a chaotic disaster, as in the old nursery rhyme,

> For want of a nail the shoe was lost.
> For want of a shoe the horse was lost.
> For want of a horse the rider was lost.
> For want of a rider the battle was lost.
> For want of a battle the kingdom was lost.
> And all for the want of a horseshoe nail.

Linear causality is so embedded in our culture that it impedes our understanding of, or even perception of, the randomness of events in our world. Many people believe that, if you win the lottery, it was not a random event, but caused by the fact that you are a good person and deserve to win. God or Fate decreed that you should win. However, the butterfly effect is not an example of linear causation. It is an example of the mathematics of chaos.[14]

The development of science was based on Newtonian mathematics that describes a world that follows clear rules. It is predictable and ultimately controllable. This is the vision of the world used by those scientists and engineers who claim that the best way to deal with climate change is to devise methods of controlling the climate. Climate engineering, like the economists' command and control economy, is one of the favourite delusions of the twenty-first century. While Newtonian mathematics works very well in a vast number of situations, there are many situations where it does not. For instance, if two objects are in orbit, it is possible to use Newtonian mathematics to predict the position of these objects at any one point in time, but, if a third object is added, Newtonian mathematics cannot predict the position of the objects. In 1889 the great French mathematician Jules Henri Poincaré could not solve this problem, but he showed that, if there is any difference, however small, between the two orbits, one body will eventually fly off. Prediction is impossible.

The advent of computers led many people to believe that all the problems in the world were soluble. All that needed to be done was to build a bigger computer. It is ironic that what revealed the flaw in this thinking was a computer.

In 1961 Ed Lorenz, a meteorologist, using a simple model of the weather, was running some simulations of weather patterns on his computer. He wanted to run the simulation twice, so he copied what he thought were the same numbers into his computer. He had not realized that, while his computer stored numbers up to six decimal places, such as 0.473208, his printer to save space shortened the numbers to three decimal places, 0.473. This was a tiny discrepancy between the two sets of numbers, less than 0.1 per cent, but this small discrepancy changed the result. At first Lorenz thought that his computer was at fault, but he came to realize that, to forecast the weather perfectly, he would need not only a perfect model of the weather but perfect knowledge of wind, temperature, humidity and other conditions around the world at one moment in time. Perfect knowledge is never possible. No matter how accurate a measuring instrument may be, there is still a margin of error. It seems very unlikely that climate engineering will be able to control the weather and therefore climate change.

In a similar way, a command and control economy, where a government guided by economists could ensure continuous growth in a country's economy and so determine that a boom could not be followed by a bust, would require the careful measure-ment and control of those factors that drive the market, including fear and greed. The great economist J.K. Galbraith recorded in some detail the inability of the majority of the players in the market to learn from experience, but even he could not plumb the depths of economists' failure to understand human nature. What they needed to learn was, in Paul Krugman's words, 'The seeming success of an economy, the admiration of the markets and media for its managers, was no guarantee that the economy was immune to sudden financial crisis.'[15]

It had always been assumed that the effect of a small error in a large system would disappear. Lorenz published his findings in 1963, and in the following year another paper showed how making small changes in the parameters in a model of the weather could produce vastly different results, transforming regular events into a seemingly random, chaotic pattern. In 1972 Lorenz gave a paper at the American Association for the Advancement of Science. He called it 'Predictability: Does the Flap of a Butterfly's Wing Set Off a Tornado in Texas?' Chaos, it seemed, was not a rare, random event but was there in the systems in which we live. It seems that the more complex a system is, and particularly where a number of systems are linked together, the more likely it is that, contained in the systems, is a sensitivity to initial events that leads to later events that cannot be predicted. The economic systems that led to the last run of boom years contained within them a sensitivity to events during the boom years and before, with the consequence that the fear, greed and stupidity of a hedge fund manager in New York led to a hard-working couple in Glasgow losing their jobs and their home.

Mathematicians working in chaos theory have developed the concept of tipping point where a system is being pushed in a certain direction, and reaches a point where it suddenly tips over into another state from which there is no return. Climatologists studying climate change see our climate being pushed by the warming of the planet to a tipping point from which it will be impossible for our climate to return to the state that supports human life as it does now. Climatologists are not agreed about how close this tipping point is, but they are agreed that the tipping point is inevitable unless drastic measures to prevent it are taken immediately to reduce the levels of CO_2 in the atmosphere. Some scientists receive support from the energy industry to deny the imminence or even existence of the danger, and some people see the current turmoil in the world as evidence of the working out of God's plan, as set out in the Book of Revelation, to bring the world, and time, to an end, before which only the true believers will be taken into heaven, while everyone else perishes.

James Lovelock, who in the 1970s devised the Gaia hypothesis which describes how the Earth regulates itself, sees the tipping point of climate change being too close for any reductions in the emissions to prevent it. He describes himself as an 'optimistic pessimist'. Most of us will not survive the heating of the planet, but some of us will. He said, 'I don't think humans react fast enough to handle what's coming up. [However] for the first time in its 3.5 billion years of existence, the planet has an intelligent, communicating species that can consider the whole system and even do things about it. They are not yet bright enough, they have still to evolve quite a way, but they could become a very positive contributor to planetary welfare.'[16]

I think that we do have the ability to overcome our vanity, and our reluctance to put aside selfish, short-term advantages in order to see long-term benefits that all can share, to abandon our delusions of being saved by some great power. However, it is an ability that we rarely use because to do so requires the courage to face uncertainty. To ameliorate climate change we need to see the whole system of the Earth in all its ambiguity. It is not as if our brains cannot deal with ambiguity. All the time our Bayesian brain is creating alternative hypotheses about our situation in the world. Semir Zeki, Professor of Neurobiology at University College, London, says that the brain has evolved in such a way that it can acquire information from ambiguous situations. We do not need certainty to make sense of the world. However, when we deny the existence of alternative interpretations and claim that the one interpretation we hold is a unique and absolute truth, we are refusing to use the ability with which we were born. We deliberately make ourselves stupid.

Chapter Three

Do You Know What I Mean?

Parents like to think that they give their children clear, unambiguous instructions. They are puzzled as to why their children seem not to understand them. 'Be home by 10 p.m.' does not have a suffix of 'or whenever it suits you'. It comes as a surprise to many parents to discover that children, like adults, do not hear what is said to them. What their brain registers is not what the parent says but what the brain interprets of what the parent says. This is the disability under which we all labour. All we can know is our interpretation of a communication, not the communication itself.

Different generations live in different worlds. Each generation's world contains a past, present and future that are different from the pasts, presents and futures of other generations' worlds. Teenagers, and those of us who can remember what it felt like to be a teenager, know how, when in conversation with our parents, we suddenly see the gulf that separates our world from our parents' world. In that moment, we experience the loneliness of living in our own individual world.

This kind of loneliness is often called the loneliness of being. It is a very valuable loneliness because it allows us to think deeply, to become absorbed in meditation, or in the contemplation of nature, or the arts, or in some form of creativity. But, when we feel that intense loneliness of being unloved by those we want to love us, or of being with people who are so absorbed in themselves that they ignore us except when they want to use us, to be told that the loneliness of being is inescapable can mean that the loneliness we feel is unendurable.

Even when we are with people who love us and are interested in us, we find that our conversations always involve misunderstandings. This too is inescapable in our own individual worlds.

Here is a list illustrating the kinds of complaints people make about a conversation in which they are or have been engaged.

'You still haven't given me any idea of what you mean.'

'He can't get it into his head that he has to do what he's told.'

'She just pours out all her feelings.'

'He gave us his thoughts about this proposal but they proved to be rubbish.'

'I can't grasp his meaning.'

'I gave him a piece of my mind but he just closed his ears to what I was saying.'

'He never takes my advice.'

In each of these sentences something is being said about a thing. To speak about a thing we use a noun or a noun clause. The things talked about in these sentences are 'idea', 'what he's told', 'feelings', 'thoughts', 'rubbish', 'meaning', 'what I was saying', 'advice'. Each of these sentences contains the metaphor of something being passed from one person to another. The linguist Michael Reddy called this the 'conduit metaphor'.[1] We think of conversing with one another, be it in actual conversation, or writing to someone, or reading a book, or watching television, as a process of passing something from one person to another. The means of passing something from one person to another is along some kind of conduit. The thing launched does not always reach its objective, as in 'His words fell on deaf ears', or 'That idea has been floating around for a long time.' The conduit metaphor assumes that the communication one person sends along the conduit reaches its target complete and intact. What you receive is what I send.

The conduit metaphor lies behind Richard Dawkins' idea of the meme, which he defined as any kind of information which is copied from one person to another. The meme I send you is the one you get. Memes, Dawkins argues, replicate like genes.

To explain why one person misinterprets the ideas another person gives him, Dawkins says that, like genes, memes are not always copied perfectly, and so give rise to new memes. He likens the memes he disapproves of, such as religious beliefs, to viruses, and thus they can be dangerous. His colleague the philosopher Daniel Dennett wrote, 'Memes now spread around the world at the speed of light, and replicate at rates that make even fruit flies and yeast cells look glacial in comparison. They leap promiscuously from vehicle to vehicle, and from medium to medium, and are proving to be virtually unquarantinable.'[2] Richard Dawkins used to occupy the Charles Simonyi Chair for the Public Understanding of Science. It is somewhat ironic that the person whose task it is to assist the public in understanding science does not understand himself how human beings communicate with one another.

Dictionaries define the words we use. If I do not know the meaning of a word you use, I can look it up in a dictionary. However, a dictionary cannot tell me the connotations you have given to that word. Connotations are the meanings we attach to words and phrases. Your connotations for a word are unlikely to be the same as my connotations for that word because your connotations are drawn from your past experience and my connotations from my past experience. Dawkins' and Dennett's connotations for the word 'meme' would be along the lines of 'good', 'intelligent', 'indubitably right', while my connotations for 'meme' are along the lines of 'what rubbish'.

Everything we say has unstated implications. The person listening to what we say tries to guess the implications for the speaker of what they hear. The invented implications are rarely the same as those of the speaker, unless the listener knows the speaker extremely well. For instance, you might say to me, 'My computer's out of action again', and I immediately assume that the implication of your statement is that you are frustrated as I would be when my computer fails to function properly. I do not know that you are secretly delighted to have such a good excuse for not answering your emails. We read into a communication much more than the words alone convey. Listening to one speaker we might be most perspicacious but with another we can be quite wrong.

These connotations and implications are part of the process of what we call, wrongly, receiving a communication. When someone speaks to us, what we hear is not what the speaker intended but our interpretation of what was said. If there were eighty people listening to my lecture, eighty-one lectures were heard in that room that night – one for each member of the audience and the one I heard in my head as I spoke. If we actually received a communication as it was given, there would be no need for literary critics to explain what a play or novel might mean; no need for political commentators to analyse what political leaders say or do; and in our personal lives we would never be mistaken in what someone communicating with us actually meant.

We make mistakes when we listen to other people, but surely when we listen to ourselves we hear exactly what we mean. We tell ourselves the truth. Isn't that what intuition is?

Even if we leave aside for the moment the popular activities of wishful thinking and lying to ourselves, the question of whether, when we listen to our internal monologue, we hear exactly what is said is not simple to answer. That kind of awareness we call consciousness is actually quite a small part of what is going on in our brain. It is difficult to decide what to call the part of the brain of which we are not aware. The words 'unconscious' and 'subconscious' are now so loaded with the often lurid connotations of psychoanalysis that they are virtually impossible to use in a discussion about the brain's functions, while 'non-conscious' seems to refer to someone in a coma. Psychologists have devised three pairs of terms to refer to aspects of the unconscious, namely, explicit/implicit, declaratory/procedural, controlled/automatic. For instance, if you say, 'I am walking down a path' while carrying out this action, the part of your brain which is operating is that which is conscious, explicit, declaratory, and controlled. If you are discussing the finer points of last night's game while walking down a path, the part of your brain which is enabling you to put one foot in front of the other without falling over is unconscious, implicit, procedural and automatic.

We need a new word for the unconscious because it has very important functions, monitoring and memory. I could create a name based on these two functions, but it has many other functions, the details of which neuroscientists have yet to uncover. So I shall use 'unconscious', but ask you to remember that I am not using this word in the ways that Freud and Jung did.

It seems that our unconscious brain constantly monitors our environment. It is interpreting the environment, and these interpretations are meanings. For instance, you might be so engrossed in watching a film that you do not consciously notice that your legs are becoming cramped. However, your unconscious notices, and creates the meaning, 'Change your position', and you do so quite unconsciously. If you do not change your position, your unconscious will, metaphorically, raise its voice until it breaks through into consciousness and you move – unless, of course, your loved one is snuggled close to you and you do not want to risk destroying such bliss. You ignore the conscious warning and ensure your future pain when the film comes to an end.

The unconscious warning function is closely allied to the memory function. Your unconscious memory is like an attic where everything you have ever encountered is stored. However, the contents of this attic are in constant movement, changing their relationship to everything else in the attic. Your consciousness is not very efficient at finding things in the attic. The more it tries to find something such as a person's name the more impossible the task becomes. If your consciousness stops looking and involves itself in another task (you say 'Jim Whatshisname' and go on with the story you were telling), a few minutes later Jim's surname will pop into your head, thrown there by your unconscious like a mother who always knows where your stuff is. In the same way, when we go into an exam for which we have prepared, if we make a conscious effort to retrieve what we have learnt, all we encounter is a blank wall, but, if we sit quietly and wait for our unconscious to think about the first question on the paper, the stream of our memory will begin to flow.

Many people are very proud of their intuition. They like to think that their intuition is always right. To believe that this is true they try to forget all those times when their intuition was wrong. It is said that a group of people interviewing candidates for a job make up their minds within the first few minutes of meeting each candidate. This is simply an example of what happens to most of us most of the times when we first meet someone. It seems that on encountering a new face our unconscious scurries around in the whirling chaos of our memory, pulls something out and presents it to us. What is presented might be quite banal, such as, 'He looks like my cousin Harry.' This might be true. We might follow this observation with, 'Harry was a liar', and that might be true. But then we can make an entirely false deduction, namely, 'Therefore this chap is a liar.'

People who place a high value on their intuition are often those people who prefer their world of fantasies to the real world in which they live. They are likely to hold the belief that 'When scientists analyse things they destroy them. My intuition and my feelings are too precious to be destroyed in this way.'

Then there are the people who subscribe to the delusion, 'I am objective in all the decisions I make.' Recently, a well-known politician had made a surprising decision about his political future. I was discussing this with another member of parliament. I mentioned that some months before I had seen a television interview with the politician's wife which suggested to me that the wife did not share any of her husband's political ambitions. Perhaps this had played a part in the man's decision. My friend scornfully rejected this. He said, 'This man made his decision on purely political grounds. The state of his marriage had nothing to do with it.'

Few men my friend's generation and older would disagree with this. When the German psychiatrist Emil Kraepelin, who in the late nineteenth century became one of the founders of modern psychiatry, wrote his memoirs (according to David Healy 'among the most tedious books ever written') he noted the death of his children as something of an afterthought and failed to name either his wife or his surviving children. 'From the point of view of science, the personal details of these people were unimportant.'[3] A hundred years later, I found that the psychiatrists I was working with considered that not only their feelings but the feelings of their patients had nothing to do with the practice of psychiatry. What these men were doing was to turn their fear of feelings – their own and other people's – into a precious belief that fed their pride. They would say, 'I am objective. I am never swayed by feelings.'

Younger generations of men brought up by mothers who were in the vanguard of Women's Liberation tend not to be frightened of admitting that they have feelings, but they find them frightening. They know that feelings are there, but they would prefer they were never mentioned. When the *Guardian* decided to send their arts writers to review sport and the sports writers to review the arts, Steve Bierley, their tennis correspondent, was sent to see the exhibition of the work of the sculptor Louise Bourgeois at the Pompidou in Paris. He wrote, 'Sport is essentially about youth, and about absolutes. Sport makes you feel elated or depressed. The works of Louise Bourgeois, 97 years old this December, make you feel unsettled, repelled . . . Sports writing demands, though often does not get, degrees of objectivity and balance. But how can you be objective about art? Sport has rarely spooked me. But Bourgeois did, all the time . . . Watch sport and you think about sport. Observe art and you discover yourself. Spirals, nests, lairs, refuges. Bourgeois leads you to dark places you are not sure you want to revisit.'[4]

No wonder so many men prefer sport to art!

From my observations of succeeding generations of men, it seems that, while younger generations of men live more easily beside women than older generations of men did, men still fear women because the threat is that women always see things differently from men. This is not to say that a woman's point of view is closer to the truth than is a man's, but simply that a woman's point of view is always different from a man's. The fact that women see things differently from men is a constant reminder to men of what everyone knows but rarely admits they know, namely, that there are as many truths as there are people to hold them, and all these truths are no more than approximations of what actually exists.

Scientists may have only recently unravelled the secrets of our brain's anatomy to show how difficult it is for us to see what is there, but wise people have always known that we see not things in themselves but our interpretations of things. Writing about Francis Bacon in his book *The Threat to Reason*, Dan Hind said, 'Bacon insists that we will only learn the truth about the world if we put away our preconceptions, whether they derive from our experience, or from established sources of authority.'[5] Yet we cannot look at the world with eyes washed clean of all our past experience. All we can do is, first, to acknowledge that this is how we see, and then set about practising how to create alternative interpretations. An alternative interpretation might prove to be closer to the truth than the first interpretation.

How can we possibly know what is true? We cannot see

reality directly but only the constructions our brain devises out of our past experience. Our brain creates a hypothesis about what is going on and builds up evidence that might increase the probability that the hypothesis is correct. Truth can be expressed only as a probability, not as a certainty. Knowledge of the past is of limited use in predicting the future. Our world and our universe are far more complex than we can comprehend. There are no fixed points in our universe. Everything is in constant change. All we have are our interpretations of the communications we receive, not the communication as it was to the sender. Most of what we know lies in our unconscious. Yet, to operate safely in the world we need to know the truth of what is going on. It is as if we are blindfolded and moving through an unknown landscape, not knowing where it is safe to put a foot, but we are impelled to keep moving on. In such a situation, finding what is true would seem to be our absolute top priority.

But it is not. For all of us there is something far more important than finding the truth.

Chapter Four

Why Lying Is Necessary

'Of course you don't mean white lies, do you?'

This was often the response when I mentioned that I was working on a book called *Why We Lie*. But I did mean white lies, and black lies, and all the shades of grey in between. I had a simple definition of a lie – words or actions intended to deceive. The key word was 'intended'. We lie because we have reason to lie.

White lies trip easily off our tongue – 'Good to see you', 'That colour suits you', 'No, I'm not busy', and that all-purpose lie, a single word and the most common of lies, 'Fine', in response to the question, 'How are you?'

Bud Goodall, whose father worked in the CIA, grew up in a family that was full of secrets and lies. He wrote,

> If I was asked a direct question, such as, 'How are things at home?' my answer was always, 'Fine'. 'Fine' was a code word for keeping secret how I really felt. It was at the very least a cover-up of something that could not otherwise be fashioned into a good story, or even a pleasant one . . . Fine usually means *not* fine at all. 'Fine' is the easy answer for those of us who have settled for something less, or have given up any hope of getting anything better.[1]

Those of us who have a chronic illness have settled for less. We lie almost every time we are asked, 'How are you?' 'Fine' we say, knowing that it is not true. If we were asked why we lied,

45

or if those who hide an unhappy marriage behind 'fine', or those who lie when they tell a friend, 'You look lovely in that dress' were asked why they lie, all of us would give the same answer. We don't want to upset people.

That is our surface reason. If our questioner went deeper and asked, 'Why is it important to you not to upset people?' our answers would fall into two groups.

Many people would reply, 'Because people wouldn't like me if I told them the truth.' If then asked, 'Why is it important to you to be liked by other people?' some people resist answering and parry the question with, 'No one wants to be disliked', or, 'That's me, I guess. I don't know why.' Others would try to put into words what they know is their own profound truth. They say, 'That's what my life is about, being with other people and being liked by them. Without them I wouldn't exist.'

Those people who do not answer, 'Because people wouldn't like me', might find it hard to describe precisely how another person's upset feelings disturbs them most profoundly. For these people any disturbance can threaten chaos, and chaos is what they fear the most. They know that the world is a chaotic place, and for them to survive in it they are impelled to create their own personal island of clarity, order and control.

All of us belong to one or other of these groups. For some of us, having relationships with other people is our most important need, and our greatest fear is being abandoned and rejected. If we are in the second group, maintaining clarity, order and control is our most important need, and our greatest fear is being overwhelmed by chaos. What scientific evidence there is points to this difference in how we experience our sense of existence being genetic, but how each of us expresses our most important need and fear depends on how we interpret the environment in which we find ourselves. Most of us know which group we belong to and do not need a psychologist to tell us, but, if you do not, you will be creating a great many problems for yourself.[2]

When we talk of surviving in this way, either by keeping people around us or by maintaining clarity, order and control, we are not talking about physical survival but surviving as a person, what we call 'I', 'me', 'myself'. What is this sense of being a person? The more neuroscience can tell us, the stranger it all becomes. Yet, if we accept this strangeness and know it to be our very self, we are able to live our life much more wisely and creatively.

'I' and 'my mind' seem to be aspects of the same thing. We talk about our mind as something we can change, make up and lose. Yet, according to Antonio Damasio, the mind is a process. He wrote, 'What we know as mind, with the help of consciousness, is a continuous flow of mental patterns, many of which turn out to be logically interrelated.'[3] We all like to think that 'I', 'me', 'myself', my sense of being a person, is solid and real, but it is not. As Chris Frith wrote, 'Another of the illusions that my brain creates is my sense of self. I experience myself as an island of stability in an ever-changing world.'[4]

Our active brain creates a torrent of thoughts, ideas, images, feelings, and out of this torrent comes a sense of there being this island of stability surrounded by the great universe of movement – 'me' and the world. However, 'me' is not the equivalent of an island, something solid and real, but the equivalent of a whirlpool in a flowing stream. A whirlpool is a pattern in a torrent, but part of the torrent, and not something that can exist separately from the torrent. The philosopher Patricia Churchland wrote, 'The brain constructs a range of make-sense-of-the-world neurotools; one is the future, one is the past and one is self. Does this mean that my self is not real? On the contrary. It is every bit as real as the three-dimensional world we see, or the future we prepare for, or the past we remember. It is a tool tuned, in varying degrees, to the reality of brain and world.'[5]

However, the three-dimensional world we see is composed of guesses that can be shown to be wrong. Our sense of being a person is composed of guesses about who we are, what our world is like, what our past was and what our future will be. All of these guesses are interconnected. Our reason for telling a white lie is connected directly to how we experience our sense of being a person. If our decision to tell a white lie is shown to be a mistake, the ideas that are an essential part of our sense of being a person tumble down like a row of dominoes.

For instance, you might decide to say to a friend who is showing off a new dress, 'You look lovely in that dress.' You predict that your friend will respond with a happy smile and a thank you, but she does not. She senses that you do not like the dress, and says, 'You're lying. You don't like it at all.'

You might protest and try to reassure her, but inside you feel the dangerous instability of mounting anxiety. If your existence as person depends on good relationships, the fear of rejection begins to loom large. If your existence depends on clarity, order and control, the fear of chaos comes upon you. To save yourself, you might resort to further lies, and perhaps with these you manage to extricate yourself from a difficult situation. Your anxiety subsides. You are safe – provided, of course, you remember what were the lies you told. Successful lying requires a good memory.

All this from a simple social interaction. What happens when you discover that you have made a serious error of judgement?

Suppose, for instance, that you have mapped out your future, which will be with one special person. Then you discover that you had got it all wrong. Your loved one had tragically died, or run off with someone else, or simply had a change of heart. In this situation we all feel that we are literally falling apart. It is a very strange experience. Our body is not falling apart but inside where 'I' resides crumbles like a wooden house caught in a hurricane. What is actually falling apart is some of the ideas which make up your sense of 'I'. These are the guesses that you created about your life, your loved one and your future. If you understand that, you know that these terrible feelings will pass, and that after a period of uncertainty you will become whole again. If you do not understand this, you are overwhelmed by the greatest terror.

The original cover of Bob Dylan's perhaps most famous album *The Freewheelin' Bob Dylan* shows twenty-three-year-old Dylan and his seventeen-year-old girlfriend Suze Rotolo walking down a snow-covered street in New York. It was nearly fifty years before Suze could bring herself to write her account of her three-year romance with Dylan and her breakdown that followed. She told her interviewer Richard Williams that, 'It was the hardest thing to write about. I was young and vulnerable and insecure. There were pressures from all around and I couldn't find my place any more. I didn't feel I had anybody I could turn to. That makes you really fall apart. And that's how I felt.'[6]

Describing the events that led to their break-up was difficult, but what she put into that six-word sentence 'That makes you really fall apart' can go beyond the capacity of language to describe. What Suze said sounds like a cliché but it is not. It refers to a life-changing and self-changing experience. Her sense of being a person fell apart, and then had to rebuild itself in a way different from what it had been before.

Had she been older, better defended and secure in herself, a romance, or rather an affair with Dylan would not have been such a profound experience. Ending it might have been unpleasant and sad, but she would have been able to tell herself that she had survived similar events in the past, and she would survive this one. However, she was very young and inexperienced. The 'pressures from all around' included the attitudes of Dylan's friends who condemned her for trying to maintain her career as an artist instead of devoting herself fully to Dylan. If her career was floundering and she was no longer loved by Dylan, she no longer fitted into any part of society and belonged there. 'Home', said Robert Frost, 'is the place where, when you have to go there, they have to take you in.' Suze had no home. Her mother and her sister disliked Dylan (imagine the 'I told you so's) and so there was no one she could turn to. In similar circumstances each of us would find ourselves falling apart. Most of us would not know what was happening to us, and we would be terrified.

The fear of being annihilated as a person is far worse than the fear of death. We can tell ourselves that when we die we shall go to heaven, or become a spirit, or return as another person. People will erect memorials to us, they will talk about us, remember us. But, if we are annihilated as a person, there will be nothing, no heaven, no spirit, no return, and no one will remember us because it will be as if we have never existed. We have disappeared like a wisp of smoke in the wind. We will do anything to stop this happening. This is why we lie. *Every lie we tell, no matter how small and unimportant, is a defence of our sense of being a person.*

We will lie over the most stupid things; tell lies that are patently, outrageously lies; build lie upon lie until they form a great, sticky web of lies. We will lie when telling the truth would lead to a better outcome; we will lie when we do not know why we are lying; we will lie to people who do not matter to us, and to people who do; we will lie to people who know that we are lying; persistently, unthinkingly, we will lie to ourselves. And all for one reason. To preserve our sense of being a person.

So much do they fear the destruction of their sense of being a person that many psychologists have avoided trying to understand just what it is that they fear. They deal with the problem of understanding what the sense of self is by hiding it in a mist of romantic fantasies, as happens in transpersonal psychology; or they talk about it in such obscure ways that no humble inquirer after the truth would dare to ask a question (ask a Freudian analyst a question and the reply is likely to be, 'Why do you want to know?'); or they believe that the sense of being a person is not something that a proper psychologist would study because proper psychology is objective and scientific. This last position is based on the popular principle that, if you don't talk about something, it doesn't exist.

Psychologists might pretend that the sense of being a person does not exist, but they cannot pretend that emotions do not exist. It is not possible to understand what emotions are without understanding what the sense of being a person is. Since this understanding is missing from much of psychology, an enormous amount of rubbish is written about emotions. Theories about emotions seem to fall into two categories. There are the 'emotions are like the climate' theories, and the pseudo-scientific theories that talk about 'the emotional brain'. Both kinds of theories make us helpless. According to the climate theories, emotions roll over us like unstoppable summer storms. According to the emotional brain theories, we are mere puppets at the mercy of the most ancient parts of our brain. Lurking in our amygdala are the emotions of fear and anger, ready to burst forth at any time. More complex emotions require a functioning cortex, but, even in that part of the brain where reason is considered to reside, emotions can override the intellect. These theories do not give us a means of understanding why, say, we are able to deal calmly with a situation involving our brother, and yet fly into a rage in another very similar situation which involves our sister. Nor do these theories help us understand why, say, we feel guilty over something that was clearly not our fault, but are untroubled by another situation where we have failed to fulfil our obligations. To understand these differences we need to know why we interpreted two of these situations as threats to the integrity of our sense of being a person, and the other two situations as being unthreatening.

If all psychologists recognized that every moment of their life they are creating meanings, and that out of these meanings come their sense of self, they would readily see that emotions are meanings, and that all these meanings relate to their sense of being a person. Emotions are rarely expressed initially in words, though they can later be put into sentences. All these sentences have just one subject – 'I'. 'I am angry', 'I am happy', 'I am envious', 'I feel guilty' and so on. Psychologists label emotions as positive and negative, but often do not see that positive emotions have to do with 'I' being safe, and negative emotions have to do with 'I' being in danger. When the world is the way we want it to be, we are happy. When there is something wrong with our world, we are unhappy. When our body or our self is in danger, we are frightened. Being happy comes in a range of intensities, from contentment to ecstasy. Being in danger can take many forms, which is why there are so many negative emotions. Being angry involves a degree of pride, 'How dare that happen to me!', while being jealous involves a certain perception of ownership. 'That person has something which is rightly mine.'

The interpretations we call emotions enable us to make decisions about what we should do. As the neuroscientist Antonio Damasio has shown, if damage to our brain prevents us from feeling emotions, that is, assessing our situation in terms of the safety or danger of our sense of being a person, we cannot make the simplest decision about what we should do. Even rational men need their emotions!

Psychologists who espouse Positive Psychology tell us that we can learn how to be happy through the use of our positive emotions. Barbara Frederickson, a Positive Psychologist, was quoted as suggesting that 'positive emotions – such as joy or love or attraction or contentment – enhance our readiness to engage with people and things, making us more attentive and open to and able to integrate the things we experience. Negative emotions, on the other hand, are believed to "narrow" rather than "broaden" the individual's reactions and openness to the world.'[7] All this could have been put more simply. When we feel safe, we open ourselves to the world and other people: when we feel we are in danger, we close ourselves off and put a barrier between ourselves and the possible sources of that danger. This quotation shows how psychologists change what people do, for instance, creating the meanings, 'I feel joyful', 'I love', 'I'm attracted to' into abstract nouns, and then talk about these abstractions (that is, ideas in our head) as if they are real things that can have an effect on the world. Anger never starts a conflict. Conflicts are started by angry people.

Our sense of being a person is always vigilant, always watching for a possible threat. However, just as a strong, well-equipped army views threats to its safety very differently from that of a weak, badly equipped army, so people who see themselves as being strong and skilled in their personal defences view threats to their safety very differently from the way people who see themselves as weak and ill-equipped do. The second group see threats everywhere, and are likely to interpret ordinary remarks by another person as a threat to the integrity of their sense of being a person. For instance, people who describe themselves as being 'sensitive' have an amazing ability to perceive an intended insult in someone's ordinary remark. In contrast, the first group are less likely to interpret another person's behaviour as a slight or a humiliation, or, if it is such, they believe that they have the means to deal effectively with such threats. People in the 'strong' group are less likely to feel the need to lie in order to preserve their sense of being a person, but they will lie in order to advance their own interests. If they believe, say, that they have the ability to become a successful

53

captain of industry, they might lie in order to become the person they wish themselves to be. It seems from the research that a completely truthful CV is rare.

The meanings, ideas, attitudes, beliefs that make up our sense of being a person form a system, and, like most systems, it has a means of defending its integrity and keeping it whole. Just as the white blood cells of our body will rush to our defence when we are invaded by noxious bacteria, so a force intrinsic to our sense of being a person will rush to our defence. For want of a better term, I call this force primitive pride, and distinguish it from personal pride. We learn from other people how to take personal pride in ourselves. For instance, most of us learn from our parents to take personal pride in being clean, or to be seen to be honest. Primitive pride seems to have its origins in those brain-based operations that lead to the development of consciousness and a sense of being a person.

When we take personal pride in ourselves we can point to something outside ourselves as evidence of our achievement and worth. Just as a two-year-old can hold up her empty plate as evidence that she has eaten all her dinner, so adults can point to an examination they have passed, the old car they have rebuilt, the sporting medals they have won, the pictures they have painted, the family they have raised. Personal pride is our way of expressing our confidence in ourselves as we operate in the real world.

Primitive pride takes no account of the real world. It always refers back to the person, and it needs no outside evidence to support it because it is a fantasy. Personal pride requires some thought, such as, 'I think I can be proud of myself for getting that degree. Working full time and studying wasn't easy.' Primitive pride is immediate and unthinking.

All of us have been in a situation where someone has insulted or humiliated us. We had to disregard our immediate impulse to strike the person down, but directly and unbidden comes the thought, 'What else could you expect from a —', and here we insert some pejorative word for the nationality, race, religion, gender, sexuality, age, or class of the person who has insulted us. We might have taken personal pride in our generous and impartial attitude to all our fellow human beings, but primitive pride can always dip into that drive to survive, no matter what, and draw from it some fantasy that proves to us if to no one else that we are superior to all other people. Primitive pride often masquerades as personal pride. When I was researching for my book *What Should I Believe?* I soon lost count of the number of religious groups I found who claimed to be God's Chosen People. Beliefs reside in our heads. Simply believing that you have been chosen by God does not make you superior to others. Getting a first in maths does entitle you to feel that you are better at maths than most people.

Primitive pride is indifferent to the truth, and very adept at producing lies that we are reluctant to see as lies. For instance, anyone who has been responsible for a young child has had the experience of the child suddenly doing something very dangerous, just at the moment when your attention was elsewhere. Perhaps the child suddenly rushed across a busy road, or fell over in his bath. You retrieved the child and no harm was done, but you were very frightened. Fear itself can be a threat to the sense of being a person, especially when the event that led to you being frightened has revealed that you are not the person you thought you were. You thought you were vigilant and careful, but you are not. Realizing this can be so destabilizing that primitive pride comes immediately to your aid. It was not your fault that the child was put in danger. It was the fault of the disobedient child. Your fear turns to anger, and you berate – or slap – the child.

What you have done is to lie to yourself and to the child. The truth was that the child was too young and impulsive to understand the possible danger, and that you were not paying attention to the child. You cannot accept this unpalatable truth, and so you lied to protect yourself.

The actual events in such a scenario are simple. The child was suddenly in danger but was saved. What created the complications that led to your lies were the discrepancies between what you thought yourself to be and what you were shown by the event to be.

Within our sense of being a person are many ideas concerning what kind of person we are. I wish I could say that we all know who we are, but I cannot. We can all describe our likes and dislikes, and what improvements to our talents and circumstances we would like to see, but, while some people are very familiar with the person that they are, there are people who experience an emptiness inside them, a space where their sense of being a person could be. They describe themselves in terms of what they do, the roles they play, but they have limited or no sense of being anything more than these roles. When in an interview the actor Bill Nighy was asked, 'Who do you think you are?' he replied, 'I have very little contact with myself. When people talk about knowing who they are or having access to their feelings, I never know what they're talking about. I have this sort of commentary that natters on in my head, which I suppose is me, but apart from that I'm just this sort of slightly misarranged organism.'[8]

Even if we start our life with a sense of who we are, the adults around us soon make it clear to us that as we are we are not satisfactory. The word 'ought' enters our life. We ought to do as we are told, eat our dinner, wash our face, not hit other children, not be greedy. In short, we ought to be good. If we have not formed a satisfactory bond with a mothering figure in the first months of our life, we might not see any reason to become what the adults around us want us to be, but, if we have formed a bond, we want to maintain that bond because then we shall be looked after. We do not want the bond to be broken, and so we try to please the person with whom we have formed the bond. We set our feet on the path of becoming good in the way the people looking after us want us to be good. Thus, most of us have a collection of meanings that we can lump together as 'the person I ought to be'. Some of us make every effort to live up to these 'oughts', while others make more of a show than a real effort, and often resort to lies to maintain the appearance of being good. The most popular lies in this situation are, 'I'm sorry', and, 'I feel so guilty.' Whether we are actually good, or pretend to be good, most of us can distinguish clearly between 'the person I am' and 'the person I ought to be'.

However, some children are so frightened by their mentors over not being what they ought to be that they lose sight of who they are. If they happen to catch a glimpse of the person they are, they condemn this person for not being good. They never feel that they are entitled to what they achieve, and, if successful, they see themselves as an imposter whose base character will soon be revealed.

When we grow up being familiar with the person that we are, we are usually aware that there is something within ourselves that needs to come into being in order for us to be fully the person we can be. Becoming the person that you are brings the greatest of all satisfactions because you no longer have to pretend that you are someone else. Failing to become the person that you are is to many people their greatest loss. Many adults who, to the outside observer, lead secure and comfortable lives, experience a kind of heartache or angst to which they cannot put a name. Often they know the cause of the heartache, but they dare not say it aloud because the family and friends would not understand. Perhaps they became a civil servant instead of spending their life experiencing the danger and exultation of climbing mountains; or they may have had just one child instead of the six they intended to have. People like these have settled for less than what they might have been. One of the most poignant scenes

57

in the history of the cinema is in *On the Waterfront* where Marlon Brando, playing Terry Malloy, a failed boxer, says to his brother, played by Rod Steiger, 'I could've been a contender. I could've had class and been somebody. Real class. Instead of a bum, let's face it, which is what I am.' Terry had been persuaded by his brother to throw a fight so that his brother's criminal boss would win a bet. In real life, Terry would have remained a bum, but in true Hollywood style, he found redemption, that is, became the person he knew he had it within him to be, not just by being courageous but by telling the truth.

In real life, some people find themselves by lying.

Tobias Wolff is world renowned for telling the truth through fiction – his great short stories and novels – but he also wrote two volumes of autobiography which are a truthful account of lies and liars. His mother's lies were fantasies of about-to-happen happiness. In the next town, when she gets her next job, when she meets the right man, she and Tobias will be happy, while all the time she moved from place to place without a clear plan or aim, working at whatever she could get, and unerringly finding the wrong kind of man. Tobias's father lied to impress others, and to avoid paying any bills. Children learn from what their parents do, and so Tobias learned how to lie. In his youth and early adulthood he lived a formless, chaotic existence, acting out his emotions and not understanding what he was doing. He knew that he was disobedient, lazy, aggressive and careless, responding without thought to whatever he encountered. He was a poor student, but in his early teens he decided to become a writer, and never wished to do anything else. Within the chaos of his life he had some misty awareness of the person he could be. He saw that if he stayed at Concrete High in Chinook near Seattle, oppressed and used by his stepfather, he did not have a future that would be worth living. So he created a plan made up entirely of lies, yet these lies contained a truth.

He set out to win a place in one or other of the best private schools in America, even though there was nothing in his school record that would recommend him to any of these schools. He wrote to each school, requested application forms, and filled them in. He wrote letters of support supposedly from his teachers. 'The words came as easily as if someone were breathing them into my ear. I felt full of things that had to be said, full of stifled truth. That was what I thought I was writing – the truth. But it was truth known only to me, but I believed in it more than I believed the facts arrayed against it. I believed that in some sense not factually verifiable I was a straight-A student. In the same sense I believed I was an Eagle Scout, and a powerful swimmer, and a boy of integrity. These were ideas about myself that I had held on to for dear life. Now I gave them voice.'[9]

Tobias was given a scholarship to Hill School and off he went. Were this a story told by some Hollywood film, Hill School would have been the making of him, but it was real life. Eventually he was expelled from the school, and soon after he joined the army, just in time to spend four years in Vietnam. His account of this war, *In Pharaoh's Army*, is one of the best books written about the ugliness and pointlessness of war. When he was discharged he drifted, then went to England to visit friends. There, after four and a half months' study, he passed the entrance exams for Oxford and took a degree in English Language and Literature. One night he was in the Bodleian library working on a translation from the West Saxon Gospels for his Old English class. The passage to translate concerned the story of the man who built his house upon a rock and the man who built his house on sand. 'And the rain descended, and the flood came, and the winds blew, and beat upon that house; and it fell; and great was the fall of it.' He later wrote, 'The winds that had blown me here could have blown me anywhere, even from the face of the earth. But I *was* here, in this moment, which all the other moments in my life had conspired to bring me to. And with this moment came these words, served on me like a writ. I copied out my transla-tion in plain English, and thought that, yes, I could do well to build my house upon a rock, whatever that meant.'[10] He returned to America and became a great teacher and writer. He became the person he knew himself to be.

Chapter Five

How We Learn to Lie

Fragile though it might be, our sense of being a person is the most important part of our life. Newborn babies show very clearly that they are determined to survive physically. If a light tissue is placed over the baby's mouth and nose, the baby will struggle to remove it. Babies also arrive in the world determined to survive as a person. They search for the one thing they need for survival – the attentive face of another person. Babies arrive in the world ready to feed, and able to single out a face from their surroundings. While it has always been known that babies need sustenance, it was not until the end of World War Two that the importance of a relationship with another mothering person was recognized. Midst the turmoil of the aftermath of the war in Europe there were children who had survived without being in the care of adults. Some were the survivors of places like the Warsaw ghetto and the concentration camps, some had been separated from their parents as they fled from the enemy, and some were the blond, blue-eyed children conceived as part of Hitler's plan for the master race and brought up in Nazi institutions, and abandoned as the Russian army advanced on Berlin. Amongst these children were those who had survived physically but, in the absence of anyone to take a personal interest in them, they had not become what we would regard as someone like ourselves. Some of these children distrusted all adults and related only to other children, while some were unable to create a relationship with any human being. To become ourselves we need other people.

Our physical makeup ensures that we can be aware of something only if that thing stands in contrast to something else. If we lived in a world where nothing ever died, we would have no concept of life because there was no death. If everyone invariably told the truth, we would have no concept of truth because there were no lies. We know our self because there is not-self – the world around us and other people, that is, other selves. It is only recently that this has been understood. Writing in the early twentieth century, William James described the newborn baby as seeing the world as nothing but a 'booming, buzzing confusion', while Freud believed that a baby cannot tell where his body ends and the world begins. (These men might have fathered babies but they did not spend much time in the daily care of them.) Studies where newborn babies are shown a number of objects, and the length of time that the baby spends looking at each object is measured, have shown that a baby is born not only knowing how to identify a face from other things but preferring to look at a face, even just a simple cartoon of a face, than at anything else. Dangle some small object about a foot in front of an infant. The baby will look intently at the object, and then reach forward with one or both arms in the attempt, sometimes successful, to touch the object. This is not proof that the baby is aware that the object is not part of his body, but it does suggest that he is beginning to understand that he can use a part of his body to reach something he can see.

The weight of evidence suggests that the newborn baby sees a world of patterns, and that some of these patterns have considerable significance, that is, meaning for the baby. Moreover, the baby is keen to discover the means whereby he can influence some of those patterns. When babies are given the opportunity to suck on a dummy fixed so that the changing pressure on the dummy switches some music on and off, they will readily learn how to do this. The patterns babies want most to engage with are faces. Moreover, right from birth, babies show a clear preference for faces that look directly at them, rather than faces that are turned away.

If you are unused to being in the company of young babies you can be quite unnerved by finding yourself the subject of a young baby's thoughtful gaze. You might even think that the baby is gravely assessing you and finding you wanting. You might hasten to decide, as many psychologists do, that this must be an illusion. How could a baby assess you when he does not yet know that he himself is a person? These psychologists know that, when mothers say that they have little conversations with their baby, the mothers are deluded. Babies might appear to converse, but, according to Michael Tomasello, babies cannot understand that they have intentions to communicate with others, and others have intentions to communicate with them, until they are nine months old.[1] Babies might seem to communicate, but this is a pseudo-communication. However, Tomasello was examining those communications where two people have a common subject that they are discussing. There is another form of communication, often used by mothers and babies younger than nine months, where the mother notices what the baby is feeling and responds to that. The baby then responds to the mother's response. In a similar way, a baby will notice that his mother is dispirited and try to initiate a conversation. Such attention from her baby can often produce a much happier response from the mother but, if the mother does not respond, the baby will try again once, perhaps twice. If the mother still does not respond, the baby looks elsewhere rather than at the mother's face. Adults often communicate in the same way. I observed a woman my age looking at a teenage girl whose need to be fashionable had quite overcome her sense of the ridiculous. As the woman shook her head and turned away, she caught my eye. I smiled, and she smiled back. Nothing needed to be said.

Psychologists will argue that there are good scientific reasons for rejecting the theory that babies are born with some degree of a sense of self and an ability to perceive a sense of self in other people. However, science is concerned with probabilities. Any statement of absolute certainty cannot be scientific. Deciding whether a particular probability is so significant that it can be acted upon is a subjective judgement. For instance, you have about one chance in fourteen million of winning the UK National Lottery. Such a probability has never tempted me to buy a ticket, but millions of people do, many on the grounds that, 'Someone has got to win it.' More often than not, whether we see a particular probability as being significant depends on whether it fits with the way we see things. There are many adults, and not only psychologists, who want to see themselves as being superior to children. When you were a child, how many adults did you meet who spoke to you as an equal? Did you try to bear this as best you could, or did you resolve that, when you grew up, you would do to children what had been done to you?

All the evidence that infants can imitate, converse, feel self-conscious, understand intention, understand humour and how to deceive others has not changed the minds of those psychologists who are devoted to the theory that children have to be about four years old before they acquire a sense of self and an understanding that other people have a sense of self. My husband, who had a somewhat tangential relationship with truth, used to say that you should never let the facts stand in the way of a good story. He could have said the same about any theory on which a scientist has staked his identity. Abandoning a theory on which you have built your career and reputation with your peers will threaten your sense of being a person, and so you are likely to deny the evidence that shows your theory to be wrong.

So rarely does a scientist gracefully relinquish a theory which built his reputation that much is made of those occasions when a scientist does just this. In his book *The God Delusion* Richard Dawkins tells the story of a respected elderly zoologist who was tremendously pleased when, in a lecture, a much younger scientist showed the zoologist that his long-held theory was wrong. Dawkins wrote, 'We clapped our hands red.'[2]

If you are the student of a well-known or an up-and-coming scientist, one of the most dangerous things you can do is to obtain research results that throw doubt on this scientist's theories. (Alternatively, one of the best things you can ever do is to produce results that disprove the theories of his competitor.) Vasudevi Reddy told the story of what happened when one of Piaget's students, Olga Maratos, made a discovery that suggested that Piaget might be wrong. From his extensive research the great psychologist had concluded that it was not until they were about eight months old that infants could imitate another person because imitation requires some understanding of oneself and another person, and this a newborn baby did not have. Olga Maratos found that, if she poked her tongue at a baby no more than a month old, the baby, seemingly with much thought and effort, poked his tongue at her. Her fellow psychologists were sceptical, but, when she showed the great man a video of her research, he said, 'Indeed they imitate!' When she asked him what she should do, he said she would either have to develop his theory, or create a different theory from the data.

When Olga had presented her work at a conference of the British Psychological Society, in her audience was a young psychologist who went on to show that what she had found was indeed the case. Babies are born knowing how to imitate.

It was Andrew Meltzoff who, having persuaded a large number of pregnant women to allow him to be at their baby's birth, established that, if you hold a baby who has just been born so that the two of you are looking at one another, and you poke your tongue out, slowly and carefully, the baby will copy you. Now, nearly a hundred studies of newborns have shown that babies within minutes of birth can imitate mouth opening, finger movement, eye blinking, and even one sound, 'aaaa'. Reddy wrote, 'The debate is just as passionate as it ever was, now having shifted to the question of whether we could actually call such acts "imitation".'[3] This reminds me of the phenomenon of 'retrospective diagnosis' which I observed in the psychiatric hospitals where I worked. The psychiatrists I worked with believed that depression was a lifelong chronic illness which could be managed by the psychiatrist with the use of antidepressant drugs. When any of my depressed patients came to the conclusion that it was their ideas that had led them to become depressed, and decided that they could change these ideas to ones that ensured a satisfactory life, the psychiatrist who had diagnosed this patient as being depressed would deny that the patient had ever been depressed. He had merely suffered from mild anxiety. Changing the facts so that your original theory still holds is a very popular form of falsehood called 'hypothesis saving'. It is not just scientists who do this.

The question of whether newborn babies can imitate is important because, as Reddy said, 'You cannot imitate that which in some sense you don't understand.'[4] To imitate you have to have some sense of self and to see something similar in the person you imitate. When the First Fleet arrived at Sydney Cove in 1788 there followed a meeting between two groups of people whose paths had diverged some sixty thousand years before. When the first groups of homo sapiens left Africa, the distant ancestors of the officers, soldiers and convicts had settled in Europe while the distant ancestors of the Aborigines had set off on a long journey that eventually brought them to Australia. The two groups developed vastly different languages and cultures. Thus, when some of their number met on the shores of Sydney Harbour they could communicate only by facial expressions and gesture. What disconcerted the whites was the way the Aborigines could imitate them. The Aborigines could echo back to the English words and phrases that the white men had used. The Aborigines had no knowledge of what were appropriate manners in eighteenth-century England, but they could understand, say, how one man might display his

66

power by the way he moved and gesticulated, and another his vanity. However, despite this and much other evidence that the Aborigines were the same species as the whites, the whites had to maintain their pride by insisting that the Aborigines were not just ignorant savages but less than human. This belief has not entirely vanished from the minds of many white Australians today. Whoever you are, if you are treated as inferior by those who have power over you, you suffer. Children suffer when the adults around them treat them as their inferiors, as many adults do. Yet it is now quite clear that newborns do not merely imitate, they are able to distinguish human beings from objects, and understand wordlessly that people have intentions but objects do not, and that other people can confirm your existence but objects do not.

It seems that we are born with the ability to be a person but that this ability requires interaction with other people in order for it to manifest itself. In the company of attentive faces, the many and various facets of being a person begin to show themselves. In her book *How Infants Know Minds* Vasudevi Reddy gives an account of all of these, but here I want to look at the aspects of being a person that relate to truth and lies.

Infants perceive and respond to another person's emotional state. They show a clear preference for happy faces rather than angry ones. What they dislike most is a blank, unresponsive face. We might not enjoy someone being angry with us or rejecting us, but at least these people are taking notice of us. Nowadays, in conversation 'blank' is used as a verb, as in, 'At the party Susie blanked Jim, and he got back at her by sending her up.' I am not sure how much of that sentence is Australian slang and how much English, but it means, 'Susie refused to acknowledge Jim's presence, and he responded by making fun of her.' Teachers must make sure that they pay attention to the well-behaved child, otherwise the child might become very badly behaved in order to get some attention. In some of the workshops

I used to run, I would ask the participants to imagine they were the sole survivor of a shipwreck. They had just enough strength to paddle their life raft to one of two islands. On one island, the inhabitants would ignore them completely. On the other, the inhabitants would notice them but only to be extremely unpleasant to them. Which island would they choose? The majority of people chose the island where the inhabitants acknowledged their existence, albeit unpleasantly. If, over a period of time, nobody takes any notice of us we start to feel that we have disappeared.

It seems that babies soon discover that, if they respond to an adult in the way the adult wants, the adult rewards them, not just with smiles, but also with saying something in a warm, encouraging tone. By the time they are eight or nine months old infants start to understand and respond to orders. At first, this can seem to be another enjoyable game, but then some of these orders become, in the infant's way of seeing things, an unwarranted intrusion into what the infant wants to do. Infants learn very quickly how not to comply to unwelcome instructions. To these they respond sometimes with noisy defiance, and sometimes more subtly with a stiffening of the back and the sudden onset of deafness.

In responding in these ways to unwelcome orders, infants show that they understand the dangers inherent in being very obedient. If we comply with an order because, if we had thought of it, we would have done what we are now being asked to do, or because we want to please the person giving the order and fulfilling that order is not difficult, we feel that we are in control of that situation. However, if we believe that we will feel guilty if we disobey an unwelcome order or that in the face of punishment we are being compelled to comply, or that complying means going against the grain of our very being, we are not in control of the situation. We want to resist, and, if we do not do so, we despise ourselves. If these last three situations often arise, we soon find that continual compliance threatens to wipe us out as a person.

We do not need a language to understand the danger of being annihilated as a person, in the same way as we do not need a language to understand that, if we touch something very hot, we must withdraw our hand immediately.

In her book, Reddy mentions what she calls the 'disintegration' of the self following bereavement or shock.[5] In psychoanalytic literature, such 'shock' is referred to as trauma. For the baby this can occur when the 'good' mother suddenly turns into the 'bad' mother. The smiling mother might suddenly become angry, or distant, or vanish and not return. Whenever we suffer a trauma or a bereavement, we discover that the world is not what we thought it was. Some of our ideas are disconfirmed, and we feel ourselves falling apart. We have to find ways of protecting ourselves from trauma, and, if this happens, ways of holding our sense of self together.

At about nine months babies discover that they can protect themselves by refusing to obey orders. However, adults are more powerful than infants, and they can punish those who disobey. When the refusal to obey fails to protect infants, they have to learn how to lie. But before they can do this, they have to discover the two prerequisites of lying.

To lie you must first know the truth.

The person you wish to lie to must be capable of being deceived.

From the moment newborn babies gaze upon the world they are in the business of discovering what is going on. They want to discover this for themselves, and, as soon as they can point at something, they want to share this information with the people around them. Reddy wrote, 'From about 12 to 18 months toddlers effortfully, selectively and appropriately inform other people truthfully about reality, often telling people things they don't appear to know or may "need" to know.'[6] They offer other people information, and they are capable of selecting among several adults those adults who lack certain information that the other adults already have.

A number of recent studies have found that even fifteen-month-old toddlers seem to be able to detect that other people can have false beliefs about reality. Well before they can tell a lie, infants discover how to deceive. They quickly grasp the principle of 'What the eye doesn't see the heart doesn't grieve over.' If your mother does not want you to do something, wait until she is out of the room. The psychologist Judy Dunn has shown that toddlers of no more than sixteen months can discover what would upset or please their mother or their siblings, and then do it.[7] Such young children fail the Piagetian tests for understanding the general principle that other people can hold false beliefs. However, the people whose minds you need to be able to read early in your life are your nearest and dearest, because they are the people who can easily annihilate you as a person, or give you the kind of affirmation that brings the greatest joy to your heart.

Most of us are born into families where the parents hold differing views on a great many subjects. It does not take us long to discover that we can get a biscuit from Dad by giving him a cuddle, whereas a biscuit from Mum comes only as a reward for doing something she wants us to do. Once we discover that our parents have very different views on what constitutes clean hands or the very last story before going to sleep, we can elaborate our tactics for deceiving our parents. However, some children are born to parents who decide that they will appear to their children to agree in their views about everything. Not being offered alternative interpretations of events, the child believes that his parents see everything exactly as it is, and are therefore not susceptible to being deceived.

In his biography of his father Philip Gosse, Edmund Gosse described how he had seen his parents in this way, and what a shock it was to him when he discovered that his father could be in error. Philip Gosse was a colleague of Charles Darwin, a painstaking biologist, and a devout Plymouth Brethren, as was his wife. Edmund Gosse wrote,

In consequence of hearing so much about an Omniscient God, a being of supernatural wisdom and penetration who was always with us, who made, in fact, a fourth in our company, I had come to think of Him, not without awe, but with absolute confidence. My Father and Mother, in their serene discipline of me, never argued with one another, never differed; their wills seemed absolutely as one. My Mother always deferred to my Father, and in his absence spoke of him to me, as if he were all-wise. I confused him in some sense with God; in all events I believed that my Father knew everything and saw everything. One morning in my sixth year, my Mother and I were alone in the morning room, when my Father came in and announced some fact to us . . . I remember turning quickly, in embarrassment, and looking into the fire. The shock was to me as a thunderbolt, for what my Father had said *was not true*. My Mother and I, who had been present at the trifling incident, were aware that it had not happened exactly as it had been reported to him. My Mother gently told him so, and he accepted the correction. Nothing could have possibly been more trifling to my parents, but to me it was an epoch. Here was an appalling discovery, never suspected before, that my Father was not as God, and did not know everything. The shock was not caused by any suspicion that he was not telling the truth, as it appeared to him, but by the awful proof that he was not, as I had supposed, omniscient.[8]

Not long after this incident, Edmund chanced upon some tools which workmen had left in the garden near a small rockery built by his father with what Edmund described as 'a pretty parasol of water'. Edmund wondered whether one of these tools could make a hole in the base of the water pipe to the little fountain. He made the hole, and moved on, thinking about other things. Several days later his father came in to dinner very angry. He turned on the tap to the fountain, and water rushed through the hole. The rockery was ruined. Edmund was 'frozen with alarm' and waiting to be blamed. However, his mother pointed out that the plumbers had probably caused the damage, and his father agreed. Edmund was 'turned to stone within, but outwardly sympathetic and with unchecked appetite'. He wrote,

> The emotions which now thronged within me, and led me with an almost unwise alacrity to seek solitude in the back garden, were not moral at all, they were intellectual. I was not ashamed of having successfully – and so surprisingly – deceived my parents by my crafty silence; I looked upon that as a providential escape, and dismissed all further thought of it. I had other things to think of.
>
> In the first place, the theory that my Father was omniscient or infallible was now dead and buried. He probably knew very little; in this case he had not known a fact of such importance that if you did not know that, it could hardly matter what you knew. My Father, as a deity, as a natural force of immense prestige, fell in my eyes to a human level. In future, his statements about things in general need not be accepted implicitly. But of all the thoughts that rushed upon my savage and undeveloped little brain at this crisis, the most curious was that I had found a companion and confidant in myself. There was a secret in this world and it belonged to me and to somebody who lived in the same body with me. There were two of us, and we could talk to one another. It is difficult to define impressions so rudimentary, but it is certain that it was in this dual form that the sense of my individuality now suddenly descended on me, and it is equally certain that it was a great solace to me to find a sympathizer in my own breast.[9]

The events in childhood that come to define who we are often are events that in themselves are insignificant. What is of immense importance are the conclusions we draw from these experiences.

In this successful deception of his parents, Edmund was made aware of both his sense of being a person and the lifelong dialogue between himself and his closest ally, himself. He learned that he could separate himself from what was going on around him. He could take up the position of being an observer, and discuss his observations with himself.

Edmund, an only child, spent considerable time entertaining himself, and so he could conduct long conversations with himself. His parents made it very clear to him that they wanted him to be a godly child, and he tried to conform outwardly to their wishes. However, he knew that he was not a godly child, and he never pretended to himself that he was. Because his parents never inflicted physical punishments, he was not placed in situations where he had to take a stand against their attacks on his sense of being a person. He did not have to defy his parents the way that beaten children do, by claiming that the parents' assaults did not hurt. He was a loving, respectful son who, somehow, never became the holy person his father wanted. Instead, he became the truthful writer that he wanted to be.

Edmund Gosse's story stands in stark contrast to the work of Paul Newton who studied the lies told by two- and three-year-old children. These children told a wide variety of lies, but there were no white lies. The children knew a good deal about the adults closest to them, but they had not yet perceived that some people wanted to be protected from the truth.

Many of these children told bravado lies. All bravado lies are aimed at bolstering the sense of being a person when it is under attack. We all resort to, 'No, I wasn't frightened', or, 'No, I wasn't upset', rather than admit weakness. However, it is children, more than adults, who receive physical punishment.

'It didn't hurt' is a lie commonly associated with school-age children, but in Newton's study Reddy recorded that 'there were some heart-rending reports of "Don't hurt" bravado'. She quoted one report concerned with a little girl of three years six months.

The mother of the child said,

> You can smack her legs until they're red raw, and if she's in
> one of her wilful moods she'll go: 'Didn't hurt!' On a couple
> of occasions when she's been threatened with a good hiding
> for misbehaviour she's even dropped her trousers for you. The
> other day she did this and then said, 'It dudn't hurt!'[10]

All parents of small children sometimes administer a punishment
of some kind far greater than the misdemeanour warranted. Some
of these parents, when they calm down, realize that they have
overstepped the mark and regret it. Wise parents acknowledge
this to the child, and apologize without blaming the child for
forcing them to go to such an extreme. Clearly this mother felt
she was justified in inflicting such pain on her child. It seems
that she preferred her child to fear and obey her than to love her.
Did she not know that fear drives out love? Even if we manage
to retain some love for the person we fear, our fear and guilt
prevent us from expressing fully and openly the love that we
feel.

With this mother and child, the daughter will always fear her
mother because her mother has threatened her with the greatest
peril, that of being damaged or broken by such a close encounter
with being annihilated as a person.

This little girl would not then, and perhaps never will, be
able to take that step back so she could see and describe what
exactly happened to her during those beatings. The Hungarian
writer Imre Kertész was older than she was when he, just
fifteen, was sent to Auschwitz. Years later he wrote a fiction-
alized memoir of his time in Auschwitz. He called the central
character Gyuri.

One of the most onerous tasks inflicted on the prisoners was
the loading of bags of cement. When Gyuri dropped a bag which
then split open and spilled its contents, the guard knocked him

to the ground, rubbed his face in the dirt and swore that he would never drop a bag again. Kertész wrote,

> From then on, he personally loaded each bag on to my shoulders each time it was my turn, bothering himself with me alone; I was his sole concern, it was me exclusively he kept his eye on, following me all the way to the truck and back, and whom he picked to go first, even if, by rights, there were others still ahead of me in the queue. In the end, there was almost an understanding between us, we had got the measure of one another, and I noticed that his face bore what was almost a smile of satisfaction, encouragement, even, dare I say, a pride of sorts, and from a certain perspective, I had to acknowledge, with good reason, for indeed, tottering, stooping though I might have been, my eyes seeing black spots, I did manage to hold out, coming and going, all without dropping a single further bag, and that, when it comes to it, proved him right. On the other hand, by the end of the day I felt that something within me had broken down irreparably; from then on every morning I believed that would be the last morning I would get up; with every step I took, that I could not possibly take another; with every movement I made, I would be incapable of making another; and yet, for the time being, I still managed to accomplish it each and every time.[11]

By carrying out the task of loading the bags of cement Gyuri was trying to demonstrate to the guard the equivalent of 'It didn't hurt', and thus preserve his sense of being a person. However, when we protect ourselves against a massive assault, we use up many of the strengths we have to defend ourselves. If the assaults are infrequent, we have time to replenish our strengths, but, if the assault is particularly brutal, or, if the assaults occur frequently as they do from parents who use physical punishments as the prime form of discipline, we might not be able to restore our sense of being a person to its former strength and cohesion. Like Gyuri, we can lose our ability to view our future hopefully. From then on, each day cannot be enjoyed but has to be endured. Alternatively, we can adopt a position of constant defiance, and each day, whatever the situation, every authority however benign has to be defied and fought. These two outcomes are found in the long-term studies of children whose parents used physical punishment. Some of these children, mostly girls, go on to become depressed, while others, mostly boys, become too wild and aggressive to be contained within society.[12] Both groups have lost the one great strength of being a person, that of feeling in charge of oneself. Rather, they feel themselves to be at the mercy of events, and of the emotions of fear, rage and guilt that drive them to act and they know not why.

It is possible to survive the physical assaults of beating and rape by seeing the assault as something separate from yourself as a person. Your body was harmed but not you. Knowing this, interrogators and torturers who want to do more than inflict pain use techniques that assault the sense of being a person. Complete isolation in a featureless cell with no control over the lighting, the temperature, or means of measuring the passing of time prevents the prisoner from imposing on his awareness of his existence any kind of structure. Anyone who does not already have the means of entertaining himself through memory and fantasy finds that kind of imprisonment very difficult to survive. Interrogators who have gone to the trouble of uncovering every small detail of the prisoner's life can use this knowledge to create in the prisoner intense feelings of shame and guilt, the very emotions that are the greatest threat to our sense of being a person. Such an interrogator will also be able to uncover the one specific thing that the prisoner fears the most, and then present it to the prisoner.

In his novel *1984*, about a totalitarian future world, George Orwell introduced the terms 'Big Brother' and 'Room 101'. Since

76

then the media have taken these terms over and demeaned them, so that now people use the terms without making any attempt to understand the horrors Orwell described, horrors that are not entirely absent from our world today. Big Brother was the leader, whose image was everywhere but the person never seen. Surveillance cameras were everywhere, even in people's homes. Disobedience was severely punished.

Winston Smith, the novel's protagonist, harboured ideas of which Big Brother would not have approved. He thought that he and his lover Julia were successful in hiding their relationship, but they were not. They were arrested, and their separate interrogations were begun.

Winston's interrogator was O'Brien, a man who was in turn charming, friendly, seductive, and hugely threatening. In the final stage of Winston's interrogation he was taken deep underground to Room 101 and strapped to a chair. O'Brien explained, 'The thing that is in Room 101 is the worst thing in the world. The worst thing in the world varies from individual to individual. It may be burial alive, or death by fire, or by drowning, or by impalement, or fifty other deaths. There are cases where it is some quite trivial thing, not even fatal.'

A guard entered the room carrying what for Winston was the worst thing in the world. Orwell wrote,

It was an oblong wire cage with a handle on top for carrying it by. Fixed to the front of it was something that looked like a fencing mask, with the concave side outwards. Although it was three or four metres away from him, he could see that the cage was divided lengthways into two compartments, and that there was some kind of creature in each. They were rats . . .

O'Brien picked up the cage, and, as he did so, pressed something in it. There was a sharp click. Winston made a frantic effort to tear himself loose from the chair. It was hopeless; every part of him, even his head, was held immovably. O'Brien moved the cage nearer. It was less than a metre from Winston's face . . .

Suddenly the foul musty odour of the brutes struck his nostrils. There was a violent convulsion of nausea inside him, and he almost lost consciousness. Everything had gone black. For an instant he was insane, a screaming animal. Yet he came out of the blackness clutching an idea. There was one and only one way to save himself. He must interpose another human being, the body of another human being, between himself and the rats . . .

. . . in the whole world there was just one person to whom he could transfer his punishment – one body that he could thrust between himself and the rats. And he was shouting frantically, over and over,

'Do it to Julia! Do it to Julia! Not me! Julia! I don't care what you do to her. Tear her face off, strip her to the bones. Not me! Julia! Not me!'

He was falling backwards, into enormous depths, away from the rats. He was still strapped in the chair, but he had fallen through the floor, through the walls of the building, through the earth, through the oceans, through the atmosphere, into outer space, into the gulfs between the stars – always away, away, away from the rats. He was light years distant, but O'Brien was still standing at his side. There was still the cold touch of wire against his cheek. But through the darkness that enveloped him he heard another metallic click, and knew that the cage door had clicked shut and not open.[13]

O'Brien did not need to open the cage. He knew that he had destroyed Winston. He had destroyed the ideas central to Winston's sense of being a person, ideas about how it was possible to have something in his life that was fine and beautiful, ideas about loving and caring for Julia. All the ideas that gave him the sense of being an integrated, whole person in whom he could take pride were destroyed. All that was left was something that walked and talked but was no longer a fully functioning human being. Thoughts still inhabited his mind, but they were fragmentary, incoherent.

Many people, including Orwell, know the experience of falling through the gaps between the stars when their expectations about their world have been invalidated. However, they have not been forced to betray what they hold dear, and many of the principles they live by remain intact. They are changed by their experience, but they remain a person.

Orwell wrote his novel at a time when all heroes were heroic – or so we were told. Now we are familiar with stories of torture. However, we rarely ask, 'From where do torturers get their ideas?' The truthful answer is considered to be unacceptable. It is from their experiences in childhood. If the guards at Guantanamo had not been taught about the sanctity of the Bible, how would they have known that their Muslim prisoners would feel intensely guilty when the guards besmirched the Koran? If the guards at Abu Ghraib had not experienced as children the annihilating shame of being exposed, naked, to cruel, mocking eyes, how would they have known their prisoners would feel annihilating shame at being forced into gross sexual acts?

Take, for instance, another example of a bravado lie given by Reddy. This concerned a small girl 'who hated a toy spider she had recently been bought and wouldn't go near it. Once when she was being naughty her father threatened her saying, "If you don't behave I'll get that spider out." The child replied, "I don't care. I've been playing with it all day" (she had not been near it according to her mother).'[14]

No doubt this father would argue that his threat to present the girl with the feared toy spider did not amount to torture, just as Dick Cheney argued that water boarding was not torture. Anyone who fears spiders to a degree very much out of proportion to the threat spiders actually pose would know that what this father threatened to do was torture. I grew up in a part of Australia where the deadly redback and funnel web spiders shared our homes and gardens. I was wary of these spiders but I did not hate all spiders. Far from it, I rather liked them. In England where there are no dangerous spiders, I met many adults for whom a cage of spiders, even harmless ones, would have produced a similar response to Winston's response to the rats. To them the spider is a mysterious creature with attributes that seem to represent all the unnamed fears they have inside them but do not want to recognize. Their fear of spiders had always made them vulnerable to bullying, and being bullied for whatever reason can have some deleterious consequences. It can severely damage the person's self-confidence, making the person timid and uncertain. Alternatively, the person might decide to defend himself by becoming a bully and bully those weaker than himself. You have to have been bullied in order to know how to bully.

Instead of threatening his daughter with a feared toy spider, this father would have been better employed in talking with his daughter, helping her to express her real fears and to find effective ways of dealing with them. He might have found that one of her fears was of 'my father, the bully'.

Many parents, including those who would not dream of hitting their children, use bullying and guilt arousal as a means of disciplining their children. The consequences of these forms of discipline can be more complex and far-reaching than the consequences of the infliction of pain. The child who is slapped and spanked can become skilled in avoiding those situations that could lead to punishment. One important skill is to develop a whole range of lies, including the bravado lie. They learn how to fake good. (Why do I suddenly think of politicians?) In contrast, bullying and guilt arousal undermine a child's self-confidence because they are attacks on the child's sense of being a person.

When we reflect on past events, we can feel regret, and we

can feel guilty. Regret and guilt are two very different emotions. Regret arises from the knowledge that there could have been an outcome to a past event that was happier than the outcome that did eventuate. I regret that my mother was more interested in herself than she was in me. If I felt guilty about this, I would be telling myself that it was my fault that she had little interest in me. I have often heard such sentiments expressed by my depressed clients. Their mothers had always blamed them for everything that was wrong in the mother's life. They accepted this lie because with it they could try to persuade themselves that their mother had actually been what they wanted her to be.

There are times when it is appropriate for us to feel guilty. We have done something we ought not to have done. Guilt is the fear of the punishment that is our due. The punishment may be simply doing what is required, that is, being truthful with ourselves and with other people. We say what we have done wrong and we express our sorrow and shame. We do not seek to excuse ourselves. It takes courage to do this, especially when by doing this we set in train unpleasant consequences for ourselves, perhaps a jail term, or estrangement from those who are important to us, or the loss of our good reputation. Acknowledging our guilt and suffering the consequences that follow can threaten our sense of being a person. To avoid this we can try to appear to be contrite, but without acknowledging our guilt, and without an apology for what we have done. When a bank acquires debts so vast that the viability of the bank is threatened, thus depleting the wealth of the bank's investors and customers, who is responsible? Surely it is the man who is paid a huge salary to manage the bank. Well, no, according to the managers themselves. The political sketch writer Simon Hoggart told how three disgraced bank managers, Sir Fred Goodwin of the Royal Bank of Scotland, Sir Tom McKillop, former RBS chairman, and Andy Hornby of HBOS, appeared before MPs to give an account of themselves. He wrote, 'They were sorry. God,

81

they were sorry. They didn't care who knew how sorry they were. On the other hand, they weren't to blame. Not personally to blame, anyway. Nobody had seen it coming. Everybody got it wrong. So they apologised, but it wasn't their fault.'[15]

Sometimes we find ourselves in a situation that we cannot control or influence in any way. Helplessness can seem to be more threatening to our sense of being a person than is guilt. Indeed, when we say we feel guilty, we are making a claim to a degree of power. We are saying that we were in control of the situation and we could have chosen to behave differently, but we did not. Choosing to feel guilty rather than acknowledging helplessness, that is, pretending to be something that we are not, is a lie.

For children to learn to be decent individuals and good citizens, their parents have to teach them to recognize those situations where the children have erred, to admit what they have done, and to feel appropriately guilty. The parents of these bankers had obviously failed to do this. To teach children when it is appropriate to feel guilty, parents should not include those situations where the child's actions arose from immaturity, not naughtiness, nor should the parents make the child responsible for those matters that are the parents' responsibility. Moreover, parents themselves need to feel guilt and show this in situations where it is appropriate to merit guilt, and to apologize to those who require an apology. If parents believe that to do this would mean that they would lose control over their children, and this would be devastating for the parent, or, if they see their children as objects against whom they can vent their bad feelings, they lie to their children by insisting that the children have erred and must feel guilty.

Parents explain the world to their children. When they fail to do this truthfully, they multiply a thousandfold the difficulty of the task the children have of arriving at a picture of the world that is close to being true. Moreover, they can prevent their children even from trying to find the truth by telling them that to question what the parents say or what is said by a person in authority is a sin.

When Jenni Murray wrote her *Memoirs of a Not So Dutiful Daughter* she called it a love letter to her mother. I would call it an account of a girl's battle to survive as a person, despite the attacks made on her by her mother who wanted to control rather than understand her, and who saw her daughter enjoying the freedoms and opportunities she had wanted but had been denied. In writing her memoirs, Jenni faced the question of not just what would her family and friends think but the thousands of listeners to BBC Radio 4 *Woman's Hour* where she was the much-loved and admired presenter. Whenever I write about my family, I am conscious of what my clients and readers would think. If I expect them to be truthful about their family, I should be truthful about mine. However, amongst Jenni's listeners would be many who were still in thrall to the Fifth Commandment, 'Honour thy father and mother so that your days be long in the land.' Criticize your parents and you're dead.

Jenni solved her problem by telling her story plainly and truthfully, but blaming herself for being a difficult child. Her book tells the story of her life, but it is also the diary of a terrible year, when her parents died within six months of one another. The day her mother died Jenni was told that her breast cancer required a mastectomy. Jenni wrote of herself, 'I had the benefit of the women's movement and the chance to go to university, have a career and a family and I escaped from my mother's control, often neglecting her but never free of her influence or the guilt I felt at my selfishness.'[16]

No one who understood how children develop, and who also knows how hard it is for a woman who has to balance the demands of a job with those of a family would say that Jenni was selfish. So where did Jenni learn to feel guilty in situations where guilt was not the appropriate response? Where most of us learn it: at our mother's knee.

Jenni said of her mother that she could be 'the kindest and most thoughtful of women and, seconds later, the most difficult, demanding and strait-laced'.[17] Such behaviour in a mother creates in her child what psychologists call 'anxious attachment'. If the mother is consistently unpleasant to the child, the child develops tactics to protect herself, and her attachment to her mother is minimal. If the mother is consistently loving, the child sees her mother as a highly satisfactory fixture in her life and takes her for granted in the way she takes the air she breathes. But when the mother alternates unpredictably between being loving and being unkind, the child tries to hold on to the loving mother while protecting herself from the unkind mother. The child's anxious attention is focused on the mother as she tries to predict when she will be safe and when in danger. If the mother always explains her unloving behaviour as being the fault of her child, the child feels guilty, and through this the mother controls the child. The child fights for her freedom, and then feels guilty for upsetting her mother.

By telling her stories without comment, Jenni lets her readers make their own judgements. One story that I thought significant, and, judging from the detail with which she told the story, Jenni did too, concerned herself, aged four, using a word she had heard her father use, 'bloody'. She wrote,

My mother was a terrifying sight. She towered over me, glowering, took hold of my arm and dragged me into the kitchen. Pants were pulled down, buttocks smacked, tears flowed, and I was sent to sit on the bottom step.

'You can sit there thinking about how unladylike it is to have such a filthy mouth and how cross I am with you until I say it's all right for you to leave those stairs.' The punishment was harsh and could last a couple of hours . . . Generally I sobbed for a while, mustered a little anger and defiance at the injustice of it all and then became quiet and conciliatory; at which point I was allowed to join her.

Her mother, passing her on the stairs, ignored her, acting as if she was not there. Jenni crept upstairs where her mother was vacuuming. She wrote, 'Through the half-open bedroom door, but, I thought, completely out of sight as she had her back to me, I pulled the most horrible face I could imagine.' But her mother had seen her. She stormed out of the room:

> 'Number one,' her voice now at its most quiet and lethal, 'I do not recall giving you permission to move from those stairs. Number two. Do not imagine for one moment that you can do things behind my back that I don't see. I saw you pulling that revolting face, you rude girl. Don't you know that mummies can see every little thing their children do whether they're with them or not?' Another smack and back to the bottom of the stairs to ponder my misdemeanour.

Jenni wrote that it took her years to work out that her mother had seen Jenni's reflection in the bedroom mirror. She wrote, 'I lived for a very long time with the entirely erroneous supposition that she really did know what I was up to all the time. It's a chilling thought I've never quite been able to shake off.'[18]

I have met a large number of people who still believed that their mother knew what they were saying and doing. When I was seeing clients, I had an office that contained three comfortable chairs. I would sit facing my client and, as we talked, I would sense that there was another person in the room. This was my client's mother, invisible to me, but real to my client, and sitting in the third chair. The mother was there, not as a supportive friend, but as a critic who punished disobedient, ungrateful children who dared to talk about family secrets and, worse, criticize their mother! My clients had never forgotten how close they had come to being annihilated by the person who had taken up residence in their head. Whenever they glimpsed the truth of their life, they dare not utter it.

Parents can tell lies to their children, and the children, trusting their parents, take it to be the truth. A lie, once uttered to others or to oneself, or heard and believed, can have endless consequences because it breeds other lies. The person becomes entangled in a web of lies from which it is impossible to escape because the person is incapable of seeing them as lies, and takes them to be the truth. Such lies are often those that are handed down from one generation to the next.

Chapter Six

The Danger of Being Obedient

Every child is born into the world of the ideas held by the adults who claim him as their own. Some of these ideas are lies. Perhaps the most popular lie that adults tell their children is that the family's nationality, race, religion, or class makes them superior to all other people. Such a lie can comfort the child when he feels defeated. However, if the lie becomes part of the framework of how he sees himself and his world, his vision becomes distorted. This was the fate of most German children in the nineteenth century and early twentieth century, and explains in part why the majority of Germans welcomed and supported Hitler.

In the years that followed the Second World War there have been many wars and conflicts, and many versions of Hitler and his confederates whose names are unknown to most of us. These terrible events took place in countries far away – in Rwanda, Congo, Chechnya, Cambodia, Burma, Tibet – and there were few written records of what occurred and who was involved. Though a few guilty men have been brought to justice in Rwanda and Cambodia, we shall never have any history detailed enough to give us a clear idea why these terrible events occurred. The Court of International Justice in The Hague has tried some of the murderers from the Bosnian War, but many of the guilty were helped to escape, while many witnesses continue to protect themselves with the lie, 'It didn't happen.'

The Nazis kept records – lists of private possessions stolen from the Jews, timetables of trains to Treblinka – and there was a long tradition in Germany of keeping records of household expenditure, of keeping diaries, of writing and keeping letters. A great deal is known of how Germans thought and lived before and during those terrible years. Some of the guilty, like Albert Speer, Hitler's architect, wrote their self-justifying memoirs, and some, like Franz Stangl, Commandant of Treblinka, talked not just to those investigating them but to writers like Gitta Sereny, who wanted, as far as she was able, to uncover the truth about these men. She wrote, 'Untruth always matters, and not just because it is unnecessary to lie when so much truth is available. Every falsification, every error, every slick rewrite job is an advantage to the neo-Nazis.'[1] All these records give us a means of understanding why some people, who are living peacefully with one another as a family or neighbours, suddenly turn against one another, and commit the most terrible of crimes, and why some people like the neo-Nazis long for the return of a dictator.

Historians look for the events, customs, ideas, beliefs and prejudices that might have played a part in what led to the conflict. What they have difficulty in finding is why one individual tried to destroy his neighbours while another individual tried to save them. To discover this the historian would have to know a good deal about the life of each individual. In Rwanda such information is near impossible to gather. Not so in Germany, and so it is possible to take one individual, read what those who knew him said of him, and what he said of himself. Did this man lie, and, if so, why? What effect did his life have on members of his family? Studying one well-documented life could help us understand the lives of people whose personal history is less well-documented, but whose lies and truth-telling had and are still having important consequences.

Gebhard Himmler would probably have led a quiet life had not his younger brother, the middle of three, become a major player in the tragic farce that was Nazi Germany. Heinrich Himmler, Reichsführer SS, was responsible for the murder of millions of people during the Third Reich. When Gebhard testified at the Nuremberg trials, he defended Heinrich and tried to minimize what he had done. In the following years Gebhard was interviewed by several people who were writing biographies of Heinrich. Gebhard's great-niece and biographer Katrin Himmler said that Gebhard talked happily about the childhood he shared with Heinrich. He insisted that Heinrich 'had been a soft-hearted, sensitive man who had always maintained good personal contact with his brothers and had never forced any relative to join the SS'. He presented Heinrich as a 'selfless, self-sacrificing servant of the regime whose only fault had been not to realize in time that he had been serving the wrong man'. Gebhard claimed to have criticized Heinrich for this.[2]

Why did Gebhard lie? Was it out of loyalty to his brother? He could have been loyal to his brother and still told the truth. He could have said, 'My brother was a wonderful man and I supported him in everything he did. I will not betray him now.' Many people regard loyalty among family members as one of the greatest virtues. They could well have applauded Gebhard for the stance he took. However, even though no evidence was ever found that showed that Gebhard, though a member of the SS, had been actively involved in Heinrich's programme of mass murder, his truthful statement could have led to many years' imprisonment. So he gave a dollop of truth, namely, 'I am loyal to my brother', along with the lie, 'I was not involved in what he did.'

As things turned out, Gebhard spent three years in internment camps. His great-niece Katrin Himmler described how in the camps 'he kept coming across "old comrades"' who, like him, had been led astray by Hitler. Gebhard enjoyed drawing, so in the camps he sketched and wrote poems. After he was released, Gebhard found 'a modest post' and had his pension as a senior civil servant restored.[3]

All of us have told lies to get ourselves out of a difficult situation. When our lie proves to be successful, most of us try never to mention the situation in which we lied again. We do not want to draw attention to it in case other people's curiosity is aroused. Further inquiries could show us to be liars. Gebhard did not do this. Like many Germans in the post-war years, he saw no reason why he should not receive his pension, but he went further than that.

After his return home, Gebhard created family albums where photographs of Heinrich at important official functions took pride of place, along with photographs of Gebhard in uniform and displaying many medals. He wrote 'Reminiscences' for his children where he carefully separated his career from the Nazi system. He did not mention that he was a member of the Party and of the Waffen SS, nor did he mention that where he worked, the Central Office of Technology, was a Party organization.[4]

Gebhard's ability to lie to others and to himself seems never to have failed him. Why should it? It was a skill he had developed from his earliest days. His most damaging lie was the lie he told himself when he would have been three or four years old. This became the centre of the web of lies he wove around himself, until he became so enmeshed that he could no longer tell what was a lie and what the truth.

Gebhard and his brothers were born into a society that believed itself to be superior to all other societies. All nationalities believe this of themselves, but, while some people hold this belief as a private conceit, Germans were expected to have a devotion to the fatherland that matched, or surpassed, their devotion to God. Wibke Bruhns wrote of her grandfather, Kurt Klamroth, 'It was an honour and a duty to serve the fatherland, and the rules of Kurt's class were fear of God, manly courage and self-control.' Bruhns had access to her father's letters, and she wrote of him, 'He's incapable of thinking outside ideas of national greatness and the harm it has suffered' (following Germany's defeat in the First World War, and in the economic turmoil that followed). Her father, Hans Georg (his family called him HG) was born into a wealthy, upper-middle-class family. He was a young officer in the First World War, and joined the Nazi Party in 1933. Later he became an officer in the SS, and his life came to an end with him hanging on a meat hook in the prison of Plötzensee, a victim of Hitler's revenge after the bomb plot of 30 July 1944.[5]

The diaries and letters of the Klamroth family show that some of the ideas central to Nazi policy had long been part of the German way of thinking. During the First World War, those convinced of Germany's superiority regarded it as right that Germany should take over the territory to their east. This was long before Hitler made his plans for Lebensraum. Bruhns noted how often members of the Klamroth family disparaged the lower classes, 'the common herd'. They did business with the Jews, but had nothing to do with them socially. In her diary Bruhns' mother Else mentions events like Kristallnacht, on 9 November 1938, when Jewish shops and businesses were attacked and destroyed, but she never shows any sympathy for the Jews, or for the inmates of the concentration camps when after the war the existence of these camps could no longer be denied.

In the halcyon days before the First World War, the Klamroth clan spent their summer holidays on the North Sea island of Juist, where the children, girls as well as boys, were organized by Kurt to take part in war games. Bruhns wrote, 'They were actually playing war. The last one had been forty years before. It was short, relatively low in casualties, and victorious. None of the players of these games [had] experienced war as anything other than flag-waving parades on Sedan Day.'[6] No wonder these children later went off to war so willingly, and were killed or maimed in their millions. In the 1920s and 1930s the first years of the twentieth century were seen as the golden age, so those who remembered the war games of their childhood were likely not to see anything wrong with their children or grandchildren being required to become members of the Hitler Youth. Towards the end of the war, boys of thirteen or fourteen were amongst the troops defending Berlin against the Russian army, while girls were drafted into the aircraft batteries that were at the mercy of the waves of bombers that were pulverizing German cities. Why didn't these children rebel? Because they were obedient.

Modern-day parents can only dream of having children who are obedient and look up to their parents. German children were certainly obedient, but, before the revolution in childcare, children generally were obedient. Apart from those who lived in poverty and wore rags, in the 1930s children had to demonstrate their obedience by dressing the way the adults wanted them to dress. As a child, whenever I saw photographs of English children, the boys with their hair cut in what was called 'short back and sides', and the girls with their well-brushed hair tied with ribbons, standing in line or sitting at their desks and putting up their hands so respectfully to answer the teacher's questions, I despised them. I could not have put what I felt into words, as I can now, but what I was seeing, fearing, and, to defend myself from this fear, despising, was the surrendering of oneself to authority. At school and at home I aimed at a degree of obedience that would keep me out of trouble and no more. In doing this, I was selecting from all the ideas available in Australian society the idea that those in authority have to earn the respect of those over whom they have authority. The notion that a person in authority had to be respected simply because he was in authority was and still is a notion totally foreign to me. I had a wider range of ideas to choose from than HG Klamroth or the Himmler boys had. How lucky I was!

Bruhns noted that, from the family history kept so diligently by Kurt and then by HG, 'No one in this family rebels.'[7] When Kurt and his wife Gertrud write about their son, words like 'good', 'well-behaved', and 'obedient' appear frequently. 'Both parents repeatedly express the wish that their son may bring his parents and grandparents "much joy" – little thought is given to the question of whether he should derive some pleasure from his life.'[8] Children were expected to remain obedient to their parents well into their adulthood, if not forever. When Kurt as a young man visited London he was surprised and envious to find that in England sons were able to express opinions contrary to those of their father. When Albert Speer wrote his memoirs, he skimmed over his childhood. His parents were loving and kind: his childhood was happy. He willingly gave up his ambition to study mathematics and took up architecture, just as his father wanted.[9] Eight years after his memoirs were published, Gitta Sereny visited him in his 'patrician family property on the hill above the Heidelberg castle'. Speer told Sereny, 'I hate this house. It is a constant reminder of the miseries of my childhood.'[10] He could tell the truth about his parents only in private to someone he told himself he trusted. He knew Sereny was a writer, and that no writer can be trusted not to use anything they are told as copy. But, if she did repeat what he had told her in confidence, he was not to blame. Thus, he could punish his parents while appearing to be the good obedient son they had wanted him to be.

Such training in obedience stood a boy in good stead if he became a soldier. Bernd Freytag von Loringhoven was born in 1914 into an aristocratic family. In July 1944 he became aide-de-camp to Hitler, but was able to leave Hitler's bunker before the end came. When he was ninety-two he was persuaded by François d'Alançon, a chief reporter for *La Croix*, Paris, to turn the notes he had made in the bunker into a book.

Von Loringhoven witnessed the way Hitler's generals accepted Hitler's increasingly delusional orders without any expression of dissent. He wrote, 'The soldier's duty of unconditional obedience had its roots in the traditional relationship of the king and his officers . . . Reservatio mentalis (closing one's mind) made obedience easier.'[11]

After the failure of the bomb plot, Hitler took revenge, not merely on the plotters but on anyone who had any connection with them. This was why HG and his son-in-law Bernard Klamroth were arrested, tried in the People's Court, and killed.

Von Loringhoven was extremely fortunate that he did not suffer the same fate. His cousin Wessel Freytag Von Loringhoven was a member of the Abwehr, the intelligence service of the Wehrmacht. A group of officers in the Abwehr had long been interested in overthrowing the Nazi regime. In a conversation with his cousin, far from listening ears, Wessel expressed his dissatisfaction with the way the plotters had designed and carried out the plot. '"You know, Bernd, with these Germanic types of the Reich, you simply can't put together a plot," he said with that Baltic accent of his. Wessel had grown up in Russia and completed his secondary education in St Petersburg. He spoke Russian fluently, and he had a deep awareness and appreciation of that country's culture . . . And from Russian history he had derived a lesson, as to how to organise a plot with skill and discretion.'[12]

The first requirement of a plotter is to be disobedient, not just once or twice in a personal history of obedience, but with disobedience as a way of thinking. That does not mean that your plots will always be successful, just that your plots will be on the firm foundation, that it is right to disobey oppressive authority.

Children are not born obedient. Why obey orders when there is a wonderful world to be explored, and marvellous things to be done? How do parents make children be obedient? Terrify them. What is the easiest way of terrifying children? Beat them.

And this parents did. After all, the Bible says, 'He that spareth his rod hateth his son: but he that loveth him chasteneth him betimes.'[13] Bruhns wrote, 'I read an entry in Gertrud's rapid hand, that "days without spanking" are rare, and HG is two at the time. Around his sixth birthday she writes, "Unfortunately the temper tantrums are very frequent, and very often the rod must come and provide a reason." Smacking "so that you've got something to cry about!" only stopped in my children's generation, if it ever did.'[14] In describing the family home where she lived as a child during the war (Bruhns was born in 1938) she wrote, 'Into the rhododendron hedge on the side of the wall I disposed of the cod liver capsules I so detested, and which were so indispensable in the time of food shortages after the war. I got a terrible beating for it.'[15]

When in 1827 Thomas Arnold took over the headmastership of Rugby School he decided that the boys should not study science. He wrote, 'Surely the one thing needful for a Christian and an Englishman is to study Christian and moral and political philosophy.'[16] To create these English Christian men Dr Arnold instilled fear. Lytton Strachey said of him, 'As the Israelite of old knew that his almighty Lawgiver might at any moment thunder at him from the whirlwind, or appear before his very eyes, the visible embodiment of power or wrath, so the Rugby schoolboy walked in holy dread of some sudden manifestation of the sweeping gown, the majestic tone, the piercing glance, of Dr Arnold.' 'When Dr Arnold considered that a flogging was necessary, he administered it with gravity.' He called flogging 'personal correction', and was disgusted with the view that 'personal correction' was degrading to the boy. Only the boys of the lower parts of the school felt the benefits of 'personal correction', and 'with a double force. The Sixth Form were not only excused from chastisement; it was given the right to chastise. The younger children, scourged both by Dr Arnold and the elder children, were given every opportunity of acquiring the simplicity, sobriety, and humbleness of mind, which are the best ornaments of youth.'[17] When Lytton Strachey was writing about the hypocrisy of certain eminent Victorians, their descendants were obediently and willingly dying in Flanders fields.

The boys' parents did not object to this regime of fear and flogging. After all, they had been beating their children, just as they had been beaten. Theirs were among the voices that were raised in praise of Dr Arnold, making him famous as an educator whom aspiring headmasters did well to emulate. One such headmaster was Gebhard Himmler, father of the Himmler boys.

In 1922 Gebhard Himmler senior was promoted to the head-ship of the Wittelsbacher Gymnasium, a well-known and highly regarded school in Munich. In 1980 a memoir by a writer who had been one of Gebhard's students in 1927 and 1928 was published with the title *The Father of a Murderer*.[18] The father in question was Gebhard senior, and the writer was Alfred Andersch, one of the founders of Group 47, whose members included Heinrich Böll and Günter Grass. The book caused an enormous stir.

Katrin Himmler summarized the two sides of the debate as those who remembered Gebhard as 'an energetic person, highly cultured and intelligent, who commanded respect', and who had been 'equally feared, revered and admired by teachers and pupils alike' and those who remembered 'his overriding desire to get on in the world, one of those types who crawl to those above them and take it out on those below'.[19] Commendable though Gebhard's list of virtues might be, the word 'likeable' was not included. Moreover, his virtues are not inconsistent with his vices. Intelligent, energetic people can be very ambitious. Commanding respect, and being revered and admired do not exclude being feared. A hierarchical society, which Germany was, teaches children to fear those in authority, and, even in our supposedly classless society, there are many people who fear those in authority, for all that the person in authority might try to be as benign as possible. What Andersch describes in his memoir is a headmaster who is highly skilled in making people fear him, especially powerless people like children. According to Andersch's account, Gebhard did not administer a beating and that was the end of the matter. He did administer beatings and other punishments, but he also wanted to humiliate his victims. He did this with great skill, but he also knew how to disconcert them by suddenly treating them with warm friendli-ness, and thus creating in them what psychologists came to call 'anxious attachment'. Thus, in future years his victims would be able to say, 'I was beaten by my headmaster and it didn't do me any harm.'

Gebhard had not been born with the desire to humiliate and hurt people, but he had been born into a family that was near the bottom of the German hierarchy. His mother was the widow of a customs officer who seems from what accounts are available not to have been the kind of man a son could be proud of. Gebhard would have suffered considerably in his childhood, and for this we should pity him. However, suffering does not necessarily improve our character. As children, when we suffer at the hands of others, we comfort ourselves with fantasies of becoming wealthy and admired, and thus 'showing them', that is, humbling those who used their power against us. Such dreams can be the springboard for ambition, but they do not necessarily make us nice people.

Gebhard was an outstanding pupil. He gained entry to university where he studied classics. On graduating he became tutor to Prince Heinrich von Wittelsbach who was so impressed with him that he helped Gebhard obtain a permanent teaching post at a well-respected school. Once his position was secure, Gebhard married the daughter of a wealthy merchant. He named his first child Gebhard Ludwig, the second name being a mark of respect to the Bavarian crown prince, while his second child was named Heinrich Luitpold, after Prince Heinrich von Wittelsbach and Prince Regent Luitpold. Five years later, Katrin Himmler's grandfather, Ernst Herman, was born in Munich where the family now lived.

It was not until Katrin Himmler's father asked her to see if there were any files on his father Ernst in the Federal Archives that she began thinking about her grandfather who had died in unknown circumstances in the chaos in Berlin as the Russian army entered the city. In her mind, Katrin had always separated 'Heinrich the Terrible' from 'Ernst the unpolitical'. She had studied National Socialism and had been particularly interested in

97

how to distinguish active Nazis from those who knew what was going on, from those who profited from it, and from those who went along with it, but she had never applied this study to her own family. From the way Katrin described her way of thinking, this seemed to be an example of how, when we want to separate an awkward truth from another truth, we try to construct a wall separating each truth from the other. However, she soon discovered that her grandfather, far from being unpolitical, had been a Nazi who helped Heinrich in return for the help Heinrich had given him in his career. Their parents, Gebhard senior and his wife Anna were ardent Nazis and made the most of Heinrich's position.[20]

All this Katrin discovered later. There was little information in the file, and her father had no interest in pursuing the matter further. However, when Katrin did have an opportunity to talk to her father about some of the questions the file threw up, for the very first time she asked him what memories he had of his father. She was astonished at his vehement reaction: 'What do you imagine I think of a father I can only remember punishing and beating me?!'[21] Did punishing include being humiliated? As a father, Ernst was treating his son in the way his father had treated him. Gebhard senior beat his sons in the way he beat his students. Gebhard junior would refer to the beatings ironically. Receiving a beating was being 'liberally rewarded'.[22]

What does it feel like to be beaten? It hurts. A child might lie defiantly and claim the beating did not hurt, but it did. What did the child feel not only as the blows were raining down but afterwards? People who have been beaten often cannot remember because they have overlaid their truthful memory with so many lies – 'I was beaten as a child and it didn't do me any harm' – and so much guilt – 'My mother was a wonderful woman: she wanted the best for me' – that the only time a memory of the unmistakable, clear feeling of rage can come into clear consciousness is when it breaks free of all the murk that is holding it in the depth of the person's unconscious memory and bursts forth in seeming madness because it is not attached to any event that explains its presence. If the person does not recognize that the rage comes from injuries in childhood, he can turn the rage against other people, and claim that his victims deserved such punishment.

The best description of how the child first feels this rage comes from Edmund Gosse, and not in connection with some assault upon his bodily integrity but on his sense of being a person. It was when his mother was dying of cancer. He wrote, 'We had no cosy talk; often she was too weak to do more than pat my hand: her loud and almost constant cough terrified and harassed me. I felt, as I stood, awkwardly and shyly, at her high bed, that she was floating out of my reach, that all things, I know not what, were coming to an end . . . I could not understand it; I meditated on it long, long upon it all in my infantile darkness; and a great, blind anger against I knew not what awakened in my soul.'[23]

This great, blind anger never goes to sleep again. Once you discover that some person or power can wrench you from your safe little world and cause you much suffering, you also learn how primitive pride can come to your rescue with its anger that says, 'How dare this happen to me!' The more a child suffers, the stronger the anger grows. Some of us learn ways of keeping it in check, but many do not. Though many people would deny it, we are always looking for a situation where we can express this anger. If we are not consciously aware that this is what we are doing, we can do great injury to ourselves and to others.

Babies are born self-centred and amoral. The parents' task is to help their child develop a concern for others and a sense of right and wrong. This is a very difficult task. If the parents are too lenient, the child is likely to become too selfish and ill-disciplined to be an accepted member of society. If the parents are too strict, the child will be burdened with a self-punitive, implacable conscience. When parents use physical punishment as their chief and frequently used form of punishment, they can break the child's spirit, and, in doing so, turn the child's rage against himself. Alternatively, the child can identify with the powerful parent and try to become powerful and able to vent his rage against others.

A child needs to discover the hard truth that his family do not always hold him in the same high regard as he holds himself. It is rare for children to arrive at this understanding quietly and peacefully. Usually the circumstances are the more dramatic scenes in family life. Ridiculous as these scenes might be, if the parent does not turn them into high drama where the child feels utterly condemned and cast out, the child can come to see himself as not being entirely satisfactory, but he is capable of making the necessary improvements. This is the truth of the situation. No one is perfect, but we are all capable of improving ourselves.

Some parents like to play the Dr Arnold as Jehovah role, and terrify the child into believing the parent's lie that the child is intrinsically bad and must spend his life trying to be good. Physical punishment is not essential in persuading a child to create this lie. Just tell him that he is, in essence, bad, that God knows his every thought, and is likely to punish him for eternity. This lie, and the fear it generates, can so lodge itself inside the child that, even when the child in later life chooses a more benign form of religion, or no religion at all, in times of crisis all adult wisdom and reason can be swept aside and the person is again gripped by the terror of his childhood.

The domestic scenes with the parent as Jehovah usually involve the child being caught in a situation from which he cannot escape. Jenni Murray's story about her having to sit on the stairs was one such scene. When we cannot escape from a very unpleasant situation, we can create a kind of escape by re-defining the situation. At present, some of the people who have lost their jobs have re-defined themselves by, say, ceasing to think of themselves as bankers but, by undertaking some training, coming to think of themselves as teachers for whom jobs are available. Some people re-define the situation, perhaps by calling it a rat-race and dropping out of it. Small children, unable to leave a situation where their parent is punishing them, see the situation accurately as, 'I am being unjustly punished by my bad parent.' All little Jenni had done was to use a word that her father had used. Instead of explaining to Jenni why the use of the word could offend some people, her mother unjustly punished her. In such a situation, the truth is hard to bear, especially when the child sees that the injustice has been perpetrated by the person on whom she relies. So the child re-defines the situation, and in so doing creates a lie, 'I am bad and am being justly punished by my good parent.'

The word 'bad' here can range in meaning from 'not entirely acceptable' to incorrigibly and essentially wicked'. Which degree of badness the child chooses to apply to himself depends to a considerable degree on what support is available to the child in this crisis. Some parents bring the punishment scene quickly to an end with a cuddle and a reassurance that the child will be able to improve his behaviour. Sometimes another adult is available to comfort and reassure the child. However, if the parents collude in punishing the child, and no one else gives the child support, he has to deal with the aftermath himself. When his rage subsides, the feeling of desolation that comes over him can be so all-encompassing that he is likely to spend the rest of his life trying to avoid finding himself in that degree of desolation ever again. Much of what is taken as ordinary behaviour in our society is an attempt to avoid that feeling of total desolation. Thus some people fill every moment of their life with work or some kind of being busy, some people expend every effort to achieve power, wealth or 'celebrity' as fame is now called, while others find themselves driven to engage in serial love affairs or opportunist fucks. Such activities are denial of the truth, the original situation and the desolation that followed. They are, in fact, lies.

The original lie 'I am bad and am being justly punished by my good parent' preserves the parent as good, but the child pays the price of having to see himself as bad. He sees himself as deserving the punishment he was given, and goes on believing this for the rest of his life, unless he manages to summon up enough courage to look at his childhood with an adult eye and see the injustice he suffered at the hands of someone he once trusted. Many people do not attempt to summon up such courage. Instead they will say, 'I was beaten as a boy and it didn't do me any harm.' Just as physical punishment is mentioned in the Klamroth family history, so it is in accounts of interviews with the children of prominent Nazis. When the Israeli psychologist Dan Bar-On interviewed Peter, the son of one of the doctors who worked at Auschwitz, Peter said, 'I used to get spanked. I mean, I got spanked and deserved it. That was the only possible way to deal with me. When I think back, I would say that [my father] was very, well, I would use the word "humane".'[24]

This lie comes with a benefit. It allows the child to feel virtuous because he has recognized his wickedness, repented of it, and accepted his punishment. However, creating this lie does not mean that the child forgets what is true. In future, whenever the child is punished unjustly and cruelly by the parent, the truth threatens to break through into consciousness. The child who is repeatedly punished has to create another lie to keep the first one in place. This lie is, 'I am bad and am being justly punished by my good parent, and when I grow up I shall punish wicked people in the way that I was punished.' The child now feels justified in punishing those whom he is entitled, for reasons of his superior virtue, to punish. His life, whatever it turns out to be, will provide him with opportunities to do this.

Not all the children who are beaten respond in this way. It depends

102

on how the parent explains what he is doing when he punishes the child. My mother came from a family well practised in scenes of high drama. They specialized in sudden, noisy rage, leaving the room in a marked manner, not speaking, and sulking. They took themselves very seriously. No one dared to call their bluff. My mother had mastered her family's specialties, and used them to control her husband and children. If a person offended her, and it was so easy to do so, she would look at the offender with one of her bone-chilling, black looks. If the offender was not a member of the family, she would leave the room in a very marked manner and not return until the offender had left. If the offender was a member of her family, she would say enough to let the offender know that he was now in what my father called 'Ella's black books'. It was easier to get out of Purgatory than have your name removed from the list of people to whom she no longer spoke. When she left the room, the not speaking and the sulking would begin. Since I was her child, I was treated differently. If I offended her, she would slap me hard, and, if we were at home, the slaps could well turn into a beating. I learned to play my part in this drama with much loud crying. I remember one occasion when I was nine or ten, when I flung myself face-down on a couch, kicking my legs and crying for my father who was away. This was not a good move, because my mother began hitting me on my back and saying that she was going to kill me and then kill herself. All my life I feared her, but by then I was big enough to defend myself. This declaration enraged me. She could kill herself if she wanted to, but not me. Suddenly she left the room, slamming the door as she left. I bolted for my bedroom where I waited until I thought she might have moved into the next phase, not speaking. If she had gone to her bedroom the not speaking might have turned into sulking, and that could last for many weeks, but, if she had gone to the kitchen, all I had to do was not speak to her or do anything that might annoy her. Sooner or later she would speak to me, and, when she did, she would not mention what had happened. All I had to do was survive her attacks. She did not say, 'I was beating you for your own good.' She did not lay on my shoulders a huge burden of guilt. How lucky I was!

As Dr Arnold liked to make clear, he was not flogging the boys because he was taking his bad feelings out on them. He was applying personal correction for their own good. Gebhard senior beat his sons and his students for their own good. The Himmler parents demanded that their children live up to the parents' expectations, and the boys tried to do this. They were left in no doubt how they should behave. When Gebhard was twelve, his father went on a trip to Greece, from which he feared he might not return. He wrote a farewell letter to his wife, and to each of his sons. His letter to Gebhard, so Katrin wrote, testified to his love and respect for his son, but 'this, however, is immediately followed by exhortations and instructions . . . If his father did not return, Gebhard was to anticipate "his mother's every wish, gladden her heart with his *industry, devotion to duty, moral purity*, and, as eldest, quickly become a support to her, esp. in the upbringing of your brothers". But above all: "Become a hardworking, religious and *German*-minded man.' (The italics are Gebhard senior's.)[25] Being a German and German-minded meant not only possessing all the German virtues but giving unquestioned obedience to those in authority.

Gebhard senior paid very close attention to every aspect of his sons' lives. He monitored their progress at school and selected their friends, choosing those who were well behaved and would in some way advance the boys socially, thus facilitating the movement up the social hierarchy that the father wanted. His wife filled the role of the 'little woman' who ran her household according to her husband's wishes. The French psychoanalyst Boris Cyrulnik wrote, 'The overbearing structure of a close family or society that is too well organized makes a child feel safe. But, because it forces children to develop along lines laid down by

104

their parents or by society, it blocks their creativity, as the only thing they learn is how to do what they have been told to do.'[26]

Thus Gebhard was forbidden even to acknowledge to himself the truth that the punishments he received were excessive and unfair. He could not allow himself the stray thought that his father was not always the moral, unselfish man he presented himself as being. He certainly could not allow himself to discover, as Edmund Gosse had done, that his father was not always right. He had to hold fast to the lies, 'I am bad and am being justly punished by my good father', with its corollary, 'When I grow up, I shall punish bad people in the way my father punished me.' Had he been born thirty years earlier, during the peaceful years between the Franco-Prussian War and the First World War when the ideas prevalent in his society were not challenged by events, he might have had an unremarkable life. His need to maintain his standards might have made him occasionally anxious and irritable, but he would have not been markedly different from his contemporaries. He would have brought up his sons the way his father had brought him up, and they would have respected him in the way he respected his father. But he was not born in peaceful years, and events allowed him to express his rage against those he had been taught to despise, and in the framework of a structure, the Nazi Party, which demanded total obedience.

On the cover of Katrin Himmler's book is a photograph of the Himmler boys dressed in their Sunday best. When I look at this photograph, and at the photographs of those young men and women whose strong sense of obedience led them to become martyrs, I feel very sad. What a waste of all the creativity and enthusiasm they were born with, all snuffed out because the vast majority of us have always failed to understand that which we should know best, ourselves.

As a schoolboy, Gebhard had found a way of dealing with any conflict between the lies he regarded as the truth and any mani-festation of the truth as it actually was. He ignored it. He preferred

105

to focus on what was pretty and delightful in his life. In 1918, mid the devastation of the war, even when his battalion on the Western Front was reduced in the fighting to thirty men, he sketched churches, landscapes, villages and towns, all idyllic scenes. In the internment camp he drew idyllic pictures and wrote poems about how he and others were innocents led astray by Hitler. In his 'Reminiscences' he described his part in the invasion of Poland as 'the headlong advance' where he and his motorized unit 'pulled off some daredevil strokes'.[27] In all, he had a splendid time.

Many people, not wanting to be troubled by the conflict between the lies they hold as truths, and the truths that challenge these lies, like Gebhard, ignore the conflict, and construct an idyllic picture of themselves and their life. If by chance they should complete a happiness questionnaire as used by those psychologists who espouse Positive Psychology, they might well score within the very happy range. They have many friends, enjoy their work, are optimistic, and their life is meaningful. What such questionnaires do not reveal is whether those who share their life also share their sunny view. Do those who construct an idyllic picture do so by ignoring what is happening to the people around them, just as Gebhard, as he invaded Poland, did not let the starving Poles and the dead and dying Jews spoil his happiness?

We might lie in order to protect our sense of being a person, but the consequences of our lying can be such that it would have been better to tell the truth in the first place. But how can we be sure that what we take to be the truth is so?

Chapter Seven

Deciding What Is True

Imagine, if you will, a large container full of some indeterminate substance. It is composed of bits that are of no particular size, shape, or colour. The only way you can get hold of any of the substance is to use one of three ladles lying beside the container. One of the ladles is made of steel, another of bronze, and the third of fine china. You and your two companions each choose a ladle. One companion chooses the steel ladle, the other the bronze, leaving you the ladle of fine china. You each push your ladle into the substance, but what each of you gets is not the substance. On the steel ladle is a heap of diamonds, on the bronze a pile of marbles, while the fine china ladle is full of white peppermints.

This is not the beginning of a fairy tale but a metaphor to illustrate how we perceive the world. Reality is some indeterminate substance. We each impose our individual structures on it, thus transforming the indeterminate substance of reality into something that is meaningful to us. Your ladleful of peppermints might not be meaningful to your companions, but it is to you.

Thus it is that, if Rowan Williams, the Archbishop of Canterbury, and Richard Dawkins, now more famous as a militant atheist than as a scientist, go for a walk in Kew Gardens, Rowan Williams sees all around him the wonders of God's creation, while Richard Dawkins sees evidence of evolution. Each man is convinced that his is the right way of seeing the world.

If from the beginning these two men had agreed that it was inevitable that they would differ in how they see the world, which

107

is indeed the case, many of us would never have heard of either of them. They would never have begun their interminable argument about which is the more valuable, science or religion, with Dawkins calling religious ideas 'a virus' and Williams claiming that Dawkins does not understand Christianity. Such an argument is as futile and ignorant as an argument about which is better, a horse or a computer. However, futile public arguments can be an excellent way of selling your books, or letting people know how important you are.

A horse and a computer belong to different categories of things. They are not better or worse, just different. Science and religion belong to different categories of things. They are not better or worse, just different ways of thinking. Religion is about myths, fantasies and 'oughts': science is about what is. Religion requires faith in what seems improbable, science requires proof of what is provable. They are different ways of thinking about the world. All of us use both. When a person dies in mysterious circumstances, we use the ladle of science to help us determine whether the person died of natural causes or was murdered. We might then wonder why, in the whole scheme of things, this person died. To contemplate the possible answers to this question we use the ladle of myth, ethics and religion. Neither ladle can show us reality itself, but each gives us a different perspective on something we can glimpse only dimly but never bring clearly into view.

When scientists launch bitter attacks on the religious, and the religious are enraged by those who dare to criticize their beliefs, they have abandoned the ladles of science and religion, and both are using that large, extremely well-worn ladle, 'I am in danger: I must protect myself.' All they do is demonstrate how little they understand themselves.

I think I have taken the ladle metaphor as far as it can go. The word to use is category. We think in categories. There are categories used by all people everywhere, such as tools, language, the story, mathematics, science, art, music, and categories we learn, such as information technology or fashion. There are categories within categories, but all categories, big or small, have only one place to reside – in our heads. They do not exist in reality. Reality is seamless. However, we cannot live in seamless chaos. We have to divide it into chunks. What is important is that, first, we remember that these chunks are in our head and not out there, and, second, what the chunks are that we are using.

It is easy to forget that we see everything through the category of our own point of view, as the biologist Steven Rose showed in his thoughtful review of Kathleen Taylor's book *Cruelty: Human Evil and the Human Brain*. Taylor was looking at cruelty in terms of what she called 'otherization', 'a universal way of thinking that separates "us" from "them", and enables "us" to treat "them" as *Untermenschen*', that is, subhuman. Rose pointed out that otherization is a term derived from Edward Said's writings, but in pursuing her interest in genetics, developmental and evolutionary history, 'Taylor seems unaware of the ways in which her own universalising "we" turns out to be a well-educated, bien-pensant, white, British post-Christian, content in her writings to otherise Jews, Muslims, Catholics . . . Abstracting herself from her own analysis does impoverish it.'[1]

Abstracting themselves from what they report on is what many academics do. To say, 'I think . . .' or 'I feel . . .' would be subjective, but subjective is all we can be. Yet we do have a choice. We can wallow in our own subjectivity, or see further and discover how the world looks to other people.

We each divide reality in our own individual way. No matter how carefully we examine and select what we think is true, the best we can say is that this seems to me to be true. In telling the truth, we can only say what we know. We may be mistaken, and, even if we are not, what we know is limited by our own experience. We rely very much on what other people can tell us, but, whatever we are told, it is limited by ideas that are prevalent in our society. Certain ideas can be so prevalent that we never stop to question the truth of these ideas. Take, for instance, ideas about how children should be treated. The psychoanalyst Boris Cyrulnik wrote, 'It is difficult to observe a river when you are swimming in it; so long as violence was seen as a normal educational method, the idea of abuse was inconceivable.' He went on, 'Infanticide was for a long time seen as a form of social hygiene.'[2] In ancient Rome a father was allowed to decide what would happen to a child he did not want, and some infants were killed or abandoned. In the Middle Ages unwanted children were drowned, smothered, abandoned, or sold. In the nineteenth century, slavery was abolished in some countries but industry took its place. Such cruelty seemed normal. It was not until the 1970s that the idea of abuse became widespread. Some women, often with the encouragement of members of the Women's Movement, began to speak out about the sexual abuse they had suffered as children. Evidence of the correlation between sexual and physical abuse in childhood and mental disorder in adult life began to be accumulated by researchers, and this, slowly, changed society's ideas about how children should be treated. If you have grown up in a society which sees children as human beings that happen to be smaller than adults, you might be unaware that there are still many people who see children as inferior beings not yet ready to be admitted to the adult world, and therefore of no value.

You might think that psychiatrists would have noticed that many of their patients reported that as children they had been sexually or physically abused. They did not report this because, if a patient insisted on talking about such events, they refused to listen. Freud at first had listened, but when he realized that, if he reported what his patients had told him, cultured, wealthy Viennese society to which he wished to be accepted would reject him, he decided to change his theory of neurosis. His patients had been reporting the sexual fantasies they had about their parents. Freud was greatly attached to his theories, just as anyone who had worked hard to qualify as a member of a profession can become so attached to the theories of that profession that they believe that they are unquestionably true. Thus many professionals learn a particular theory, stick to it for the rest of their life and deny all evidence against the theory. Paul Krugman ended his book *The Return of Depression Economics* with, 'Some people say that our economic problems are structural, with no quick cure available; but I believe that the only important obstacles to world prosperity are the obsolete doctrines that clutter the minds of men.'[3] Our financial future depends on whether new ideas about how banks should function are accepted, or whether the doctrine of the free market and lightly regulated banking should continue to prevail.

After I arrived in England in 1968 I worked for many years with psychiatrists who in their training had been taught a theory about madness that had changed little since the nineteenth century when the German psychiatrist Kraepelin had described what he called the mental illnesses of depression and dementia praecox, later called schizophrenia. He said that these illnesses had as yet unknown physical causes and were incurable. The task of the psychiatrist was to diagnose the illness and then manage it with certain drugs and electroconvulsive therapy. All that was needed to diagnose a patient was to ask certain questions, and these questions should elicit from the patient evidence of certain symptoms. Any further discussion with the patient was unnecessary. It was inconceivable to them that their theory was wrong. As I had little to do other than listen to the patients I soon accumulated considerable evidence that this theory was indeed wrong. There was no doubt that these people were suffering immense mental distress, but this distress arose from how they had interpreted the terrible things that had happened to them. The psychiatrists did not wish to hear any of this. Years passed

111

without a discovery of a physical cause for these mental illnesses, but, like the faithful who daily expect the return of the Messiah, the psychiatrists believed that the cause would be discovered. These psychiatrists were using the idea of a simple linear cause, while those of us who criticized their theory were developing an understanding of a complex network of causes that leads to severe mental distress.

Cause is an important category we all use. We find it hard to think of an event just happening without there being something that caused that event. The notion of a random or chance event whose cause, if there was a cause, is unknown, creates so much uncertainty that we will accept the most nonsensical notion of a cause. There are poltergeists or spirits, or the force of the Just World that ensures that good people are rewarded and bad people punished. We can understand linear cause, but chaos is far too complicated. We could argue that, if Gebhard senior had had parents who were wealthy, kind, loving and never punitive, he would have been unfailingly nice to his sons, and they would not have had within them such rage that becoming a Nazi appealed to them. However, that line of reasoning ignores the effect of the dominant ideas in Germany, and the consequences of the Treaty of Versailles on the German economy, or the degree to which Germans became fascinated by Hitler, and so on. To understand why we do what we do we need to be able to think about cause in terms of a network of causes that includes what goes on inside a person as well as what goes on around him. There are situations where a simple linear cause is an adequate explanation, and situations where it is not. The answer, 'I overslept', can be an adequately truthful answer to the question, 'Why were you late this morning?', but it is not to the question, 'Why are you late every morning?' Much more needs to be taken into account.

Whenever we encounter something new, we look for something this new thing is like, and then we can examine what is new about this thing. When mobile phones arrived, we first saw that they were like the phones we were used to, and then we saw what was new – the mobile was not attached to anything – and with this discovery we could see that we could use the mobile in ways that we could not use landline phones. Most of us would agree that what I have just said about mobile phones is true. However, sometimes we see a similarity that arises, not from what actually exists, but from our own individual way of seeing certain things. In his book about his work with prisoners in Guantanamo the lawyer Clive Stafford Smith told how a journalist, David Rose, had noticed the unfavourable attitude that certain members of the medical personnel had towards the prisoners. He described how one young man was chained to a bed and was being force-fed through a tube inserted into a nostril. This is such a dangerous and painful way of treating a prisoner on hunger strike that in many jails it is forbidden. However, the doctor in charge of this prisoner, Dr Louis Louk, a naval surgeon from Florida, explained to Rose, 'He's refused to eat 148 consecutive meals. In my opinion, he's a spoiled brat, like a small child who stomps his feet when he doesn't get his own way.'[4]

Dr Louk used a simile, whereas the Nazi doctor Fritz Klein used a metaphor when he answered Ella Lingens-Reiner, a physician and survivor of the concentration camps, when she asked him how he reconciled the incinerators in the camp with his Hippocratic oath. He replied, 'Of course I am a doctor and I want to preserve life. And out of respect for human life, I would remove a gangrenous appendix from a diseased body. The Jew is the gangrenous appendix in the body of mankind.'[5]

Both Dr Louk and Dr Klein would say that they were using a simile or a metaphor to illustrate the truth of what they say, but each figure of speech here is based on the lie, 'I am superior to other people.'

When the Obama administration took over from the Bush administration, nothing changed in the fighting that was going on in Iraq and Afghanistan, while the search for al-Qaeda continued. The situation had not changed but the words used for talking about it did. The new administration sent an email to senior Pentagon staff, 'This administration prefers to avoid using the term the Long War or Global War on Terror (GWOT).' The term they were to use was 'overseas contingency operations'. This seems to be one of those phrases used by government officials when they do not want to commit themselves to anything, but it does sound much less worrying than War on Terror.[6]

Telling the truth requires a very careful choice of words. Wily politicians and public relations people often use what the BBC presenter John Humphrys called 'Words of Mass Deception', thus echoing those words aimed at deceiving those who might oppose the War on Terror, 'Weapons of Mass Destruction'.[7] Words of Mass Deception might begin their life as a popular shared joke, but then are used by individuals to hide the truth from themselves.

During the later part of the Second World War vast quantities of supplies were being moved from place to place as the Allies slowly recaptured the territories that had been invaded. The Allies were said to be liberating Europe and the Far East. At the same time the people who had access to the supplies were often busy, as it was said, 'liberating' some of them. After years of rationing and austerity, the supplies of 'liberated' goods were greatly welcomed by service people and civilians alike. Being given a pair of nylon stockings or a bar of chocolate was a great thrill, but the truth was, these things had been stolen. No one used that word because no one wanted to think of themselves as being a thief or a receiver of stolen goods.

In situations where terrible things happen, truthful words disappear. The writer Kevin Myers, in his account of the Troubles in Northern Ireland, told how in the summer of 1972, a particularly terrible year, the language of Belfast changed. ' "Dry your eyes" became the standard sneer – in other words, feel no pain, mercy or remorse. To execute someone at point-blank range was to "nut" him. The dead were merely called tatey-bread, and the verb "to romper" entered our vocabulary. This was a satanically mordant wordplay on a BBC children's programme called *Romper Room*: but in the loyalist parlance, a rompering was a truly terrible beating that was given to a man, usually a Catholic, before he was murdered.'[8]

In the first Gulf War we discovered that troops who were killed by their own side did not die because their comrades were careless, stupid, lazy or incompetent. They died in 'friendly fire'. At Guantanamo attempted suicide was 'manipulative self-injurious behaviour', and torture 'advanced interrogation techniques'. These lying words are so grotesque that perhaps the only people who are taken in by them are those who use them. However, lying words are used in great abundance in the professions. Because professionals are supposed to be experts, non-professionals assume that the words used by professionals must be truthful, when in fact professionals can use them to deceive. Often the professionals themselves do not realize that they are doing this. To them they are using the language of their profession, and, since the theories they have learnt must be true, so the words they use must be true.

To become a member of a profession you have to pass qualifying examinations where you are tested on your knowledge of the theory, practice, and language of the profession. Completing this can take many years and a great deal of hard work. We all hate that feeling of having wasted our time, and so, once they are qualified, many professionals are very reluctant to let themselves see when they use their professional language to deceive. Amongst themselves, they argue the finer points of theory or the value of a particular piece of research, but they cannot bear to allow themselves to see the untruths in what they do. Thus, they deceive others, and they deceive themselves.

The language we use in ordinary life is remarkably well adapted to talking about what we do. After all, we have been using it to do this for thousands of years. As our knowledge about the world has increased, occasionally we have had to create words so we can speak about something new. Nuclear physicists who have discovered things the like of which most of us will never comprehend have had to invent a great many words. Medical science has required the invention of new words. However, ordinary language is well adapted to talking about people. Law, education, psychiatry, psychology, sociology, and economics are all about people and what they do. Why should they need a special language?

When nuclear physicists needed to invent words, they chose ordinary words like string and black holes. Some of the words they chose tended to be whimsical, like quarks, charm, gluons and the elusive Higgs boson. The words used in law, education, psychiatry, psychology, sociology and economics are not ordinary or whimsical at all. They are usually words of more than one syllable, and, even when a word seems to be an ordinary word, its meaning can be different. Take the word 'leverage'. It can mean the action of a lever, or a mechanical advantage given by using a lever, or, metaphorically, having an advantage over other people. Describing how the word is used in the financial world, Gillian Tett said that, 'it refers to the process of using investment techniques to magnify the direction or force of a market trend'. One way of doing this is to borrow money. In recent years, 'borrowing itself has often come to be called "leverage"'. In the derivatives market investors can be markedly affected by changes in prices, and this too can be referred to as 'leverage'. Tett explained, 'Using leverage in the derivatives world is the financial equivalent of a property developer who buys ten houses instead of five; owning more properties will leave that developer more exposed to losses and gains if house prices rise or fall, particularly if the properties are financed with debt.'[9] 'Leverage' in the financial world is a Humpty Dumpty word: 'When I use a word it means just what I choose it to mean – neither more nor less.'[10]

The reason for this fiddling with words (as in 'fiddling the books') lies in how we define who is in my group and who is outside. Very few of us feel that we are well informed about physics. Hence physicists do not have to worry about being overrun by people claiming to know as much about physics as they do. Whereas, the subject matter of law, education, psychiatry, psychology, sociology and economics is something we all know about. How can these professionals protect themselves from being overrun by the hoi polloi, the non-professionals? By creating a language that only they can understand. They can then use their language to imply that they are privy to matters that are incomprehensible to non-professionals, and that nothing that a non-professional knows overlaps in any way with what the professionals know.

On the opening page of William D. Cohan's book about the fall of the investment bank Bear Stearns in 2008, Bennet Sedacca, president of the investment management company Atlantic Advisors, is quoted as saying what a firm in Bear Stearns' position is supposed to do. 'You're supposed to cut your dividends, you're supposed to raise equity, and you're supposed to shrink your balance sheet.'[11] Sedacca's statement is true, but, unless you are familiar with the language that economists and financiers use, you would not be able to tell. Yet, if it were in ordinary language, not only would you know it was true, but that Sedacca's advice was what you would give a friend who had lost his job. Instead of telling him, 'cut your dividends' you would say, 'Stop giving money to your layabout brother, even though he is your best friend.' Instead of 'raise equity', you would say, 'Do something that earns you money.' 'Shrink your balance sheet' would be, 'Pay off your credit card and then cut it up, collect all the stuff in your home that you never use and sell it on eBay.'

Bear Stearns did not take Sedacca's advice. Instead, they borrowed even more money, so much that the size of their debts far outstripped their assets. Say that in ordinary language, and everyone can see how stupid the men in charge of Bear Stearns were.

The professional language used by psychologists serves the same purpose as the language the bankers used – to exclude and to deceive.

I have found that many of my psychologist colleagues are keenly interested in new words, and even more keen to use old words in new ways. Many of these words come from the public relations and advertising industries. The language used by members of these two industries is not always tied to the truth, and, as often as not, old words are used in new ways in order to deceive the public. Surely, psychologists would be aware of this?

Psychologists who wish to give the impression that they are knowledgeable and important are never given a task. They are tasked with doing something. Why change the noun 'task' into a verb 'tasked'? These psychologists never give anything to anyone. They gift it. The first time I heard the noun 'gift' being used as a verb was in connection with a will. At first I thought that 'gifted' must have had some legal significance. Fortunately, I have reached an age where I no longer need to pretend that I know everything, and so I asked what 'gifted' meant. The psychologist who had used the word had the grace to look shamefaced. He knew that he should have said, 'given'.

Many psychologists and sociologists seem to be unaware that the language they use is unnecessary and deceitful. Kathleen Taylor, whom I quoted earlier, used the verb 'otherize'. I do not know how long sociologists have been using this word, but it certainly is unnecessary. It does take more words to say that we often exclude and denigrate those people whom we do not want in our group, but these words spell out clearly and accurately what we do, while 'otherize' hides what we do. It might act as a kind of shorthand for those who know what it means, but it can become like all those abstract nouns beloved by those who want to deceive.

At school you would have learnt that there are three kinds of nouns – common nouns that name things, proper nouns that are the names of special people and things, and always begin with a capital letter, and abstract nouns that are ideas that have been abstracted from real situations. Thus, we can observe in the slums of, say, Nairobi that there are many poor people. From this observation, we can abstract the idea of poverty.

Poverty does not exist. It is an idea in our heads. When you were wandering Nairobi you would not see lumps of poverty lying around or hovering above people's heads. All you would see were poor people (unless you felt it was indelicate to call people poor, in which case you would refer to them as 'financially disadvantaged').

Psychologists love abstract nouns. Their books and learned papers are full of abstract nouns. To become a psychologist you have to learn how to talk and think in abstract nouns. You might come to believe that these abstract nouns actually exist in reality, and then you can waste years of your life trying to measure intelligence or creativity, when the only material you have at hand to study are people behaving intelligently or creatively.

Psychologists might argue that abstract nouns like intelligence and creativity have within them the concept of a person. However, these words do not actually draw our attention to people or anything real. Rather, they have been cut adrift from reality. They are in danger of becoming weasel words, words that have had all meaning drained out of them the way that a weasel sucks an egg and leaves only the shell. Don Watson wrote, 'Weasel words are the words of the powerful, the treacherous and the unfaithful, spies, assassins and thieves. Bureaucrats and ideologues love them. Tyrants cannot do without them.'[12] In the House of Lords in March 2009, the Liberal Democrat peer, Lord Smith of Clifton, criticized phrases such as 'extraordinary rendition' and 'quantitative easing', pointing out that there was 'an increasing reliance of ministers on weasel words and euphemisms to obfuscate reality'. He was answered by Lord Davies of Oldham, speaking for the government, who said, 'Fresh phrases come into use and "quantitative easing" is a very clear expression of what is being developed in terms of additional resources for the economy.'[13]

Lord Davies was speaking at a time when most people were trying to save what money they had because the future was uncertain. However, the government was trying to persuade people to start spending by 'quantitative easing', that is, giving them money to spend. The government did not actually print money, though the Australian Federal Government did print its equivalent – the substantial cheques that were sent to all but well-off Australians. The British government reduced the amount of Value Added Tax, which left people with more money to spend. Lord Davies, speaking independently and truthfully, could have added, 'The world economy runs on spending, consuming and debt. This mightn't be the best way of organizing the economy, but it's the only way we know, and none of us is brave enough to try something new.'

The language used by politicians and professionals enables them to hide the truth when they believe it is not in their interest to reveal it. Some of my psychologist colleagues use their professional language in discussing their work because using ordinary language would reveal how trivial it is. Many psychologists do research that is scientifically respectable but avoids acknowledging the irresolvable dilemmas and inevitable misery of human life. Many of the psychologists who write for the general public seem to assume that the general public are incapable of understanding anything complex, and will fall apart if presented with any kind of unhappiness for which there is no cure. Bereaved people are assured that they will find 'closure', after which they will 'get on with their life'. As every parent whose child has died knows, there are some losses for which there can be no closure and no kind of amelioration. There is no 'getting on with our life'. We have to live with that sadness as best we can for the rest of our life.

There are some psychologists who face the truth and write about it in a way that we can all understand. Neuropsychology and psychoanalysis are two very different and complex ways of trying to understand why we behave as we do, and each has its own professional language. The neuropsychologist Chris Frith and the psychoanalyst Boris Cyrulnik are able to write about what they have discovered very simply and clearly. Disparate though their approaches might be, if you read Frith's *Making Up the Mind* and Cyrulnik's *Resilience* you will discover that, even though neither writer mentions the other, each book illuminates the other. Frith tells his truth in such a witty and beguiling way that we might not at first realize what a terrible truth it is, that we have no certainty about who we are and where we are and what we are experiencing. We live our life *as if* what we perceive is real, while knowing (or perhaps refusing to admit we know) that our life is real in a way we cannot perceive. That is, our existence is real – we are part of everything that exists – but we perceive our existence *as if* it is real. We try not to lose our nerve, though often we do some unwise things in order not to lose our nerve. Frith keeps reassuring his readers that they can achieve their aim, as evidenced by the fact that they do this every day. Cyrulnik sees his readers as being capable of bearing his truth, and learning from it. Yes, we can be resilient, but not without cost.

Categories of Truth

The touchstone of truth is real, lived experience. We can ask ourselves, 'What is it that I am experiencing?' 'What is it that I am seeing, hearing, touching, smelling, in the here and now?' We are aware that we are living in the present moment, and taking account of the interaction between ourselves and the world around us.

We can ask ourselves, 'What am I feeling?' We can be aware that we are feeling something. We turn our attention inward. Perhaps we are angry, or frightened, or happy. If we are truthful with ourselves, we can be very precise in knowing what we are feeling, but, if you believe, say, that you ought not to be angry, you can lie to yourself and call your feeling of anger fear.

We can ask ourselves, 'What is it that I know?' This is a more difficult question to answer than the questions about what we perceive or feel, because it takes us back to the category of religion, myth and ethics, and the category of science. We can speak the truth in each category, but they are different kinds of truths.

Religion, myth and ethics contain the multitude of ideas that we have created over thousands of years about what we might call the whole scheme of things, the place of human beings within that scheme, and how we ought to behave. We can say, 'This is how it seems to me', and speak the truth, but it is our own individual truth. It is true for me, but not necessarily true for you. Your experiences have been different from mine. When we use the category of religion, myth and ethics, much of what forms our truth we have taken on trust. We believe what certain people have told us, and disbelieve others. We see as being true matters for which there can never be any proof. For instance, I believe that we are born with the capacity to live peacefully and wisely with one another. Evidence supporting this belief is scant, and the evidence against it is abundant, but, that is what I believe. Some people might say they share my belief, but, if we explored the implications of our beliefs, big differences in our beliefs would emerge. Religious communities always claim that members of that community share the same beliefs, but, if that were the case, the history of religion would not reveal endless schisms and bitter arguments, often fought out brutally and without reconciliation and forgiveness, that arise from different interpretations of the ideas to do with religion.

The knowledge that we are puny beings in a vast world over which we have little control can be too much for us to bear. Perhaps when we were infants we were able to take for granted that we were being watched over, and so we could play like the fox cubs tumbling on my lawn, never needing to check that their mother was there, watching over them. We never forget this feeling of security, and, once it has vanished, in moments of weakness, we long for its return. We want to be looked after, protected and advised what to do. We long for someone else to take responsibility for us, yet we soon learn how limited the power of our parents is. To comfort and inspire us, we imagine beings who are like our parents and other people we know and admire, but much more powerful and farseeing. We weave stories about these beings or gods, using the knowledge and wisdom we have acquired from our own experiences, and pass this on to our children by telling them these stories. We see events in our world as being influenced by our gods. When our life, as lives do, has its ups and downs, our beliefs about our gods can comfort and support us. However, when there are events that suggest that our gods have not answered our prayers, and that they can be capricious or forgetful or unjustly punitive, we might doubt the truthfulness of our religion and its myths. This leaves us standing alone facing the unknowable. We might cling to one another, but, ultimately, with our own individual vision of our situation, we have to face the unknowable alone, and take responsibility for ourselves.

This is the greatest challenge to our sense of being a person. Many people face this challenge and learn how to live with the unknowable with all its uncertainty. If we are able to live with the unknowable, we are able to accept the uncertainty that brings us an infinite number of possibilities. We are not imprisoned by absolutes. We are free.

Many people cannot find the courage necessary to live in an unknowable, uncertain world. Some people dare not even try because they believe what they have been told, that their gods will punish them if they doubt or question. The primal fear of falling apart as a person and disappearing drives them back to the myths about some transcendental power. Just as the child who is being unjustly punished by his parent has to try to strengthen his denial of this truth, so those who want to see their myths and fantasies about their gods as being true have to try to strengthen their belief by claiming that what they believe is absolutely true. Moreover, they will punish anyone who denies this absolute truth.

'Death to the infidel!' is with us still. In most of Christendom infidels are no longer burnt at the stake, but, as I discovered when my book *What Should I Believe?* was published, the cold ferocity of the anger directed at me by those who present themselves as the well-mannered godly astounded me.[14] Over the years I had no doubt that I had angered many psychiatrists by criticizing their theory and practice. They might have discussed together the possibility of getting me deported back to Australia, but they did not try to effect this. When talking to me, they were unfailingly polite, and were often helpful. However, they were not attached to their theory and practice by fear, need and denial as were the godly attached to their religious beliefs. They were attached to their theory by habit and laziness. Over the years, their theory makers did modify their theory. They dropped the words 'chemical imbalance', but did not broadcast the fact that they had, not even to the members of their profession. As a result, many psychiatrists still use this phrase when talking about the cause of depression.

Unlike religious beliefs, scientific beliefs can be shared because there is evidence to be found in the outside world to support them. There is fairly good evidence that the sun will rise each morning. We have our different connotations attached to the idea that the sun will rise each morning, but we all share the idea that it will rise because we have evidence that it does. We all have and use scientific beliefs. If, say, you are charged with a crime, you can state your truth in terms of scientific evidence, 'I was outside this country when this crime was committed', and produce your stamped passport to prove this.

However, scientific truths can be stated only as a probability. The jury, in deciding whether you were guilty or innocent, would have to take into account the possibility that you might have an identical twin who was using your passport when you committed the crime. When a scientist wants to prove a scientific truth, he can test only a small sample of what he wants to study. If I wanted to prove absolutely that the buses on the No. 4 and No. 19 routes that go past my home always travel in pairs, so that, if I miss the No. 4, the No. 19 will be so close behind that I will miss it too, I would need to note every bus that went by. This would be an impossibly onerous task so, rather than attempt this, I resort to noting, say, two instances of these buses travelling in pairs, and then feel that this is a large enough sample for me to complain about the buses to my fellow passengers. Probability is a subjective matter.

However, in the scientific world there are arguments that have all the hallmarks of a religious war. People might not be murdered, but reputations can be ruined and prestigious jobs and research grants lost. What is going on here has nothing to do with science. When a scientist builds his sense of being a person on the theory he is investigating, much in the way that a religious person builds his sense of being a person on his religious beliefs, evidence that could show that his theory is wrong

125

can result in the scientist believing that his sense of being a person is about to be annihilated. To prevent this the scientist will fight as ferociously as the godly do.

Truth can cease to be important when the sense of being a person is at stake.

Chapter Eight

How Important Is the Truth to You?

To find the truth we need to be sceptical.

When working out what seems to be true for us in terms of religion, myth and ethics, we need to question what we have been told by those in authority. In recent years, many Christians have rejected the once popular idea that the Christian God was a fearsome, jealous, punitive God and have turned instead to the idea that their God was kind, loving and benevolent. Similarly, at the risk of being called unpatriotic, many people have found that they can be fond of their country without having to accept the myth that their particular country is the best in the world. All it needed was a change in the law and the stroke of a psychiatrist's pen to change homosexuals from being mad and bad to being no madder or badder than the rest of us. Homosexuality ceased to be a mental disorder when it was removed from the psychiatrists' bible, the *Diagnostic and Statistical Manual*. However, there are still many people who regard homosexuals as being bad.

Sometimes we think we believe something when in fact we do not. We need to question ourselves by asking what it is we take to be true. We should ask, 'Is that really what I believe?' Some people never question the religious beliefs and the myths of their own society because to question is to undermine their sense of security and certainty. Others might not question because they fear discovering the truth, which is that they do not share the beliefs of those people with whom they wish to belong. I have been impressed by the number of people I know, all of them parents, who, having never shown any interest in religion, suddenly discover a faith in the Anglican God who is responsible for a local primary school that has a reputation for being the best in the district.

The only way to arrive at scientific truths is to be sceptical. Unpleasant though it often might be, what is actually going on is what we have to examine. When others tell us that this or that is true, we have to ask, 'What is your evidence for that?'

In an article in the *Skeptical Intelligencer* Nikos Petousis, Greek Honorary Consul in New Zealand, set out clearly what being sceptical is. He wrote, 'In the Greek language, the noun "skepsis" means deep and critical thought, reflection, contemplation, debating with oneself, activities which occupy those with some intelligence. It is natural for human beings to be curious and to learn. It is ignorance and superstition which stifles this innate tendency.' Sceptical people must have always existed but, if any of these became powerful, they must have kept this to themselves. Leaders, then and now, need to act as if they know what is true. In early civilizations, only special people – the religious or royal elite – could possess knowledge. Some of this knowledge was scientific, and some was magical, in particular, how to influence the gods. These were the only people to receive an education. This really has not changed a great deal over thousands of years. Even in countries considered to be enlightened, people with little money are given a less than adequate education, and what they do get is usually aimed at making them useful rather than enabling them to think clearly and critically. If you are a working-class girl or boy, no matter how hard you study and what excellent exam results you obtain, you cannot take for granted that you will be given a place at Oxford or Cambridge University.

The Greek city states in the seventh century BCE excluded most women and all the slaves from education, but the acquisition of knowledge was not restricted to the religious or royal elite. Moreover, sceptical inquiry was not prohibited. Such a society produced the philosopher who is regarded as being the first scientist, Thales, who searched for knowledge for its own sake. Other scientists followed, the most famous being Archimedes. The knowledge and critical thought produced by the ancient Greeks and those who followed in their footsteps perhaps justifies our calling ourselves 'homo sapiens'. However, those who strove to destroy this knowledge and critical thought showed that we do not merit this title. Christianity became the official religion of the Roman Empire, and, for the first time in their history, Greek subjects were required to bow before the priests. They had to learn about sin and everlasting punishment in hell. The philosophical inquiry that had been such an important part of their inheritance became heresy and was punished. Petousis wrote, 'Subsequent emperors enacted laws which resulted in the destruction of anything that stood for freedom of thought and expression. Theodosius, for instance, decreed that books should be burnt, the Olympic Games should cease to exist, and the academy of Athens and the theatre should close, and he ordered the destruction of anything which stood before in the Hellenic world.' How like the Taliban these Christian men were!

In this ancient world, one great treasure was the library in Alexandria. When the bishop Theophilus burned down the library of Alexandria, Theodosius sanctioned his action. 'Thus ended', wrote Petousis, 'a period of burgeoning of human inquiry and achievement initiated by the Ionian inquiring mind. All that had been built up and developed during those productive years was destroyed, defaced or taken over by the Christian Church. The flowering of the Ionian mind was crushed, trampled and engulfed by the Church, causing the gradual decline into barbarism and the Dark Ages.'[1]

That was not the end of it. 'The Catholic Inquisition insisted that there could be only one belief and spent 600 years (from the thirteenth to the nineteenth century) using fire and sword to destroy all trace of those who did not think along the same lines.'[2] The men who propagated Catholicism, like the men who propagated all the other religions, claimed to be in possession of the absolute truth. The existence of so many absolute truths simply demonstrates how each of us sees the world in our own individual way.

As individuals we might hold certain ideas for many years and never change our mind. For each of us, many of our ideas are reliable. We do not change our mind about them. Being reliable does not prove that these ideas are true. In scientific terms, for any statement to be true, it has to be both reliable and valid. That is, a belief is reliable if the person who holds it does not proclaim it true one day and not true the next. For a belief to be valid its degree of truth has to be verified, that is, it has to relate to something outside of itself. As I write, a nasty form of flu, swine flu, is in the news. Scientists have demonstrated that this form of flu is new because the virus that causes this flu differs from the different viruses that cause other forms of flu. The existence of this virus is outside the statement, 'This is a new form of flu.'

In contrast, the *Diagnostic and Statistical Manual* is a reliable document because the committees of psychiatrists agreed on what disorders should be included. However, apart from where it deals with demonstrable brain injury, the DSM is not a valid document. None of the mental disorders included in the DSM has been shown to have a demonstrable physical cause. Psychiatrists might talk about 'chemical imbalance in the brain' and genes that cause depression or schizophrenia, but there is no scientific evidence to support these ideas. The DSM is a collection of opinions. When the committees of psychiatrists change their opinions, a mental disorder might be removed from the DSM and some new one included. Different groups of interested people sponsor a new disorder and lobby for it to be included in a forthcoming revision of the DSM. For instance, in 1985, an American psychologist, Dr Richard Gardner, who had specialized in litigation involving parents and children, coined the term Parental Alienation Syndrome (PAS) to refer to the way some of the children of divorcing parents seem to show a preference to stay with one parent rather than the other. The preferred parent is deemed by the rejected parent to be influencing the child in making his choice. Some of the people who believe in the existence of this disorder have been lobbying the psychiatrists who are responsible for the production of the next revision of the DSM to include PAS in the DSM IV. Parents who battle over the children caught in the parents' divorce always cause their children distress, and children who are distressed often do not behave well, but to say that the children have a mental disorder is monstrously unfair to the children. As no virus or brain lesion can be shown to cause PAS, whether it will be included in the DSM IV depends on the opinions of the men and women who are deciding what will go in the new volume. Let us hope that none of them has gone through an acrimonious divorce that left them feeling bitter and vengeful, and that all of them really care about children.

Believing in the DSM is much the same as believing in, say, the doctrines of the Presbyterian Church. Both sets of doctrines are reliable. Neither is valid because neither can point to evidence that supports the doctrine and lies outside the doctrine itself. Presbyterians might point to the words of the Bible and of men like Martin Luther, John Calvin, John Knox, and other notable men, but this is hearsay, not scientific evidence. It is possible to believe in both the DSM and be a Presbyterian, but it seems that the popularity of the DSM amongst psychiatrists, psychologists, social workers, administrators, nurses, mental health workers, academics who teach Mental Health, lawyers, health insurance companies, and the families of mentally distressed people who do not want to be blamed for their relative's distress could well exceed the total number of Presbyterians!

Truth always causes problems. Parents might feel that they ought to teach their children to be truthful. After all, if your children are

131

truthful, they have to be obedient or suffer more punishments than they would if they were effective liars. However, truthful children will tell neighbours and relatives what you might not wish them to know. They will comment, usually unfavourably, on your appearance and behaviour, and they will draw your attention to the number of times you lie. Nevertheless, there are parents who demand that their children always tell the truth. In doing so, they forget that, whatever parents do, it always attracts the attention of the law of unintended consequences.

Rosemary Edwards, a lovely fifteen-year-old schoolgirl, disappeared from her home after an argument with her parents. They had discovered that she had lied to them when she told them that she had left her part-time job. In fact, she had been sacked for doing something of which her employer disapproved. Three weeks later her body was found in the woods ten miles from her home. The police said that there were no suspicious circumstances.

Her father told a journalist that he and his wife had punished Rosemary for lying by imposing 'a short ban on accessing the Internet and a longer ban on horse riding'. He explained, 'As parents we didn't want this [lying] to be the start of Rosemary going off the rails.' He added that, having read the texts and emails she had sent in the days before her disappearance, he now realized that she had been going through 'some kind of torment in her head'.[3] Mr and Mrs Edwards told the BBC that they would love to know why Rosemary died but, because they cannot, they must live with the consequences. 'We don't want her [death] to become a focal point of our lives,' Mrs Edwards said. She told how she and her husband with their other children had been to the place where Rosemary's body had been discovered. 'All four of us thought it was a weight that had been lifted and it is something I would recommend if it should happen to others.'[4]

Edmund Gosse's mother believed that to compose a fictitious narrative of any kind was a sin. She had been taught this by her Calvinist governess, who, like all good Calvinists, was against

132

all forms of pleasure. Loving mother though she was, she never sat Edmund on her knee or tucked him into bed and told him a story. He wrote,

> Never, in all my childhood, did any one address me with the affecting preamble, 'Once upon a time!' I was told about missionaries, but never about pirates; I was familiar with humming birds, but I had never heard of fairies. Jack the giant killer, Rumpelstiltskin and Robin Hood were not of my acquaintance, and though I understood about wolves, Little Red Ridinghood was a stranger even by that name. So far as my 'dedication' [to the Lord] was concerned, I can but think that my parents were in error thus to exclude the imaginary from my outlook upon facts. They desired to make me truthful; the tendency was to make me positive and sceptical. Had they wrapped me in the soft folds of supernatural fancy, my mind might have been longer content to follow their traditions in an unquestioning spirit.[5]

In case you might think that you have now discovered a way of making sure that your children follow in your religious beliefs, I have to tell you that, from my earliest days, the best part of my life at home was the endless fund of stories that my father told me. Sceptics have no difficulty in living in their imagination.

When Tony Blair became prime minister in 1997 he spoke with an appealing ring of truth in what he said. Everyone wanted to believe him. They had no reason to disbelieve him. Then came the tragic farce of the Weapons of Mass Destruction and the special relationship with George Bush, and they understood what Paddy Ashdown famously said, that, whatever Tony Blair says, he means it at the time.[6] Blair's government ran on spin, which is a message that has a tiny kernel of truth inside a thick husk of lies. Often the kernel of truth is missing.

In marked contrast to Tony Blair is Edzard Ernst, the Professor of Complementary Medicine at Exeter University. In 1993, the news that this post had been created, the first in Britain, attracted considerable media attention. There seemed to be the assumption that this showed how important complementary medicine is, but Professor Ernst quickly showed that this was not the case. His research showed that complementary medicine could have adverse effects. About 13 per cent of patients have reported adverse effects from acupuncture, while chiropractic spinal manipulation could have serious effects. Ernst and his team developed an effective research design to study spiritual healing and showed that it had impressive placebo effects but nothing else. In his studies of homeopathy he showed that the popular remedy Arnica that is used for bruising and other trauma had no advantage over placebo in reducing postoperative pain, bruising and swelling in patients undergoing elective hand surgery.[7]

In 2008 Ernst summarized what his research has shown in an interview with Michael Bond for the *New Scientist*. He said, 'Practitioners of complementary and alternative medicine (CAM) often fail to explain what the evidence shows and does not show. It is a triumph of advertising over rationality: many of the 40 million or so websites on alternative medicine promote outrageous lies. People seem quite gullible.' Bond remarked that, whether Ernst was dealing with the practices of the Austrian medical establishment during the Second World War or of complementary medicine now, he seemed to be driven to search for truth. Ernst replied that he was. 'My wife tells me I'm driven that way and she must be right. It is probably my personality. I cannot easily do things halfway; I have to go all the way. It does get me into trouble. I am stubborn – either that or I'm just a good scientist.'[8]

Tony Blair and Edzard Ernst illustrate a universal difference about which I have written at length in earlier books.[9] Many psychologists talk about extraversion and introversion, but these are abstract nouns and exist only in a psychologist's head.

However, there are extravert people and introvert people. Blair is an extravert and Ernst an introvert.

Extraverts experience their sense of being a person in relationship to other people. What they fear most is being completely rejected and abandoned. Other people are in the world around them, and so they turn (vert) outwards (extra). Introverts experience their sense of being a person in terms of gaining and maintaining a sense of clarity, organization, control, and a sense of achievement in terms of getting something done. These ideas and feelings are inside them, and so introverts turn inwards.

Every decision we make is ultimately based on the way we experience our sense of being a person. Both extraverts and introverts can be ambitious, but extraverts believe that, if they are successful, people will like them. Introverts want to be successful because for them being successful is what life is about. Thus, extravert actors aim for the adulation and applause success will bring them, while introvert actors want to be the greatest actor ever. Provided he has people round him who give him support, an extravert can deal with a situation where he has lost control and everything is falling apart, but finds himself close to disappearing when he is rejected. An introvert can be hurt and angry at being rejected or betrayed but still stay an intact person, whereas he shatters and crumbles when he fails to achieve and loses control in what he sees as chaos.

Tony Blair's reaction to rejection was played out on our television screens. He had thought that everyone in the UK would be as flattered and thrilled as he was with his special relationship with George Bush. He was sure he could charm everyone into agreeing to an invasion of Iraq. When most of the country turned against him, his puzzlement and confusion showed on his face. His face had always shone with a boyish gloss, but the boyish confidence disappeared, and he visibly aged within weeks. Many extraverts, in a similar situation and feeling themselves falling apart and disappearing, would have dealt with it by accepting the truth of their situation. Had they been prime minister, they would have resigned, and earned the respect, if not the love, of others. Blair could not manage to do this. Instead, he tried to hold himself together with a fantasy. It was one that most of us used when we were children and beset by unpleasant critics and enemies. Its theme is about revenge. 'I'll show them and then they'll be sorry.' Delicious and comforting though this fantasy is, most of us realized that, even if we did show them (parents, siblings, friends, teachers) they would never say sorry for hurting and humiliating us. So we left our fantasy behind with all our childish things. Not Blair. In desperation he tried to reconstruct himself, and, while his colleagues organized to force him to resign, he appeared almost nightly on television, trying to explain away the failure to find the WMDs, and to justify himself with, 'I believed I was right.' In everything he said there was a hint of a threat, 'One day you'll discover that I was right and you were wrong. You'll come to me on your knees and beg for my forgiveness.'

Margaret Thatcher was an introvert and, apart from creeping up behind the political journalist John Sergeant, who was talking live to camera, and simultaneously terrifying him and making him famous, she did not let us see how oddly she might behave as her power and control slipped away and she started to shatter and crumble. Perhaps her tears as she left Number 10 were carefully staged to win the public's sympathy and punish those who had forced her to leave. Many introverts use a carefully chosen display of emotion as a weapon. Tragically, she had built her whole identity and her life's project on gaining power and control, and thus winning her father's approval. When all this slipped away, she had nothing to put in its place. Our sense of being a person is not separate from our body. When it crumbles, our body crumbles too. (The reverse is not necessarily true, as many frail old people demonstrate.)

Our sense of being a person, our ideas, memory and emotions form our internal reality, and the world around us our external reality. When life is going along smoothly, the two realities have the same degree of 'realness'. When life is not going along smoothly and we are beset by a crisis, we retreat into what we experience as the more 'real' reality. If you are an introvert, you are familiar with how, when something quite unexpected and untoward happens to you, the world around you becomes not quite real. Your brain fails to convince you that the picture it has constructed of your external reality is actually there. What does not change is the 'realness' of your internal reality. You retreat into yourself, limit how much you talk to others, and seek solitude until external reality becomes real again and you can deal with it. If you are an extravert, you are familiar with how, when something quite unexpected and untoward happens to you, your internal reality becomes unreal to the point of almost vanishing. Your external reality remains real, and so you seek out people to talk to, and you busy yourself with whatever comes to hand.

If your external reality can turn unreal and, if you are frightened of chaos, then the security and clarity of truth is very important to you. On the other hand, if your sense of existence depends on having good relations with other people, you might not want to run the risk of alienating them by telling them truth they do not wish to hear. Extraverts like to be liked by everyone, and are faced with the problem that it is impossible to be universally liked. For introverts, as long as a small group of people whom they have selected likes and approves of them, they are satisfied. I have encountered Edzard Ernst only once, at a conference, and found him to be kindly and well-mannered, but, when he spoke, he had naught for the comfort of those whose work he had examined and found wanting. In doing this, he has managed to offend the entire community of complementary medicine practitioners, most of their patients, and Prince Charles himself, despite the fact that Ernst dedicated his latest book, *Trick or Treatment*, to the prince.[10]

Nothing of what I have written here should be taken to mean

that all extraverts are liars and all introverts invariably tell the truth. Far from it. Many extraverts care about the truth and struggle daily with the problem of telling the truth while not offending people. Some of them have perfected the art of telling unpleasant truths in the gentlest, kindest way.

Many introverts make lying their way of life. Some have the attitude that, as long as they know what the truth is, it does not matter whom they lie to, if lying will further their interests. Others create a theory that they are sure is the absolute truth. They lie in order to force their theory on to others. Margaret Thatcher believed in the theory of monetarism, and forced it on the public by lying about the benefits it would bring to everyone. Thus she helped lay the foundation of the present financial crisis. Hitler, another introvert, developed his theory about the inherent supremacy of Germany, and punished those who did not accept his lies.

Seeing the Truth in Front of Us

We can assess the particular situation we are in and see it quite accurately. Then the situation changes, but we fail to acknowledge that it has changed. We can be so attached to our view, our own particular truth, that we fail to notice that our perception of our situation has ceased to be true.

In early February 2009, in the state of Victoria in Australia the temperature each day was climbing past 38 °C. The state had entered its eleventh year of drought, and it was the bushfire season. The fire authorities issued the warning, 'The confluence of heat, dry and wind is unprecedented. The state is baking. Be prepared.' John Brumby, Premier of Victoria, warned, 'Don't go outside your house, unless you absolutely must.'

What do Australians do on a summer weekend? They go to the beach or the bush. On the evening of Friday, 6 February, many people – the precise number is not known – packed their cars and prepared to drive to Maryville, a delightful town deep in the bush. Some of the local people were concerned about the possibility of bushfires, but most of the beds available for tourists had been booked and few people had cancelled. Moreover, an unknown number of people would be coming for the day, and they would need feeding. The local people, who worked as usual, believed the story that Maryville had never burned and never would. But on this occasion it did. Apart from the historic Crossways Country Inn, the town was destroyed. It is thought that around 170 people died. The fires were so fierce that few identifiable remains could be found of anyone caught in the blaze.

A month later the journalist Kate Legge was able to talk to some of the people who had managed to escape. They spoke of lolling by the swimming pool, barely glancing at what they took to be black clouds heralding an afternoon cool change. What they were actually seeing was 'a mass column of grey and yellow smoke billowing upwards, a kilometre or more and cascading over itself, as it flowed towards the town from the north'. Photographs exist of bathers on Thai beaches on Boxing Day 2004 wading into the surf while in the distance a great wall of water – a tsunami – is coming towards them. At Maryville people had heard the warnings but, as one woman said, 'We'd spent $200 on accommodation.' The temperature moved upwards, and people dozed, waiting for the cool of the evening.

Some people did see the danger. The owners of the Kerami Guest House saw what they called 'the rust and red sky', and told their guests to leave, as they themselves were doing. Why do some people recognize a calamitous new situation while others do not? Were they so attached to their original assessment of the situation, 'a relaxing weekend', that they could not see that the situation had changed? Did these people cling to the belief that, 'Nothing bad can happen to me'?[11]

The belief that nothing bad can happen to me derives from a

bargain many of us made when we were small children. We would give up being ourselves, making our own decisions about what we would do, and do as we were told, that is, we would be good in the way our parents wanted us to be good. In return some person or organization would take care of us. This bargain meant that, if we were good, nothing bad could happen to us. Parents soon prove to be too fallible to provide such care, and so we look further for some great power. If we happened to be born in Germany in the 1920s we could, like so many Germans at that time, see Hitler as having the power to protect us. In the same way, had we been born in the USSR or North Korea, we could see the State as having the power to protect us. For nearly two thousand years, Christianity has offered millions of people this bargain. Which bargain we choose depends on when and where we are born, but, once we choose, we have to acquire a particular set of beliefs that becomes the filter with which we interpret everything that befalls us. We can come to believe that this filter is the truth, a totally accurate account of what is going on. We forget that it is, like all our ideas, a theory. When something happens that threatens to disprove our beliefs, we can resort to that popular lie, 'It isn't happening and it hasn't happened.'

How else for the last sixty or more years in Ireland many Christians must have known, yet denied what they knew, that the children they cared about were being physically and sexually abused by priests and nuns? In what was virtually a theocracy in Ireland, Catholic parents closed their eyes and ears to their children's suffering, while the hierarchy of the Catholic Church not only knew that such abuse was endemic in church institutions but they did everything they could to protect the abusers. Everyone wanted to go on believing that the Church was incapable of error.[12] If the Church erred, it and its God could not be trusted to protect them from all harm. The bargain they had made with the Church where they had to be good in the way the Church defined good had cost them dear. Being a good Catholic involves

140

considerable pain and sacrifice. They could not bear to contemplate that all their effort had been wasted. To protect their beliefs they sacrificed the children in their care.

To the men in charge of Britain's biggest banks it must have been inconceivable that anything bad could happen to them or their banks. They had enjoyed so much power, wealth and government favour for so long that they must have felt it would last forever. They failed to understand that in all budgets, big or small, the size of the debt must not outweigh the assets. They believed that they could handle the risks involved. After all, they were the masters of the universe, and they could force reality to accommodate itself to their desires. Speaking of such attitudes, Jon Moulton of Alchemy Partners said, 'Incomprehensibility and aggression is a combination that leads quite often to spectacular failure.'

In his short television series *Crash: How the Banks Went Bust*[13] Will Hutton, journalist and executive vice chair of The Work Foundation, told the story of the near-failure of the British banking system in the first week of October 2008. He revealed how, so confident and aggressive was Sir Fred Goodwin that he was extraordinarily slow in recognizing that his bank, the Royal Bank of Scotland, had lost the confidence of the wholesale markets and, accordingly, the other banks were becoming increasingly unwilling to lend RBS money. It was not until the Thursday of that week that the truth dawned on Goodwin that something bad had happened to him, and that everything he had achieved at RBS was in danger of being lost. There was only the coming weekend when the RBS and the whole UK banking system could be saved. Of all the banks, RBS was in the worst position. After desperate negotiations with the Treasury, RBS was forced to sell a majority stake in the bank to the government, or rather, the taxpayer. Later, Goodwin described what had gone on as 'less than a negotiation, more of a drive-by shooting'.[14]

Goodwin's apology to the Treasury Select Committee had all

Why We Lie

the hallmarks of expensive public relations advice rather than of true contrition. It is unlikely that his explanation to himself of what caused the disaster is in terms of 'I was wrong'. Sometimes the truth can be too much for a fragile but well-defended person to bear. The cause of the disaster has to be construed in terms of a fantasy, or a precious belief, or a delusion, or a lie.

Chapter Nine

Fantasies Are Important

Some Definitions:

A *truth* is a theory that is tied as closely as possible to the real world. It has evidence to support it, and is always a statement of probability based on the amount of evidence to support it. An absolute truth can only be a fantasy.

A *fantasy* is a theory that uses elements from the real world to tell a story that explores possibilities in the real world, or entertains us, or comforts and supports us. Some fantasies draw heavily on the real world so we can examine what could or might come into being, while other fantasies select aspects of the real world to create something new. All of our fantasies come out of our past experience. We have nothing else to draw on.

A *belief* is a theory that can be either a truth, as in, 'I believe the trains to Richmond leave on the hour', or a fantasy, as in, 'I believe that the energy from crystals can cure cancer.'

A *delusion* is a theory that has no connection to the real world, but only to the fantasies, memories, needs and desires of the person who holds it and who insists that the delusion is the truth.

Fantasies

It seems likely that our ability to fantasize developed when our homo sapiens sapiens ancestors developed self-consciousness. When we measured our puny self against the vastness of the world, we saw how powerless we were. We had to create

143

fantasies in order to survive both physically and as a person. What we did was to make our world meaningful by creating stories.

Moment to moment, what we all experience are the individual pictures that our brain creates. Sunlight on a wall, a gate clanging, a man's voice – all snapshots without connection. If your childhood has been relatively ordinary, where events recurred and were explained to you by adults, you discovered how to turn fragments like these into a story. Now you do this all the time. However, amongst those children who have experienced the extremes of suffering and cruelty – the numbers of these children now run into many millions – are children who are themselves no more than the fragments of their experiences. What should have been their self, a single whole, is a vaguely shifting collection of fragments. Their life has been one of extreme events, where little has been replicated and nothing explained. Thus they have been unable to fit these fragments into some kind of life story that they can tell to themselves and to others. Because they have no story to tell, they are deprived of the reactions of other people to their story, whereas we who do have a life story to tell constantly modify our idea of ourselves so that the meaning of our self is in constant change. Is it not tragic that the extensive knowledge we now have of how our self arises out of the functioning of the brain has come in large part from the work of neurosurgeons and neuroscientists who have studied the head injuries caused by the violent conflicts in the world, and from the work of psychoanalysts such as Boris Cyrulnik who work with the child victims of these conflicts?

The purposive behaviour of species other than our own suggests that these species have an ability to weave the fragments of their experiences into a simple story of perhaps no more than 'hungry – food – get'. It may be that the split between our immediate predecessors, the homo sapiens and us extremely intelligent beings, the homo sapiens sapiens (Oh, the blind vanity of those

144

men who named us!), came when some of our ancestors began pondering the question, 'Who is it that is thinking, "hungry – food – get"?' Thus we acquired self-consciousness and, along with that, fantasies. Let me tell you a story.

Imagine that one day a small group of our ancestors went for a walk, and happened upon a patch of dirt on which was a pattern of indentations. To make this pattern of indentations meaningful, they had to put it in a story. One man said, 'I think that this is the footprint of a lion that has passed this way.' Another added, 'It came out of the bushes there and it was going to the stream.' Their story was now complete. It had a beginning, a middle, and an end. No one had actually seen the lion, so their story was a fantasy. The first man decided that they should use their fantasy scientifically. They would hide near this spot to see if the lion was going to return this way, thus proving that their fantasy was true. If it were, they could then use their spears to kill the lion. This was actually a risky proposal, because in those days the lions that roamed Europe and North America were much bigger than they are today, and, having longer legs, ran much faster when chasing their prey.[1] However, let's suppose that our scientific ancestor not only was right but survived the encounter by killing the lion.

Ancient lions went around in prides, and so it was not surprising that one day another man on his way to the stream encountered a lion. He ran towards the nearest tall tree. He could see that the tree's lowest branch was certainly beyond his reach and the tree impossible to climb, but, when he jumped up as high as he could, his fingers closed over the branch and he was able to pull himself to safety. It seemed (perhaps he thought of this later) that the tree had bent down and scooped him up. When eventually he thought he might be safe to descend, he felt that what he had experienced was more than ordinary, everyday luck. He had been saved, and by this special tree. It seemed to him that the tree was invested with some mysterious quality. It was far more than

145

an ordinary tree. He patted the tree, and then stepped away from it and bowed, thanking it for saving his life.

The man who speared the lion and the man whose life was saved by the tree had great stories to tell around the tribe's fire. The scientist spear thrower might have polished up his story just to make sure that he got the praise he deserved. It was thanks to his skill rather than mere chance that he had brought the lion down. Moreover, even if he never killed another lion in his life, he had been shown to be right. In the future people would listen to his opinions about the world. The man saved by the tree had a choice of implications for his story. His tree was not an ordinary tree. It had special powers. It could do more than just stand there being a tree. How could he develop this story?

Perhaps he had an interest in entering into bargains that would lead to him getting certain advantages. Perhaps he already knew that, as Seth Godin put it in his book *All Marketers Are Liars* thousands of years later, 'Successful marketers are just the providers of stories that consumers choose to believe.'[2] What if he told, as a sequel to his story, how he had discovered that his tree had certain medicinal qualities disclosed to him and him alone by the tree. However, he could obtain certain things from the tree, a twig, or perhaps a leaf, which, carefully preserved and carried on the person, would give the same protection that the tree had given to him. Obtaining these parts of the tree was not easy, and so there would be a small charge, but the benefits would be enormous.

Perhaps he was more ambitious. The tree was more than a tree. It was part of the vast powers that controlled the thunder and lightning, that caused the sun to rise, the snow to fall, and the spring to return. The tree had chosen him, and now he could contact the powers beyond, indeed, perhaps he was part of those powers. This was a story that so many people wanted to believe.

Or perhaps the tribe was made up of sceptics who told him where to go with his stories. We sceptics must have had some ancestors.

We spend much of our time creating fantasies, and not merely in daydreaming. Memories are the fantasies we devise about our past. The future is made up of our fantasies about what will happen. When we mentally list our tasks for the day and the order and manner in which we will carry them out, no matter how carefully and realistically we created our fantasy, it usually proves to have remarkably little to do with the real world and what actually eventuates. Life, I find, is made up of interruptions.

Fantasy plays an enormous part in science. Every hypothesis is a fantasy until it acquires enough evidence for it to be called a truth. When it is not physically possible to carry out certain experiments, scientists conduct what they call 'thought experiments', as Einstein did when he rode on a beam of light, and Schrödinger put his cat in a box. Scientists use fantasy to find reality. Good writers start with the reality of lived experience and turn it into a fantasy that reveals a deeper truth. Ernest Hemingway's biographer, Jeffrey Meyers, writing about the principles that Hemingway used to guide his work, said, 'The first – derived from newspaper experience which had trained him to report only what he had witnessed directly – was that fiction must be founded on real emotional and intellectual experience and be faithful to actuality, but must also be transformed and heightened by the imagination until it becomes truer than mere factual events.'[3]

There is no point in telling a story if no one wants to listen. Engaging an audience and telling the truth requires considerable skill, particularly if you put the truth you want to tell into some kind of fantasy. You have to make sure that you never lose sight of the difference between the truth you want to tell and the fantasy. Only then can you control both elements of your material. In the early part of his career, Hemingway saw this distinction clearly, but all too soon it was lost in what became his most time-consuming work, the creation of his fantasy about himself, Hero

147

as a Man of Letters. Hemingway played a character who was larger than life and who never let the truth get in the way of a good story. He built upon his childhood fantasies to create a whole mythology. Meyers told how, 'Everyone believed that Hemingway had Indian blood, was kept out of school for a year to play the cello, ran away from home, injured his eye while boxing, associated with gangsters . . . Yet virtually all the drinking, boxing, hunting, fishing and fornicating were exaggerations or fantasies.'[4] He created his fantasies, and then he told himself that they were true.

Hemingway saw his lying as an essential part of the writer's art. He wrote, 'It is not *unnatural* that the best writers are liars. A major part of their trade is to lie or invent and they will lie when they are drunk, or to themselves, or to strangers. They often lie unconsciously and then remember their lies with deep remorse.'[5] Here Hemingway is presenting the self-justification 'everybody does it' as profound advice about how to write.

Whenever we make a practice of lying, or fail to distinguish between our fantasies and the truth, disasters follow. With his success as a writer and great personal fame, Hemingway could not maintain the high standard he achieved in his early work, and what followed was a tragic tale of how he destroyed his relationships with all who cared for him. Depressed, Hemingway fell into the hands of a Dr Rome at the Mayo Clinic in Minnesota. Dr Rome's fantasy was that electroconvulsive therapy (ECT) cured depression, when all it does is destroy memory. There is a photograph of Hemingway taken after two courses of ECT. Meyers wrote, 'Hemingway's dazed and vacant stare reveals that the shock treatments at the Mayo Clinic have damaged his memory. He has become a frail old man.'[6] It is hard to see in this sad old man the once strong and vibrant features of the younger Hemingway.

Dr Rome seemed not to know that he should be suspicious whenever a very depressed patient suddenly seems better and wants to go home. The patient has not recovered but made an irrevocable decision to end his life. Such a final decision brings a certain calm. Hemingway had already told his friend Hotchner, 'If I can't exist on my own terms, then existence is impossible. That is how I have lived, and that is now how I *must* live – or not live.'[7] This is the reason that people kill themselves. They feel that they cannot live their life on their own terms, and so they will die on their own terms.[8] So Hemingway went home, where his wife Mary had locked his guns in the basement of their home but absentmindedly left the keys to the basement in the kitchen where Hemingway could find them.

Mary, the fourth and last of Hemingway's wives, here demonstrated how a wish we dare not turn into a conscious fantasy can make its presence felt. In her marriage to Hemingway Mary had showed an infinite capacity for self-sacrifice, looking after Hemingway devotedly while often being the object of his cruel selfishness. Anyone who has witnessed the long, drawn-out death of a loved one knows how the wish that the person's suffering would end can so easily come into your mind, and even the wish that it were possible to help the person have a peaceful death, but, when a person has to bury this wish in their unconscious, more than a simple wish is being denied. Perhaps Mary felt that she had to deny all the fantasies of revenge a long-suffering wife has to create in order to survive the insults her husband heaps upon her. Denial and repression are two of the means whereby we lie to ourselves.

Fantasies that help us survive can be our most important fantasies. They provide the means whereby we can be resilient. These fantasies are stories that begin with what the person sees as his weakness, and what follows is how he triumphs over this weakness. The greater the weakness, the more glorious must be the triumph. For many of us, creating these fantasies and telling ourselves these stories over and over again until they cease to be interesting is all we need to give us courage to face each day.

In bed at night, we triumph over our parents, siblings, teachers, classmates, and next morning, no longer needing to murder them all, we get up and go to school. However, for some people their weakness is too great and the assaults too continuous to be dealt with by imagination alone. They have to turn their fantasies into actions.

In his biography of Hemingway, Meyers lists all the accidents Hemingway had, even more than would be expected for such an active man, and refers to him as being 'accident prone'. At different times in my life, I had a relative and then a colleague, both of whom had what seemed to be an excess of accidents. These appeared to be random, but actually there was a pattern. Like Hemingway, both these men were extraverts whose need for attention became especially keen when their self-confidence had received a blow. Having an accident can bring a great deal of satisfactory attention, but for these two men there was a deeper meaning. Whenever his life was going well, my relative grew increasingly anxious. He would be waiting, as he sometimes told me, 'for the blow to fall'. Whenever the blow was slow in coming and nothing else was available, he had an accident. It seemed that he believed that his fate was to suffer, and, in doing so, to scorn those who had life easy. My colleague's accidents, as all of us who knew him agreed, were self-punishment. He actively sought them out, and then displayed his injuries much in the way Christian martyrs might have displayed their wounds.

In their childhoods each of these men had suffered the kind of unthinking cruelties that families can inflict while believing that they love the child in their care. In some ways it can be easier for a child to make a meaningful story out of consistent rejection by their families than out of shows of affection and casual cruelties. Rather than blame their families and risk being rejected, each man created a story where he was the hero of a tragedy. Both believed that their fantasy was the story of their life that they could do no other than live out. They did not see that they were living a fantasy, and that they were free to change it. Their circumstances would have allowed each of them to live the life of a successful professional man. However, they did not want this. They despised men who led ordinary lives. No matter how much they suffered, they wanted to be spectacularly unique.

The great advantage of an accident is that you can claim that it was not your fault. It was caused by fate, or God, or other people. Hemingway never blamed himself for anything. He always looked for a scapegoat. He could not bear to add to the burden of blame he had been carrying since early childhood.

Hemingway was born into a religious Protestant family. They said blessing before meals, had morning family prayers, and went to church every Sunday. Hemingway sang in the choir. Meyers wrote, 'The Sabbath was strictly enforced at home; all games and play were forbidden. When the children were spanked by their father, they had to kneel down and ask God's forgiveness.'[9]

Hemingway's mother Grace, being more interested in the arts than in domesticity, left the care of the children to a nursemaid and cook, and domestic matters to her husband Ed, who was a doctor. Meyers described him as being 'extremely rigid; he saw everything as black or white, and refused to recognize the grey ambiguity. Both parents, when Ernest was a boy, were foes of dirt and disorder. They brought up their children to follow strict schedules, stand inspection, and be scrupulously neat and tidy.'[10]

Hemingway was born into a prosperous family at a peaceful time in a prosperous country. Eccentric though his parents might have been, their marriage worked quite well. They loved their children and wanted them to do well. As a child Hemingway was presented with a wide variety of ways of interpreting the world, not just from his parents, sisters and younger brother but from his grandparents and an uncle, a missionary in China. He had a comfortable home and frequent access to the wilderness. All of this was wonderful material for the imagination of an inquisitive, active boy. However, over it all loomed the Protestant

151

God who saw all and disapproved. Many Protestants today like to claim that their God is cuddly and accepting, but to believe this you have to ignore the existence of the Old Testament. The God Hemingway was taught to fear was the God of the Old Testament.

Having an exceedingly critical parent is difficult for a child, but at least you have a chance of surviving by doing all you can to keep yourself separate from your parent. Saying very little is one useful technique: lying is another. But a critical God who regards most of what an ordinary boy does as a sin (Ed believed that masturbation led to blindness, insanity and death) and is all-seeing is inescapable. Life becomes a prison against whose walls you can rain blows but from which you can never escape. Hemingway spent most of his life raining blows on the walls of his prison, but, as his biographer said, he 'always retained his hard-working, self-reliant, conscientious, anxious and guilt-ridden Protestant inheritance'.[11]

The fantasies that can help us become resilient are but frail barques that can carry us over stormy seas to solid ground. These fantasies might entertain and amuse us, fill us with joy, inspire us with ambition, encourage us to explore, learn, and, most important of all, to be brave, but they can never be the truth. The truth – real life – is always different from our fantasies.

Chapter Ten

The Delights of Shared Fantasies

Sometimes we share a fantasy with other people, or so we like to think. However, our fantasies, like our perceptions, are individual. When two people fall in love, they tell one another that they share the fantasy of a happy life together, but, in fact, their fantasies about what this life will be are very different, as their squabbles and arguments soon show. If one partner regards his or her fantasy as the truth that must emerge over time, disappointment is inevitable. If their partner is unfaithful, betrayal comes as a double blow to the person and to the beloved fantasy.

Sometimes the couple create a fantasy of their life together that, according to how each person interprets the fantasy, allows each of them to feel secure and supported, yet able to pursue the aims of their individual interpretation of the shared fantasy. Conventional marriages often work well in this way. Perhaps the woman tries to fulfil her childhood fantasies of having children and giving them what she felt was missing from her childhood. The man continues to maintain his sense of being a person through his competition with other men, but now he can do this from a secure base where he appears to be in charge. This appearance might not actually be the reality, but his wife is happy to let him think that this is so.

Trying to live a fantasy always involves lying to yourself and to others because a fantasy can never become real life. Life, as John Lennon famously said, is what happens while you're making other plans. If we construct a fantasy that is closely modelled on reality, little lying is needed in order to live that fantasy. When

153

the fantasy is revealed to be a fantasy, as such fantasies always are, we can discard it without too much pain. But when our fantasy is far removed from real life, when we have filled it with wishes impossible to fulfil and aims impossible to achieve, the fantasy becomes an integral part of our identity. We cannot abandon it without damaging ourselves.

The current fame of Victoria and David Beckham is as nothing compared to the heyday of Jean-Paul Sartre and Simone de Beauvoir. The Beckhams do little more than be beautiful, while the words that Sartre and Beauvoir uttered in public, and their every public action were reported on, analysed, criticized and absorbed into the intellectual and political life of that time. When Sartre died in 1980, the journalist Walter Schwartz was in Paris and writing for the *Guardian*. He quoted a writer in *Le Matin* who said, 'You really had to be twenty in 1954 to know what it could mean to a whole generation to have this man who dared, all on his own, to insist that the only important action was justice to the oppressed, that the violence of the colonized against the colonizer was justified, that a man could be right even against his country in the name of a superior ideal which is man himself.' He also quoted Sartre's publisher, Pierre Nora, who said that Sartre was one of those men whose 'ideas of truth rested on their own sensibility that was profoundly moral and political'.[1] In 1954 I was twenty-three, and much more interested in Sartre's political opinions than in his philosophy. I felt oppressed, and in more ways than I had yet realized. Like other left-wing politically-minded Australians, I saw Sartre as someone to admire. With Robert Menzies as our prime minister, we needed a hero.

Sartre and Beauvoir might not have been as beautiful as the Beckhams, but, like them, they knew how to control their image. Controlling your image is one way of trying to make your fantasy reality. Sartre and Beauvoir wanted to appear to be unafraid of ignoring convention, but there was much in their lives that, even though it was well known to their friends, they did not wish

154

to become common knowledge. Unconventionality might be forgiven but extremes of selfishness rarely are. We all have been the victims of other people's selfishness, and we know how it hurts. It is only recently that certain documents and correspondence relating to Sartre and Beauvoir have become available to biographers. This material reveals the inconsistencies between what Sartre and Beauvoir advocated as the way to live and how they actually did live. In her biography *A Dangerous Liaison*, Carole Seymour-Jones called Beauvoir's memoirs 'her most fictive work'.[2] Having used the German occupation of Paris to further his own ambitions, Sartre, after the liberation of Paris, presented himself as a hero of the Resistance. Henri Noguères's definitive history of the Resistance does not mention Sartre, but 'in later years Sartre created a false history, writing that he had "taken an active part in the Resistance on the barricades of Paris". By then he probably believed it.'[3]

Of course, he was not the only Frenchman that did this. I recall how, in the 1950s, it was difficult to see how the German occupation of France could have lasted so long when every French man and woman had joined the Resistance! In Marcel Ophüls' film *Le Chagrin et la Pitié*, former Resistance fighters had only the greatest scorn for those neighbours who pretended that they had been in the Resistance. Mockingly, one man told how men he met would say, '"Monsieur Gaspar, if only you knew what we did for the Resistance." I stay calm . . . Sometimes I have to listen to a song and dance of some guy who shows me a drawer and gets his wife to confirm there was indeed a revolver which he was supposedly ready to use on the Germans only he never used it.' Another Resistance fighter said, 'They claimed they didn't know how to get in touch with the Resistance. Somehow an old fool like me knew how, and they didn't.' Although this film was made in 1969 it was not shown; it was banned in France until 1981.

In 1929, after Beauvoir had managed to escape from her family home and live by herself, she and Sartre made a pact of '"essential love" which allowed secondary affairs intended to guarantee their "reciprocal liberty"'.[4] It was to be *la vie contingente*, a life that welcomed chance. They believed that, 'Life would bend itself to their will and, with the arrogance of youth, they already believed that, by virtue of contingency, *it* had chosen them.'[5] In her book *Fool's Gold* Gillian Tett, writing about the group of young men responsible for developing the derivatives sector of the investment bank J.P. Morgan in 1994, said, 'They were all convinced, with the heady arrogance of youth, that they held the secret of transforming the financial world, as well as dramatically enhancing J.P. Morgan's profit profile.'[6] In fact, they were creating the explosive device that brought down the banks. The combination of intelligence and youthful enthusiasm rarely produces wisdom.

By 1929 Freud's *The Interpretation of Dreams*, published in 1900 to no acclaim, had acquired considerable fame among the intelligentsia. Sartre and Beauvoir read it and decided that Freud was quite wrong about the existence of the unconscious. They believed in Descartes' *cogito ergo sum* and their conscious 'I' was in control. Through their free will, they could make reality yield to their ideas. They concentrated on these ideas while ignoring the Wall Street Crash and the emergence of the Nazis in Germany. Beauvoir said, 'Public affairs bored us.'[7] Not realizing that they were boring, public affairs continued on their way.

Sexual relationships are always about a great deal more than sex. In 1934 Beauvoir discovered that Sartre was having an affair. She wrote in her memoirs, 'This affair neither took me by surprise nor upset any notions I had formed concerning our joint lives, since right from the outset Sartre had warned me that he was liable to embark on such adventures. I had accepted the principle, and now had no difficulty in accepting the fact.'[8] The truth was that Beauvoir was in turmoil. Had she acquainted herself with her unconscious, she would have known that what she feared the most was rejection and abandonment, and why this was so.

156

When war was declared on 3 September 1939, she wrote to her lover Jacques-Laurent Bost, someone who was very important to her but whom she failed to mention in her memoirs, and said, 'I have the impression that *I* no longer exist.' This is what extraverts feel when faced with what they see as complete abandonment. When both Bost and Sartre had joined their army units, Beauvoir had a panic attack while travelling on the Metro. She described feeling that she was nothing but an anonymous face in the crowd, 'drowned by the war'.[9] The terror of being annihilated as a person is what psychiatrists call a panic attack. This is the equivalent of calling the collapse of the bank that holds all your savings 'a bit of a bother'.

Sex is an excellent way of keeping someone close to you without having to explain that you are terrified of being alone, or of having to cope with the messiness of a relationship. It also allows the acting-out of many kinds of fantasies. As a child, Beauvoir's closest relationship was with her younger sister Poupette, whom she enjoyed teaching. Later, as a teacher in a girls' secondary school, Beauvoir discovered the pleasure of dazzling her students with her brilliance. She took a special interest in the girls who fell in love with her, and went on to make close relationships with a series of vulnerable young women. She seduced them, and then shared them with Sartre. When they were tired of these girls, they discarded them. One Jewish girl, Bianca Bienenfeld, was abandoned by them while she was desperately trying to find some way of not being rounded up by the French police working with their Nazi occupiers and sent to a concentration camp. She managed to survive the war by marrying a non-Jew. Later she said of Sartre and Beauvoir, 'I carried the weight of that abandonment my entire life.'[10]

When we construct a fantasy, we decide what roles other people should play in it. This does not matter when the fantasy is enacted only in the theatre of our mind, but, if we try to turn our fantasy into reality, we ignore the fact that other people will not necessarily act in the way we want them to act. After all, they are the central character in their own life story. They do not wish to be part of our fantasy, unless they see some advantage to themselves in doing this. Hitler's henchmen accepted roles in Hitler's fantasy in order to advance their careers and status, but they found that Hitler was oblivious of their thoughts and feelings, except those of betrayal. They had no way of controlling their role in Hitler's fantasy, and they paid dearly for their own fantasy that they could.

Those who were caught up in the fantasy that Sartre and Beauvoir had constructed suffered greatly. Beauvoir wrote a great deal about feelings, but the only feelings she took account of were her own. After the war, her American lover, Nelson Algren, was enormously hurt when, after many comings and goings, and many protestations of great love, Beauvoir rejected him. Unbeknownst to him, she put him in her novel *The Mandarins*. Algren saw this as the ultimate betrayal.

Had Beauvoir and Sartre lived in peaceful times, their biographers would have used these tales of sexual encounters to enliven what might be a straightforward account of their work. However, Beauvoir and Sartre did not live in peaceful times. They were at the centre of the storm that overtook Europe. The German occupation of France presented the French with huge moral issues. Many French people behaved courageously with supreme concern for the welfare of other people, but so many did not that when Frederic Spotts wrote a book on how French artists and intellectuals survived the Occupation, he called his book *The Shameful Peace*.[11]

The defeat of France was a central part of Hitler's fantasy of world domination. However, he viewed France very differently from the way he viewed Poland and the USSR. To him the Poles and the Russians were of no more value than the Jews were, and could be eradicated. The French were different. In the years leading to the war, France was seen as the world leader in the arts. Hitler wanted to make French culture subservient to that of Germany. Moreover, 'In the arts he saw a narcotic to be used to pacify the French and make them amenable to collaboration while he was busy with his war in the Soviet Union. So he not only allowed but actively encouraged a rich artistic life.'[12] Spotts went on, 'The Wehrmacht's policy was to allow just that amount of cultural freedom that would make life bearable but not undermine the absolute imperative of civil order. The *musae*, far from being silent, were to be encouraged to speak. But – a huge but – they would say only what the Occupier allowed. In reality cultural freedom was therefore a tactic in a stratagem of repression.'[13] As a result, right-wing artists and intellectuals actively collaborated with the Germans, while others thought that they could pursue their careers unhindered, ignoring what was going on around them. Sartre and Beauvoir were amongst this group. It was left-wing artists and intellectuals who understood the reality of the Occupation. Some joined the Resistance, while others, knowing they were in danger, fled the country.

In 1941 Henri Matisse was seventy-one and very ill. Such was his fame that, had he decided to collaborate with the Germans, he could have lived out the war in great comfort. That thought never crossed his mind. This was the third war with Germany in his lifetime, and he knew what the Germans could do. His biographer Hilary Spurling wrote of how Matisse was 'appalled by his country's capitulating, sickened by the continuing slaughter, and consumed with fear for his family'.[14] He wrote to his daughter Marguerite, 'Each one of us must find his own way to limit the moral shock of this catastrophe . . . I am trying to distract myself from it as far as possible by clinging to the idea of the future work that I could still do, if I don't let myself be destroyed.'[15] He had nothing but contempt for Vichy France, and was greatly distressed by the round-up of Jews and foreigners. His wife Amélie and daughter Marguerite joined the Resistance. When they were caught by the Germans, Amélie was imprisoned and later released, but Marguerite disappeared. Severely tortured, she was close to death, but survived and was released into the chaos of liberation. Later, when she told her father about what she had suffered at the hands of the Gestapo, 'Matisse recognized the philosophy of endurance he had taught his daughter carried to lengths even he had never imagined.'[16]

Matisse had applied his philosophy of endurance all through the war years, when he suffered a series of serious illnesses, but kept working. He had his family to support. In January 1941, while awaiting colonic surgery, Matisse sorted out his affairs, and wrote to his son Pierre. In this he 'reviewed the results of the bargain he had made between life and art. It was a dispassionate, honest and accurate reckoning, deploring the suppression and secrecy that had turned his family relationships into a minefield, attributing many of his children's subsequent difficulties to pressures imposed by his work when they were young.' He ended 'by reiterating his deep and abiding love for his family, including his wife'.[17]

This letter is based on Matisse's lifelong respect for truth, here the truth about himself as a parent. A great many parents can never bring themselves to face such a truth in their own life. They want to cling to the fantasy that they were perfect parents, and that any difficulties their children experience were caused by other people, or by the children themselves. They, the parents, are not to blame. Adult children often find that they are rebuffed by their parents if they ask questions about events in their childhood. Many know better than to try. In all the lectures I have given, nothing creates more discomfiture amongst my audience than any suggestion that a parent could do something that might have a deleterious effect on their child. The split in consciousness that clinging to a fantasy can cause is shown in the intense public anger when a parent has been extremely cruel to a child, and the refusal by the British government to change the law to give children the same protection against assault that adults enjoy. If you hit me,

160

you have committed a crime, but, if you hit your child, you are merely exercising parental privilege.

Matisse took no special pride in being truthful. It was simply part of his being, part of that clarity of vision that produced such magnificent work.

Beauvoir and Sartre were sucked into the evil of the Wehrmacht because they were lost in their fantasy that they were supremely intelligent, destined for great fame, and able to live their lives free of conventional rules. To them there was nothing in the Occupation that required them to make a moral judgement and act on that judgement. This was a bizarre idea. At present, with the turmoil of the global financial crisis and the wide-ranging implications of climate change, it is very difficult to see what is the best plan to follow. Should we return to the old financial system, but with more regulations, or should we change completely how we see the role of money? Is nuclear power too dangerous to use, or is it the solution to our need for energy? In 1940 it was quite clear what we should do. If we treasured our independence and democratic government, Hitler had to be defeated. As individuals, we all needed to decide what we should do in what was called 'the war effort'. Many people realized that, if you lived in Germany or any of the occupied countries and were unable to take part in the Resistance, you lived quietly, inconspicuously and as decently as you could in those terrible times. When Marshal Pétain, the hero of Verdun, signed the armistice with Hitler, those who saw clearly what this meant defined it as, 'Give me your watch and I'll tell you the time.'[18] Amongst those who lived quietly and decently there were many acts of unobserved and unrecorded heroism. However, unobserved heroism never makes you famous. Beauvoir believed that the Occupation would last for twenty years. She and Sartre joined their likeminded friends at the Café de Flore on the Left Bank, and looked for what opportunities the Occupation might bring.

Sartre was intensely ambitious, and envious of other writers.

161

In 1940–41 the anti-Semitic laws passed in France meant that over a thousand jobs in education became vacant. Amongst those Jews forced out of prestigious posts was Henri Dreyfus-le-Foyer, great-nephew of Captain Alfred Dreyfus who, in what became known as the Dreyfus Affair, suffered greatly at the hands of anti-Semitic army officers. Henri fled to the Free Zone where he joined the Resistance. At that time, Sartre was teaching at the Lycée Pasteur. There was no need for Sartre to leave the Lycée, however taking Dreyfus's job would not only improve his status but give him more time to write.

With the first German troops to enter Paris were the officials and journalists who immediately took over the French National Radio and the news agencies. Amongst the journals set up by the German Propaganda Department was the cultural review *Comœdia* with René Delange as editor. Sartre offered to write a weekly column and had an article on Melville and *Moby Dick* in the first issue. After the Liberation Sartre claimed he had never written for *Comœdia*.

The article on Melville was Sartre's only contribution to the journal, but he kept in close touch with Delange. When, in 1943, Beauvoir needed work, Sartre spoke to Delange who arranged for her to become a features editor on Radio Vichy. Radio Vichy was soon taken over by la Radiodiffusion Nationale, which was part of the German propaganda machine based in Paris and under the control of the prime minister Pierre Laval who had agreed to meet Himmler's deportation quota for Jews, 100,000 from France. 'Beauvoir stepped into the heart of collaboration, into studios thronged by Germans in well-cut uniform or civvies.'[19]

Meanwhile, 140 French publishers had signed an agreement that made them 'major executors of the German cultural strategy for France'. 'They retained their firms, their staff and their lists, and placed them in a position to make solid profits by publishing books acceptable to the Invader. Nothing was lost save honour.' Spotts described this as 'one of the most disgraceful acts in the cultural sphere during the whole of the Occupation'.[20] Both Beauvoir and Sartre benefited from this deal.

Beauvoir's first novel, a barely disguised autobiography about a threesome, made Beauvoir a literary celebrity. The book was well reviewed in the pro-Nazi press. Sartre's *Being and Nothingness* attracted little attention at first when it was published in 1944. The basic thesis of the book was that human beings create meaning and impose it on a world that has no intrinsic meaning. Sartre had no interest in science, so he had not acquainted himself with what was known then, admittedly not much, about how our brain creates meaning. He could see that our freedom lies in being able to choose how we interpret what we encounter.

Rather than explore the infinity of implications of this freedom to choose our meanings, Sartre let himself be overwhelmed by a fear of being responsible for the choices he made. He wanted to be told what the world meant. He could not accept that the world simply exists, and takes no account of our existence.

Sartre had rejected religion, but as a child he had been introduced by his mother and grandmother to a kindly version of Catholicism that had beautiful music, and to the stern absolute certainties of Lutheranism by his grandfather. The longing to return to such beauty, safety and certainty was buried in his unconscious, but, as he did not have an unconscious, or so he thought, he had to content himself with writing about alienation.

When in 1940 their old friends Charles Dullin and Simone Jollivet told them they had decided to collaborate with the Germans, Beauvoir and Sartre declared that they were disgusted. However, Sartre had no objection to Dullin asking Gaston Gallimard to publish Sartre's book *Nausea*. Dullin, an actor and producer, also brought Sartre's plays to the notice of the Propaganda Department. It was this department that launched Sartre's career as a playwright.

When Matisse was invited to join a group of artists and writers to go to Germany as the guests of Goebbels, Matisse refused.

Other artists and writers did not. Beauvoir wrote, 'When writers and painters went to Germany to assure the conquerors of our intellectual support, I felt personally betrayed.'[21] On 16 July 1942, nearly 13,000 French Jews, including 4,000 children, were rounded up and sent to Auschwitz. Beauvoir did not mention this in her memoir *The Prime of Life*.

It is possible to measure how desperately a person needs to be the centre of attention by counting the number of times that person inserts himself into other people's stories. Celebrities in need of publicity have themselves photographed with a starving child – even going so far as to adopt one. The artists and writers who accepted the invitation to visit Germany might have betrayed France, but, far worse, they had betrayed Beauvoir. But how can you insert yourself into the story of deportation to Auschwitz? Beauvoir had more sense than to claim to be there when French police lifted little children into the cattle trucks bound for Auschwitz. Nor could she have identified with the people being deported. What they felt as they were pushed into the trucks is beyond the imagination of those of us who live safe lives, while commenting unfavourably on the deportations could have brought her to the attention of the Occupiers in a way she did not want. So she stayed silent and looked for other ways to be centre stage. I have known a great many people who were very skilled at getting centre stage in other people's stories. Start telling them a story in which they do not feature, and their eyes glaze over with boredom.

Sartre and Beauvoir must have witnessed the operation of the Service d'Enquête et de Contrôle (SEC) whose job it was to arrest Jews and foreigners. They often 'set their ambushes in the corridors of the metro, at the entrances of cinemas or the exits of theatres'.[22] The members of the SEC were French, and under the control of Louis Darquier. In her study of Darquier, his wife Myrtle and their daughter Anne, Carmen Callil wrote, 'The SEC did what they liked and became looters, the private army Darquier had always wanted . . . Fear of denunciation and consequent internment meant that SEC could make money from both Jew and Gentile.'[23]

'As Commissioner for Jewish Affairs, [Darquier] was the longest serving official of the Vichy state appointed to deal with the elimination and despoliation of the Jews in France . . . He was a professional man who used Jews as a way of making a living. More than that, he was a con man, one who was in his turn used by the Vichy state and the German occupiers as their puppet.'[24] For him, 'Jews were not human beings like the rest of us. In the minds of men like Louis Darquier they become mysterious bodies, another species altogether, creatures of enormous power controlling ordinary mortals through international finance and international communism.'[25]

Given the opportunity to fulfil his fantasies about the murder of the Jews, Darquier could not face the reality of the deportations in July 1942. He stayed in his office writing letters, hiding away from the terrible scenes as families were torn apart, and then men, women and children were crammed into the Vel' d'Hiv' to await the trains to Auschwitz.

In 1942 over 6,000 children were sent to Auschwitz, a thousand of them less than two years old. Callil wrote,

There are no accounts of the experiences of these children. We know that, whether aged nine months or thirteen, they had no food, no water, no air and no light on the journey to Auschwitz. As they could not be put to work, it is most probable that the children who did not die on the way were immediately exterminated, or taken, as many children were, for medical experiments. We do know that none of the Vel' d'Hiv' children returned to France.[26]

Darquier met and married Myrtle Jones from Tasmania. Myrtle saw in Darquier the man of her dreams, a sophisticated, man-about-town, aristocrat, none of which Darquier actually was. It was just one of the roles he played. She wanted to be rich and live in grand hotels, and this he supplied by carrying out scams and running up debts. There was no place for a child in their lies and fantasies, so they left their baby daughter Anne with her nurse, Elsie Lightfoot. Callil made a detailed study of the families from which Darquier and Myrtle came. She wrote, 'The Darquiers of Cahors were by no means as blind or loving as the Jones family of Launceston. Otherwise the two families had much in common. Their unsteady hold on respectability and professional achievement demanded silence, the forgetting of disturbing facts, and gave birth to children who escaped into fantasy worlds, and therefore wrought havoc.'[27] Much the same could be said of the Beauvoirs and the Sartres.

At the end of the war the simplicity of who were the good countries (Britain and her empire, the USA and the USSR) and who the bad (Germany, Italy and Japan) vanished. Now there were only two great powers, the USSR and the USA. Neither country was ready for another war, so each set out to win hearts and minds with propaganda. The propaganda of one side or the other appealed to those who believed the fantasy that 'my enemy's enemy is my friend'. So much did they want to believe that in this world evil is always balanced by good they refused to see that your enemy's enemy can be your enemy too. Wonderful though the USA might have been in many respects, there were many powerful Americans who indulged themselves in a fantasy of world domination, a fantasy for which we shall be paying the price for many years to come.

Writing about Nazi Germany, Spotts said, 'One of the cunning practices of totalitarian governments is to take advantage of the naïveté, gullibility and vanity of artists and, step by devious step, to manipulate and corrupt them.'[28] After the war the USSR spent a great deal of money and effort in the attempt to corrupt artists and intellectuals, and so did the American CIA.[29] Sartre and

Beauvoir accepted the patronage of the USSR and, with that, all the propaganda put out by the Communists. It astounds me that they could do this. Carole Seymour-Jones considers that Sartre saw in Communism a substitute for Christianity 'to which he clung with all the fervour of the convert'.[30] How did this illusion survive his visits to the Soviet Union? This shows the power of a dearly held fantasy, here the fantasy that there is somewhere a Power great and wise enough to fill the emptiness inside left by a lonely childhood.

I went to East Germany in 1971 as the guest of the Karl Marx Psychiatric Clinic in Leipzig. I was paid for my lectures, but I had to spend the money before I left. This was a difficult task as there was little to buy in Leipzig. At the clinic, I was told that I could not use any word that began with 'psyche', an extremely difficult order for a psychologist who worked as a psychotherapist to obey. Everywhere I went I found people who were afraid. The director, whom I had met when he visited the clinic where I worked in England, showed me around his clinic, including a very silent ward in which there were two lines of beds on each of which lay a comatose body covered by a blanket. These were the patients undergoing deep insulin coma therapy. He knew that I knew that this kind of therapy had been discontinued in the UK in the 1950s, not only because it did not cure schizophrenia, but, if it did not kill the patients, it severely damaged their health. The director said nothing, but his manner was apologetic, seemingly suggesting that he had no choice but to use this kind of therapy.

The psychologists working in the clinic were keen to talk to me. When I learned that they had no access to English psychology journals, I offered to send them the journals I read and then threw away. They begged me not to do this as they would not be allowed to receive these journals, and just being sent such material would reflect badly on them.

I was taken to meet various people involved one way or another in the clinic. It was obvious who were members of the Party, and at what level. The more senior they were, the more they had travelled abroad and the more books and journals from foreign publishers they had. On one visit, I met a man who must have been a very powerful Communist. There was no apparent connection between him and the clinic, but I felt I was there to be inspected. His apartment, and the conversation we had (he spoke excellent English) were similar to the apartments I visited and the conversations I had when in later years I was in the USA visiting American academics. However, when I was with the Americans I relaxed, and in East Germany I never did. This was not because I feared being arrested and imprisoned. My hosts supervised me gently but effectively. My fear stemmed from something I had known since I was a child: that the most dangerous people in the world are those who believe that they know what is best for other people. If you fall into their hands, and are terrified into obedience, these people will not only prevent you from being who you are but they will stop you from becoming all that you might have been. I could leave East Germany, but most of the people I met there could not.

Sartre returned from the Soviet Union full of praise for his hosts. Years later, he insisted that he had lied about this. Lies always require a reason, and he could give no consistent reason for lying. He could not tell the truth, that he had been deluded by his fantasy that he was so special that he was exempt from the standards of conduct expected of ordinary mortals. Even after Beauvoir and Sartre read Alexander Solzhenitsyn's *The Gulag Archipelago*, 'It is doubtful,' wrote Carole Seymour-Jones, 'whether, even with eyes wide open, they [were] courageous enough to admit to each other the part they played in prolonging the agony of Russian and Chinese people by propping up a bankrupt system.'[31]

After the Liberation, when Bianca returned to Paris, Beauvoir remembered how she had belittled Bianca for being so frightened

of being arrested by the Germans. She told Sartre, 'It's important to see a lot of her, and I'm going to try, because I'm filled
with remorse.'[32] Accordingly, from 1945, Beauvoir took Bianca
out once a month for forty years. This, however, was not an
undiluted pleasure for Bianca. Deciding to publish Sartre's letters
to herself, Beauvoir told Bianca that she would include in this
volume the letters Sartre wrote to Bianca, and which Beauvoir
held. Very reluctantly, Bianca gave Beauvoir permission to do
this, but asked that afterwards these letters should be returned to
her. Beauvoir promised that she would do this, and from then
until her death, Beauvoir would meet Bianca, but each time she
had forgotten to bring Bianca's letters.

When Sartre and then Beauvoir died, they were buried together
in Montparnasse cemetery. Some 5,000 people attended each
funeral. At the time of their deaths it seemed that their fame
would live forever.

Yet Carole Seymour-Jones found that, 'At the Exposition Sartre
of 2005 in Paris, the comprehensive exhibition celebrating his
century, I wandered almost alone among the exhibits . . . Fame
seemed to have morphed into infamy since Marcel Ophüls' film,
Le Chagrin et la Pitié.'[33] Time distils works of art, leaving a
residue of truth in some, in others nothing but a pile of dust.
Over the hundred years since its publication, Edmund Gosse's
book *Father and Son* has shone truer and truer. The same cannot
be said of many of the works of Sartre and Beauvoir.

Inside each of us is a world of ideas. Words, sounds, images and
sensations swirl around, each linked by some force of association
to the others. One small part of this world is consciousness where
ideas come and go. When we repress and deny, that is, lie to
ourselves, we create barriers within this world. In order to lie, we
need to know the truth. When we say to ourselves, 'That didn't
happen' we know that it did. We have to put a barrier between
knowing that something happened and telling ourselves that it did
not. Then we have to expend energy in keeping that barrier in place.

Barriers prevent the intermingling of diverse ideas that not only allows us to be creative but to be the whole person that we could be. Barriers within ourselves deform and cripple us.

Good artists have always known that all you need to create is to become highly skilled and knowledgeable in your craft, and then you potter around until the ideas begin to flow. Sartre and Beauvoir did not understand this. So vain were they about their intelligence that they rejected Freud's attempts to understand some of the processes occurring in our inner world. Freud's vanity prevented him from seeing many important aspects of his clients and of himself, but his work does show how foolish it is to think we can ignore what goes on inside us. Had Sartre and Beauvoir allowed themselves to see how there is much more to a person than skill in passing examinations, they would not have been satisfied to write novels and plays that were little more than representations of their own experiences. They would have let their experiences merge into their inner world, and waited quietly until something better, something truer about their lives, emerged.

The shared fantasy that Sartre and Beauvoir believed was the truth, that they were special people, damaged only themselves and some of the people close to them. Here is another shared fantasy that was taken to be the truth, and went on to damage millions of people.

On 16 May 2003, on the television programme *Meet the Press*, Vice-President Dick Cheney said,

I really do believe we will be greeted as liberators. I've talked with a lot of Iraqis in the last several months myself, had them to the White House. The President and I have met with various groups and individuals, people who've devoted their lives from the outside to try and change things inside of Iraq. The read we get on the people of Iraq is there's no question but that they want to get rid of Saddam Hussein and they will welcome as liberators the United States when we come to do that.[34]

170

The Delights of Shared Fantasies

The Bush-Cheney administration brought together the fantasies of fundamentalist Christianity with that of world domination by America. In all his speeches George Bush appealed to the emotions of his American audience. His key words were freedom, America, and God. He wasted no time reflecting on the complex issues facing America – an economic boom that was leading to a bust, an economy increasingly dominated by China, the unwinnable wars he had started in Afghanistan and Iraq, and climate change. Instead, he appealed to the emotions of his listeners by calling on the myth they shared about the American people, God, and the American dream. As Cyrulnik had said, 'The mere fact of experiencing a shared emotion, of worshipping the same representation and observing the same rituals together, gives us a delicious feeling of belonging. But we have to be careful. Lies are not the enemy of truth but myths are. We distrust lies and try to repress them, but we love myths and ask for nothing better than to surrender to them.'[35]

When fantasies become the myths that comfort and support us, and protect us from the truths of the world in which we live, we call them 'beliefs'.

Chapter Eleven

Special Fantasies: Beliefs and Delusions

When we say, 'I believe the trains to Richmond leave on the hour', or 'I believe that Canberra is halfway between Sydney and Melbourne', we are uttering a truth but making it clear that what we have said is a statement of probability. There could be evidence that our belief is wrong. This is very different from the statement 'I believe that the energy from crystals can cure cancer.' Here the speaker is not interested in notions of probability or evidence. The act of believing provides all the evidence that is needed. The speaker wants crystals to cure cancer, and so they do.

People who believe that crystals cure cancer or that their god takes a keen interest in everything they do can be very offended when their beliefs are called fantasies. It is an insult to the sacred, they say, when what has been called into question is their vanity. Dearly held fantasies flatter the holder, while plain, unvarnished truth can be very dull. When J.P. Morgan merged with Chase it became JPMorgan Chase. Then in 2004 it merged with Bank One, and Jamie Dimon of Bank One became chief operating officer for JPMorgan. Dimon's attitude to banking shocked those colleagues who had a high regard for themselves. Gillian Tett wrote,

The old J.P. Morgan bankers might have believed they were part of a quasi-noble financial guild, while the young derivative turks of the late twentieth century were driven by the belief that they were building a brave new cyberfinance world. Dimon took a purely pragmatic approach. To him, bankers were neither noble nor Masters of the Universe, they were just business people doing a job, pushing money around the economy as efficiently and effectively as they could. The point of a bank was simply to do business.[1]

Truths take no account of our wishes. Right now, I wish that tomorrow will be fine and hot, but I believe that it will rain for most of the day. I have listened to the weather forecast put out by the Met Office, and that is what it said. Beliefs that need no evidence are fantasies that the believer wants to be true. The greater the need for the believer to believe that his fantasies are true, the more he gets angry when anyone suggests that his belief is a fantasy. Many religious people get extremely angry when someone fails to shows the respect they feel their beliefs deserve. The television presenter and conservationist Sir David Attenborough told how he gets vile emails and letters from people angry that in his programmes he does not give God the credit for creating the wonders of nature. He said, 'They always mean beautiful things like hummingbirds. I always reply by saying that I think of a little child in East Africa with a worm burrowing through his eyeball. The worm cannot live any other way, except by burrowing through eyeballs. I find that hard to reconcile with a benevolent creator.'[2]

Sometimes when we are in a situation of great danger and there is little we can do to keep ourselves safe, we adopt or create a fantasy that we treat as being true in order to enjoy the illusion of being safe. We use an old superstition or create a new one. Writing about his experiences in the army in Vietnam, Tobias Wolff showed how what he knew was a fantasy became a belief that he took to be true. He wrote,

We were all living on fantasies. There was some variation among them, but every one of us believed, instinctively if not consciously, that he could help his chances by observing certain

173

rites and protocols. Some of these were obvious. You kept your weapon clean. You paid attention. You didn't take risks unless you had to. But that only got you so far. Despite the promise implicit in our training – *If you do everything right you'll make it home* – you couldn't help but notice that the good troops were getting killed right along with the slackers and shitbirds. It was clear that survival wasn't only a function of Zero Defects and Combat Readiness. There had to be something else to it, something unreachable by practical means . . . I carried a heavy gold pocket watch given to me by my fiancée . . . It went with me everywhere, rain or shine. That it continued to tick I regarded as an affirmation somehow linked to my own continuance, and when it got stolen toward the end of my tour I suffered through several days of stupefying fatalism.[3]

Scientific truths change with the acquisition of evidence. Beliefs change when people's ideas and fantasies change. Writing about the differences between Judaism and Christianity, Howard Jacobson pointed out that Jesus was a Jew. His way of behaving, as described in the New Testament, is the way a Jew would behave. He was a Jew 'in his relentless ethicising, in his love of quibbling and legalistics, in his fondness – frankly, to the point of tiresomeness sometimes – for extended metaphors and sermons wrapped in parables, and in the apocalyptic urgency of his teaching.' However, you would not gather this 'from nativity narratives, from hymns and carols, or the art that fills the churches of Christendom. The last thing Jesus looks on the cross is Jewish.'[4] The existence of so many different kinds of Christianity shows how fantasies change when ideas change. The Jesus who told the rich young man, 'Sell what you have, give the money to the poor, and follow me' is now, according to some preachers, the Jesus who, if you give yourself to him, will make you rich.

Fantasies and beliefs that are fantasies easily encompass inconsistencies. When Ken Ham had the fantasy of building the

Creation Museum in Petersburg, Kentucky, he wanted to show that Darwin and the theory of evolution were wrong, and that Genesis was right. However, he ignored the fact that, to be consistent in rejecting science, he should not use the inventions that science has produced. But a museum lit by candles was not what he had in mind. He wanted extensive lighting, captivating animatronic displays, and computer-generated information screens, all of which were the work of scientists.

People who reject science often claim that science is a faith in the same way that their religious beliefs are a faith. Science is not a faith. As Don Engel wrote in *New Scientist*, 'Science is the only method so far devised with the ability to explain the explainable.' He went on, 'Science, properly applied, is a self-correcting mechanism for seeing the world as accurately as possible.'[5] Science is not carried out only in laboratories. We are thinking scientifically when we try to see the world as accurately as possible.

When Tony Blair was prime minister, the words 'religion' and 'religious' had taken on very negative connotations. Terrorists were 'religious fanatics', and suicide bombers believed in a religion that said that as martyrs they would go to paradise. Even though his adviser Alastair Campbell had told him, 'We don't do God', Blair had seen George Bush using religious platitudes to create that pleasant feeling of sharing myth. Blair replaced the words 'religion' and 'religious' with 'faith' which he used dripping with sentimentality and implied virtue. He spoke of 'faiths' and brought the leaders of the different religions together as if they were all happy bunnies playing together in a sunlit meadow. There was no mention of heretics and infidels, or whether there was one God or a multitude of Gods. Blair praised and promoted faith schools, and conveniently forgot not only the madrassas that taught Islamic fundamentalism but the division in Northern Ireland between Catholic and state schools. This maintained the separation of the two communities, and it was this that caused the Troubles to which Blair himself had devoted much time and effort to bring to an end.

In trying to prettify religious beliefs, which are by their nature fantasies and myths, not truths founded on evidence, Blair revealed a lack of understanding of what religious beliefs entail. Many people hold kindly, comforting beliefs based on a benevolent God or a reliable friend called Jesus. Such people rarely become religious fanatics puffed up with pride, first, because they care a great deal about other people, and, second, they know that theirs is a personal belief and not necessarily shared by others. However, there are those who are certain that the beliefs they hold are absolute truths. Edmund Gosse said of his parents,

> Here was perfect purity, perfect intrepidity, perfect abnegation; yet there was also narrowness, isolation, and absence of perspective, let it be boldly admitted, an absence of humanity. And there was a curious mixture of humbleness and arrogance; entire resignation to the will of God, and not less entire disdain of the judgement and opinion of man . . . So confident were they of the reality of their intercourse with God, they asked for no other guide. They recognised no spiritual authority among men, they subjected themselves to no priest or minister, they troubled their conscience about no current manifestation of 'religious opinion'. They lived in an intellectual cell, bounded by the walls of their own house, but open above to the very heart of the uttermost heavens.[6]

Philip Gosse was a well-respected geologist and naturalist, and author of a number of books. Charles Darwin valued his work. Edmund Gosse wrote,

> As a collector of facts and marshaller of observations he had not a rival in that age; his very absence of imagination aided him in this work. But he was more an attorney than a philosopher,

176

and he lacked that sublime humility which is the crown of genius. For, this obstinate persuasion that he alone knew the mind of God, that he alone could interpret the designs of the Creator, what did it result from if not from a congenital lack of the highest modesty which replies 'I do not know' even to the questions which Faith, with menacing finger, insists on having most positively answered.[7]

Tony Blair was sincere. He did sincerity so well you would almost think he had got it made. But sincerity, even if the person is being truthfully sincere, does not prove the truth of what he is being sincere about. Columbus was sincere when he assured Ferdinand and Isabella that, if he sailed westward, he would come to China. When Blair talked about faith, he implied that having a faith is in itself virtuous. This is a conceit in which many religious people indulge. Beliefs are ideas. They are in our head. They are neither virtuous nor wicked until we act on them. Once we have acted, other people can judge whether our actions were virtuous or wicked. For instance,

Archbishop José Cardoso Sobrinho received Vatican backing for his decision to excommunicate the mother and the doctors of a nine-year-old rape victim who received an abortion. Brazil is the world's largest Catholic country and has tough anti-abortion laws, allowing the procedure only in cases of rape and health risks to the mother. The doctors believed that the young girl met those criteria but the Church argued that the preservation of life was paramount. The girl became pregnant as a result of sexual abuse by her stepfather. He was not excommunicated because the Church regards his crime as a lesser offence.[8]

Do you assess the archbishop's actions in the same way as he and the Vatican did?

It seems that the archbishop was confident that he had made the right decision based on his Catholic beliefs. Here we come to one of the most difficult aspects of forming our judgements. People speak glibly of 'self-esteem' without any recognition of the dilemmas involved in arriving at a degree of self-confidence that gives us sufficient confidence to face life's many difficulties but, in doing so, not relying on fantasies, particularly fantasies that are held as beliefs.

When Gillian Tett described the people that made up the team at J.P. Morgan who created the credit derivatives that removed risk from the bank's books, she talked of their talent and their confidence in themselves. Initially such confidence was not misplaced. However, they took the credit for their success, and, in doing so, they changed their initially true assessment of their ability into a fantasy that they alone were responsible for their success in making money. They overlooked how much chance plays in our lives. As Nassim Nicholas Taleb said, 'Nobody accepts randomness in his own success, only in his failure.'[9] They did not recognize that their fantasy was a fantasy. They saw it as the truth. Tett quoted the journalist Paula Froelich who had said, 'When you heard these guys speak, you realized that they really believe this stuff. They thought they were the smartest guys on the planet.' Their team leader Bill Demchak later recalled with a wistful smile, 'We had an amazing team spirit, it was just an amazing time. And, of course, we assumed it would last forever.'[10]

Nothing lasts forever. The team, being young, believed the myth that all of us believe when we are young, that everything that matters has happened since we were born. Why should the team remember anything that happened before they were born, such as the Great Depression and, before that, the South Sea Bubble? One member of the team, Terri Duhon, did remember a saying from the earliest days of computers, 'If you put rubbish in, you get rubbish out.' To create a model that will predict the outcome of what you are doing, you have to find good data on which to base your model. When she tried to find data concerning mortgage defaulting that covered several business cycles, she found that there was none. The pattern of financing housing changed over the years. She discussed this with her colleague Krishna Varikooty, a gifted mathematician who wanted to get things right, but who sometimes infuriated those colleagues who were impatient to make deals. Varikooty was concerned about what correlations there might be among the different risks of defaulting when a number of mortgages were bundled together. If Mr Jones was unable to pay his mortgage, would this connect to Mrs Smith's mortgage, making the chance of her defaulting greater or less, or would it be unchanged? House prices had been rising steadily. What would happen if, across the country, house prices fell? There was no data, so no one knew.

When our self-confidence is based on a fantasy that we tell ourselves is the truth, we can make big mistakes.

When Darwin's *On the Origin of Species* was published in 1859, many Christians protected their beliefs by ceasing to regard the Bible as being literally true. It was a book of myths and legends, open to many interpretations, and from which much wisdom could be drawn. Such a view creates enormous uncertainty, and many people cannot bear uncertainty. Philip Gosse was one of these. Edmund Gosse wrote that he 'allowed the turbid volume of superstition to drown the delicate stream of reason. He took one step in the service of the truth, and then he drew back in agony, and accepted the servitude of error.' He decided to 'have nothing to do with the terrible theory, but to hold steadily to the law of the fixity of the species. By a strange act of wilfulness, he closed the doors on himself forever.' He wrote a book that claimed that 'God hid the fossils in the rocks in order to tempt geologists into infidelity.' Edmund Gosse wrote, 'My Father, and my Father alone, possessed the secret of the enigma; he alone possessed the key which could smoothly open the lock of geological mystery. He offered it, with a glowing gesture, to atheists and Christians alike. But, alas! Atheists and Christians alike looked at it and laughed, and threw it away.'[11] What Philip Gosse threw away was the opportunity to work with Darwin by carrying out some of the painstaking, detailed research the theory of evolution required. If he had, we would, in 2009, be celebrating him along with those who worked with Darwin. But his vanity required glory in his lifetime, and so we know his name now only because his son, who had disappointed him greatly, wrote a book about him.

In *My Father's Country* there is a photograph of the Klamroth children singing and holding up their arms in a Hitler salute while their father plays the piano. Their mother Else wrote in their diaries, 'We are singing Hitler songs with Father'. The eldest child, Barbara, became a devotee of Hitler. His fantasies were to her the truth. In November 1944, aged twenty-one, Barbara wrote, ' "I cannot abandon him and my faith in him, whom I served, whom I wanted to serve my whole life long. So fully do I belong to this man who murdered my father that no clear thought has yet dared rise against him." And a little later: "Mein Führer, I was one of the most faithful. I am still not free of you, Mein Führer – still I want to stand before you, captured by your gaze, then order me to do what you will, I will die for you." '[12]

The strength of totalitarian regimes lies not in their military might but in those individuals who take the fantasies on which the regime is based to be the truth. They make the fantasy an essential part of their identity. When the regime's fantasy is shown to be a fantasy, as happened when Hitler was defeated, or Stalin's USSR fell apart, the individuals who had believed the fantasy were faced with reconstructing their whole sense of identity or creating more fantasies in the process of rationalizing their beliefs. Rather than blame themselves for believing Hitler's lies, devotees blamed the defeat of Germany on traitors within Germany and those who had supported them, namely the

Communists in the USA, Britain and the USSR. Their thinking on this was far from clear.

Bruhns was telling the story of her parents, so Barbara features in it only rarely. However, she ended her book with one of her first memories of after the war. 'I got slapped hard in the face. I can't remember who did it, Else or Barbara. I just remember coming flying through the kitchen. I had to become an adult before I understood why. Half-pint that I was, I had asked out of the blue, "Where did all the love for the Führer go? Why does nobody say Heil Hitler anymore?" Perhaps I should have asked, "Why did anybody ever say it?"'[13]

Why indeed? Why are we so willing to see fantasies, even other people's fantasies, as truth? Why have we not yet learnt that when we try to impose the fantasies we take to be truths on other people, there are consequences, not the consequences we intended, but consequences that could have been foreseen, had we not been blinded by our own wishes and desires?

In 1092 Pope Urban II preached a sermon which called on Christians to take up the mission to free the Holy Land from the Turks. Anyone who went on this crusade would have the Church's blessing, and anyone who fell in battle would go straight to heaven. At the end of his television series on the Crusades, Terry Jones said,

It took two hundred years for the crusades to create this Islamic fanaticism but they had done it. It was an imitation of their own intolerance. I suppose that one of the great gifts of religion is that it provides us with certainty in this uncertain and temporary situation in which we find ourselves called life. The only snag is that religion seems to make some people so certain that they're prepared to do terrible things to other people. This is the story of the crusades. Most crusaders set out with the intention of doing good, yet they ended up perpetrating one of the great crimes against humanity. What's more, the entire enterprise was a total failure. The net result of all their efforts was the exact opposite of what they'd set out to achieve. Islam, far from being destroyed, learned to imitate Europe's rage.[14]

Delusions

A delusion is a fantasy that has little relationship with the real world but rises out of memories, needs, fears and desires. Psychiatrists regarded delusions as a symptom of psychosis. Just to say you heard voices was enough to get you a diagnosis of schizophrenia. Psychiatrists were not interested in the content of a patient's delusions, and they did not ask their patients to talk about what their delusion meant to them. Had they done so, they would have discovered that, if a person had a delusion of, say, the voice of a witch screaming curses, this was a memory of some past events where the meaning, 'My mother was like a witch when she screamed at me' became 'My mother was a witch who screamed at me', and then, 'A witch is screaming at me.' What the witch said evolved from what the mother had said when she was angry with the child.

It was psychiatric patients, and not psychiatrists or psychologists, who saw how important the meaning of the delusion was. One of these, Patsy Hage, forced her psychiatrist, Marius Romme, to listen to her and her fellow patients. Impressed with this, Romme and his partner Sandra Escher embarked on the research that provided the evidence that Patsy Hage was right. What the voices said mattered. Out of this came the Hearing Voices Network, run by voice hearers for voice hearers.[15]

Many of us hear voices. If we were lucky enough to have had a reasonably pleasant life, our voices speak pleasantly to us. When we hear such a voice, the auditory part of our brain lights up. Managing our memory is an important part of leading a peaceful life. Being able to say to ourselves quite firmly, 'I am not going to think about that right now', is important. We acknowledge that something has happened, but there is a time to think about it, and a time to think about something else. The first step in managing our memory is to be truthful about remembering the past, and distinguishing between what are truths and what are fantasies.

There is no clear demarcation between sanity and madness. Sanity is behaviour that society will allow, and madness that behaviour that society will not allow. Homosexuality was madness, and then the law was changed, and homosexuals were sane. In times of war and conflicts certain behaviours are allowed that would never be allowed in peacetime. Whenever I hear complaints about what 'the youth of today' are doing, I recall how, as a teenager, I witnessed outrageous behaviour by the then 'youth of today'. Those antics were ignored or pardoned because the youths were soldiers defending our country. Immediately after the war, I went to university where the majority of students were ex-service men and women. War changes people, and not for the better. When I read Kevin Myers' book *Watching the Door* about the Troubles in Northern Ireland in the 1970s, I was reminded of the stories these student ex-service men and women told. They had been involved in much that was far from ordinary life. Such extremes of experience left many of them with extreme ideas that could easily become delusions. I found this again when, in the years that followed, I met migrants to Australia who had spent their formative years in wartime Europe.

One of the themes running through Myers' book is drink and being drunk. Many of my fellow students had drunk their way through the war, and they continued to do so at university. To them it was part of normal life. Alcohol made the conduct of the war possible. Wibke Bruhns told how, in his letters from the front, her father would describe the officers' parties where they drank 'themselves stupid in the middle of the war'. She went on,

'They all drink, Bernard and his baby-bride Ursula, when they're together, start the day with Cointreau – of all things! Barbara, not yet twenty, describes orgies of cognac in Munich, in the bar at the Bismarckplatz all the soldiers who are home on leave, or wounded on furlough from the military hospital, knock back the hard stuff like water.'[16]

Drunk or sober, many of my fellow students talked about the war, telling the kind of stories that had never appeared in the media, or did not appear until many years later. I listened, my curiosity always overcoming my feelings of horror or revulsion. I learned how people behave when they are very frightened and the rules that governed the society they grew up in no longer apply. These experiences and their constant fear created in many of them an instability that did not dissipate when they returned home. The people for whom they had the greatest hatred and contempt were not the people they had been fighting, but those on both sides who were responsible for the war, and the people, supposedly on their side, who planned and organized the whole military venture. The lies and incompetence of these armchair warriors were unforgivable.

Myers wrote, 'Contrary to what the Scriptures command and the good believe, grief does not soften but hardens: bereavement begets bereavement. For all those who declare that they don't want others to suffer as they have done, there are many more for whom death merely steels the human soul. Violence is a virus that colonises the human heart, and transmutes all emotions into steady, focused hate.'[17]

Hate creates myths. Myers observed,

As in every war it has fought, the British army believed that it killed more of its enemy than it actually was. Therefore, in the absence of many public funerals in the North, it believed that secret republican burials were occurring in the Republic. But the same story was told the other way round: IRA men were also convinced that they had killed more soldiers than had been acknowledged, and that in English towns soldiers were buried without ceremony, the local press sworn to secrecy. These myths became, remained and persist as abiding 'truths'.[18]

Such 'truths' have continued to flourish in Iraq and Afghanistan.

Myers described impartially the delusions of the Loyalists and the Nationalists. One night he went to interview Seamus Twomey, a senior IRA figure. Twomey blamed the English for everything. Twomey told Myers that uniformed British soldiers had been seen carrying a bomb into McGurk's bar. This bomb had caused the deaths of fifteen Catholics. When Myers queried why the soldiers would wear uniforms to carry out such an act, Twomey snarled, '"They were bluffing." What on earth could this bluff be? Twomey's eyes flashed. "Because they're British, and they realised that if they wore British uniforms dupes and eejits like you would say, British soldiers wouldn't wear uniforms doing something like this, so they must be people *pretending* to be British, aye, *pretending* and then people – aye, dupes and eejits like you – would blame the Protestants and say it's the backlash, BUT THERE IS NO BACKLASH BECAUSE DEEP DOWN THE PROTESTANT PEOPLE WANT A UNITED IRELAND," – a brief pause as his anger subsided and his voice lowered – "only they don't know it yet."'

Myers commented, 'This was like talking to a man who thinks that Martians run the post office and are stopping his mail.' He went on to say that Twomey was 'a man indoctrinated in the ways of death, who had repeatedly and casually caused men to be murdered. These deeds meant nothing to him: his eyes were not cold but angry, as if he lived his life in a permanently homicidal rage. His soul knew no pity, his conscience no sin.'[19]

In his memoirs, Albert Speer told how he had always thought that 'it was a most valuable trait to recognise reality and not pursue delusions. But when I now think of my life up to and including the years of imprisonment, there was no period in which I was free of delusory notions.' This sounds very commendable, but what he does not say is that anyone who was habitually suspicious of those who seek power would have recognized right from the beginning that Hitler's policies were dangerous fantasies bordering on the delusional. Some Germans did see this, and they did what they could not to be drawn into the drama Hitler wanted enacted. What Speer saw was the opportunity to fulfil his own fantasies. It was not until he saw the terrible end that he and his colleagues were facing that the full import of their fantasies dawned on him. Having had years in prison to ponder on this, he could write,

> In normal circumstances, people who turn their backs on reality are soon set straight by the mockery and criticism of those around them, which makes them aware that they had lost credibility. In the Third Reich there were no such correctives, especially for those who belonged in the upper stratum. On the contrary, every self-deception was multiplied as in a hall of mirrors, becoming a repeatedly confirmed picture of a fantastical dream world which no longer bore any relationship to the grim outside world. In those mirrors I could see nothing but my own face reproduced many times over.[20]

Hitler had been a soldier in the First World War. For the participants, war is a combination of terror and boredom. In those periods of boredom, soldiers ponder upon the miseries and conflicts in their own life, and in the wider world. Many, in some places most, of the young men and women who are recruited into the fighting forces are uneducated and know nothing of the politics of the conflict in which they are now involved. They learn the politics of those who command them, and they might learn different views from older comrades. They see, and perhaps take part in, cruelties and disasters. They try to blot out their fears with drugs and alcohol, but nothing can erase their memories or give them an inner stability. They ponder on all this, and fantasize about their future. Not all arrive at an inspirational dream of democracy. Many acquire 'a steady, focused hate'. Many become a version of Seamus Twomey. Many see the opportunity to become an Albert Speer, or a Heinrich Himmler. Such men are in their untold numbers in all the conflict areas around the world. In their early days of boredom, they could see that their fantasies were fantasies, but, as they experience terror upon terror, privation upon privation, with no end in sight, no promise of better things to come, all visions, even memories, of an ordinary life vanish. From then on, they have to find some other way of giving themselves comfort and courage. They turn their fantasies into delusions that promise to wreak havoc on their enemies. They can no longer distinguish between what is truth and what are lies. They form a large part of what is our future.

Chapter Twelve

Varieties of Lies

Lies are words or actions intended to deceive other people or ourselves. Often, when we lie to other people we also lie to ourselves.

'Lie' is such a short, sharp word. It seems so judgemental. We look for softer words, like 'fib' or 'white lie', and phrases like 'economical with the truth'. Phrases like 'half-truth', 'near-truth' suggest that a mixture of truth and lies is not as bad as a plain lie. However, a dose of arsenic stirred into a slice of rich fruit cake will kill just as surely as the dose all by itself. Our anxiety about what we call a lie arises from our unwillingness to see how often we do lie.

Societies differ in how they grade the wickedness of different kinds of lying. When he was addressing the students at Luiss University in Rome, Luca Cordero Montezemolo, president of Ferrari and chairman of Fiat, said, 'I was the world champion copier when I was in school. I think I had no rivals for technique and sophistication. I always found a way to sit near someone clever and generous who would let me copy.' Reporting this in the *Wall Street Journal* Frances X. Rocca commented that American students might plagiarize material on the Internet, but copying from another student and presenting this work as your own is seen as very reprehensible. He explained that in Italy copying was an expression of loyalty and fraternal solidarity. 'While cheats never prosper, copiers can, if they do it with flair.'[1]

For many people, lying is a matter of what they think they

can get away with. We have seen this in many of our politicians, but this is a practice that can start early in childhood. A teacher at a private school in Sydney talked to me about the eight-year-old boys in her class. She said, 'I see one of them bop another boy on the head. I say to him, "You bopped that boy on the head." He says, "No, I didn't." I say, "I saw you do it." He'll go on and on saying, "No, I didn't", and I'll keep saying, "I saw you." Then suddenly he'll switch and say, "He made me do it."' This is a wonderful example of how to go straight from the lie to the excuse for lying without a sign of contrition in between.

Some lies are clear and plain, and so we have no hesitation in calling them lies. Anyone who had seen what this teacher had seen would agree with her that the boy was lying. However, there are many ways of lying, and people will not necessarily call you a liar. You can be silent, and thereby withhold information, or let someone go on believing that such and such is the case when you know that it is not. You can lie to yourself, and then lie to others in order to keep the first lie in place, thereby creating a web of lies so big and complex that other people take it to be the truth. You can create a certain presentation of yourself that has within it an excuse for the lies that you tell. You can claim that you lie in the service of a higher principle or higher power. In all these ways of lying, you can be successful in your deception because others might not be perceptive enough to recognize your lies, or they might be too frightened to name your lies as lies.

Family life provides a hothouse for the lies of silence. Many silences are based on the principle of 'Least said, soonest mended.' In some silences this principle proves to be wise guidance, but in most what is actually needed is a tactful way of telling the truth. Often the silence is a weapon wielded by the person who wishes to be the most powerful person in the family. In my family this person was my mother. In the silences she inflicted on my father and me, her desire to punish us and to prevent us

189

criticizing her were obvious, but I also suspected that there were matters about which she was deceiving me. There were many secrets in her family, most to do with who had fallen out with whom, and what particular grievance my mother was nursing. Her family wished to be seen as being respectable, but they had a terrible secret – a convict grandfather and a grandmother who had deserted her two daughters, one of whom was my grandmother. My father knew what these secrets were, but my parents often colluded in lying to me about a great many things. This did not trouble them because they believed that it was appropriate for adults to lie to children.

In his book *Legacy of Silence*, the Israeli psychologist Dan Bar-On told the story of his visit to his grandfather's house in Heidelberg. His grandfather had committed suicide when Bar-On's father was fourteen. The family believed that the grandfather had 'inherited suicidal tendencies'. This has always been a popular theory about the cause of suicide because it seems to absolve the family of all guilt. We often read in newspaper reports of a suicide, especially the suicide of a young person, how the deceased had always been smiling and happy, and the family loving and close. However, there are always other consequences. Bar-On wrote, 'I cannot say I did not suffer from my father's own biological theories. He first told me about my grandfather's fate only when I was approaching forty. I remember being very angry that he had not mentioned it to me before. As a child I had sensed my parents' fear but could never understand it as anything but my own naughtiness.'[2]

Parents who have a secret that they keep from their children like to think that they are protecting the children, but what they are doing is hiding their own shame. Children can cope with the truth, provided the parents present it within the framework, 'This is terrible, but we are brave and strong and can cope with it.' Left ignorant of the truth, children interpret their parents' silence in ways that the parents might not want. My mother's silence increased my fear of her, while Bar-On saw himself as the cause of his parents' fear.

Bar-On was in Germany to interview some of the now grown-up children of senior Nazi officials. One of these, Manfred, whose father had been stationed at a death camp, talked about Germans he knew who were about his father's age. He said, 'I have discovered that these ordinary people, these normal people, don't have a biography for the years between '33 and '45. Yes, suddenly people become very innocent, unblemished, although they have been junior officials in '33 and even high ranking ones in '45.'[3] Our life story is an essential part of being a person. If there are gaps in it, our identity becomes fragmented, incapable of providing the solid base for our self-confidence and peace of mind. I have often heard people who have had a course of electroconvulsive therapy speak angrily about the gaps in their memory caused by the ECT. They cannot engage in those kinds of conversations where we say, 'We had a lovely holiday that year', or, 'I always remember what Billy did on his sixth birthday.' We celebrate the unity of our life and our identity when we talk about our memories, something the Germans about whom Manfred spoke prevented themselves from doing.

Life in Nazi Germany could be very difficult, but, as long as people kept any negative opinion of the regime to themselves, they were unlikely to put themselves in danger. It was very different in the USSR. In his study *The Whisperers*, Orlando Figes told how, under the Tsars, denunciation of officials who might have misbehaved was regarded as a virtuous act. He wrote, 'Under the Soviet regime, the culture of denunciation took on a new meaning and intensity. Soviet citizens were encouraged to report on neighbours, colleagues, friends and even relatives . . . Party members were instructed to inform on their comrades, if they believed that their private thoughts or conduct threatened Party unity.'[4]

191

He went on,

There was nothing in the private life of the Bolshevik that was not subject to the gaze and censure of the Party leadership. This . . . was unique to the Bolsheviks – there was nothing like it in the Nazi or the Fascist movement, where the individual Nazi or Fascist was allowed to have a private life, as long as he adhered to the party's rules and ideology . . . This mutual surveillance . . . encouraged people to present themselves as conforming to Soviet ideals whilst concealing their true selves in the private sphere.

Informed upon, people would be arrested and sent to one of the many gulags, perhaps never to be seen again, or only after many years. Often the informers were neighbours or relatives with a petty grudge or prejudice, secure in the knowledge that, in making their complaint, truth was not required.

In such regimes parents have to be very careful in what they say in front of their children. The daughter of a middle-ranking Bolshevik official recalled, 'There were certain rules of listening and talking that we children had to learn. What we overheard adults say in the whisper, or what we heard them say behind our backs, we knew we could not repeat to anyone. We would be in trouble if we let them know that we had heard what they had said . . . No one explained to us that what was spoken might be dangerous politically, but somehow we understood.'[5]

In regimes that require only an outward show of conformity, people can be truthful with themselves while lying to others, but when the regime pries into people's thoughts, being truthful with oneself becomes much more difficult. The watchful eyes of informers might see when our private truths reveal themselves in slips of the tongue and small actions. In such situations, people might feel that it is preferable to believe what the regime wants them to believe, rather than know what their own truths might be. Such people exist in all societies, not just totalitarian ones. They are frightened by people who are critical and sceptical of those in power, and call critics and sceptics radicals and revolutionaries. However, in the world we live in, truth is always revolutionary.

Most destructive of the individual are those regimes that claim that those in charge always know what the individual is thinking and feeling. Thus many small children are taught that God knows their every thought. Since God speaks directly to the Pope/priests/ministers/imams/parents, the child can assume that these powerful people know what the child thinks. Mothers faced with the task of working out whether their baby is crying because he is hungry or wet or lonely can become quite skilled in deducing correctly from the child's behaviour what he is thinking with regard to certain matters. However, a mother who tells her child, as Jenni Murray's mother did (page 85), that she always knows what he is thinking is inflicting on him a grievous injury. The suspicion that his parent knows what he is thinking becomes a worm in the bud, undermining his confidence in the only secure, complete privacy he has.

Fortunately, some children are wise enough to work out that, when they are told that God knows everything, they are being deceived. Edmund Gosse told the story of how his father would often preach on the sin of idolatry, particularly the sin of worshipping pieces of wood or stone. Anyone who did so would make God very angry. Having questioned his father in considerable detail about this sin, Edmund waited until his parents were out before carrying out a scientific test of his father's belief. He wrote,

> I was in the morning room on the ground floor, where, with much labour, I hoisted a small chair on to the table close to the window. My heart was now beating as if it would leap out of my side, but I pursued my experiment. I knelt down on the

193

carpet in front of the table and looking up said my daily prayer in a loud voice, only substituting the address 'O Chair' for the habitual one.

He waited to see what would happen.

It was a fine day, and I gazed at the slip of white sky above the houses opposite, and expected something to appear on it. God would certainly exhibit his anger in some terrible form, and would chastise my impious and wilful action. I was very much alarmed, but still more excited; I breathed the sharp air of defiance. But nothing happened; there was not a cloud in the sky, not an unusual sound in the street. Presently I was sure that nothing would happen.[6]

This result did not lead Edmund to question the existence of God, but it did reduce his confidence that his father knew the mind of God. This raised the possibility that God might not be angry if he prayed for 'toys and sweets and smart clothes as well as for the conversion of the heathen'.[7]

Early in his life Edmund came to value what he later called, 'a human being's privilege to fashion his inner life for himself'.[8] He had learned that he must resist the Trojan horse of believing that someone else could know the contents of his mind. Alas, many children do not come to understand this for themselves. They grow up believing that God knows what they think. They fear to think their own thoughts, and believe implicitly everything their religious leader tells them. Some people in adult life might discard their religion, but they continue to harbour the fear of being punished for what they think and feel. Should they become depressed, all the terrors of God's punishment fall upon them, threatening to crush them. They cannot escape from their avenging God until they are able to gather the strength to resist these memories from the past.

Varieties of Lies

In her memoir *Giving Up the Ghost* Hilary Mantel showed
how such a fear could be instilled in a child by preventing the
child from fashioning his inner life for himself. She wrote,

> Each month, from the age of seven to my leaving at eleven we
> walked up the hill from the school to the church to go to confes-
> sion and be forgiven all our sins. I would come out of church
> feeling, as you would expect, clean and light. This period of
> grace never lasted beyond the five minutes it took to get inside
> the school building. From about the age of four I had begun
> to believe that I had done something wrong. Confession didn't
> touch some essential sin. There was something inside me that was
> beyond remedy and beyond redemption. The school's work
> was constant stricture, the systematic crushing of any spontaneity.
> It enforced rules that had never been articulated, and which
> changed as soon as you thought you had grasped them.

When adults tell children that they are too young to understand
something they have encountered, some children are tempted to
be lazy and not think, but others are wise enough to know that,
when adults say this, there is something in the situation that the
adults want to hide. Mantel was a wise child. She realized that,
'You must not accept that things were beyond your understanding
because they told you they were; you must go on trying to understand them. [For me] a state of inner struggle began. It took a
huge expenditure of energy to keep your thoughts intact. But if
you did not make this effort you would be wiped out.'[9]
  Whenever I see pictures of large numbers of North Koreans
performing obediently in some kind of gymnastics I wonder how
many of them gave up trying to understand what was going on,
and, accordingly, were wiped out as an individual. The only
meaning they can give to their existence is to be obedient.
  In a dictatorship, the leader decides what his subjects are allowed
to discuss. Philip Gosse decided what his family could discuss.

195

In the household I grew up in, my mother decided what could or could not be mentioned. In the Gosse household God's punishment for mentioning the unmentionable was, to say the least, erratic, but in my mother's household her punishment of wrong doers was immediate and more terrible than any God could inflict, or so it felt to me. However, these experiences gave me a good grounding in understanding how power operates. I acquired, as Gillian Tett did when she studied anthropology, 'a sense of scepticism about official rhetoric'. She wrote, 'In most societies, elites try to maintain their power not simply by garnering wealth, but by dominating the mainstream ideologies, both in terms of what is said, and also what is not discussed. Social "silences" serve to maintain power structures in ways that participants barely understand, let alone plan.'[10]

In 1994 two groups of men, on either side of the Atlantic, were planning to change the world. In England the Labour Party was still in opposition, but those members who called themselves New Labour were planning to win the next election. Part of their plan was to abandon Labour's traditional suspicion of businessmen and bankers, and instead work closely with them. On Florida's Gold Coast a group of bankers linked to J.P. Morgan met to create a new means of increasing the bank's derivatives business and, most importantly, finding ways of controlling the risks the bank took when dealing in derivatives. What they did not notice was that their methods of controlling risk could also amplify it. However, the bank was making money, and the other banks joined in, making even more money and creating even more versions of this new product, all bearing mystifying names like collateralized debt obligation (CDOs) and structured investment vehicle (SIV).

House prices were rising steadily and mortgages were easily available. Banks had always expected that anyone who applied for a mortgage would be able to supply evidence that they would be able to meet their payments, but in the USA mortgages were being given to people who had little chance of paying even a fraction of what they owed. These were called subprime mortgages. Salesmen, being interested only in what bonus they would get for a sale, told fanciful lies about their contracts. Some of their customers were people who had not had the necessary experience of what mortgages entailed to recognize that they were being deceived. There were others who ought to have known better.

One of these was Edmund Andrews, an economics reporter for the *New York Times*. In his book *Busted: Life Inside the Great Mortgage Meltdown* he told how, divorced and paying alimony, he wanted to buy a house for him and his second wife and her children. He went to American Home Mortgage where he was told, 'What mattered more than anything was a person's credit record. Investors had become steadily less interested in the details of a person's financial position. If you had always paid your debts on time before, the theory went, you'd probably do so in the future.' Andrews was a reporter. He must have covered hundreds of stories where an unexpected catastrophe occurred. Yet, as he said, 'I thought I could beat the odds.'[11] The odds were based on the belief that house prices would continue to rise. They did not, and in 2007 American Home Mortgage filed for bankruptcy.

Anyone who had mastered the concept of a mortgage – you borrow money and pay it back with interest, but, if you cannot pay, you lose your house – could see the danger in these subprime mortgages, but not, apparently, senior bankers and politicians. The bankers who dealt in CDOs and SIVs and the like talked about them in their exclusive jargon. It was the story of the Emperor's New Clothes all over again. The senior bankers and politicians apparently believed, as many men do, that, if they admitted that they did not know something, their two most precious possessions would drop off. They had spent a lifetime not reading the manuals of the equipment they had bought, and, when they were lost, not asking the way to go, and they were not going to change now. They pretended to understand the jargon, and insisted that everything was under control.

George Bush and Tony Blair, who believed that they knew everything they might ever need to know, wanted to take the credit for a booming economy. Moreover, they needed money for their wars. The economy was going through a twenty-first-century version of the South Sea Bubble, but nothing was said. Gillian Tett wrote,

> Most mainstream newspapers all but ignored the credit world until the summer of 2007. So did politicians and non-bankers. It was a classic area of social silence. Insofar as any bankers reflected on that silence (which very few ever did), most assumed that it suited their purposes well. Freed from external scrutiny, financiers could do almost anything they wished. Locked in their little silos, few could see how the pieces fitted together, or how bloated the future was. [12]

The lies we tell ourselves blind us to what is actually going on. As Simon Hoggart once said, 'You can fool some of the people some of the time, but you can usually fool yourself whenever you want to.'[13]

A biologist who wants to make a name for himself can search for a new species of insect or a new kind of cell, and a chemist a new element, but it is extremely difficult for a psychologist to find some new kind of human behaviour. Our circumstances change, but we go on, generation after generation, behaving in the same old ways. If the great philosophers and historians have not written about some aspect of our behaviour, Shakespeare has. However, in the second half of the twentieth century, some psychologists seized on the twin ideas of publicity and a brand name. They would choose some small aspect of behaviour, give it a brand name, claim to have found something new, and present it to the public, usually by writing a popular psychology book, and issuing a press release. There are now as many brand names in psychology as there are brands of mobile phones, but one of the first was Cognitive Dissonance which appeared in 1957. It was created by a psychologist called Leon Festinger, and it proved to be a very successful brand name, not quite as successful as Microsoft, but it still provides a living for a number of psychologists.

Joel Cooper in his *Cognitive Dissonance: Fifty Years of a Classical Theory*, defined it as, 'the holding of two or more inconsistent cognitions arouses the state of cognitive dissonance, which is experienced as uncomfortable tension. The tension has drive-like properties and must be reduced.'[14] The best example of cognitive dissonance that I have come across is the one by Groucho Marx, 'My mother-in-law going over a cliff in my Cadillac.' Mother-in-law jokes are not as common as they were then, perhaps because mothers-in-law are so busy with their careers they do not have time to harass their son- or daughter-in-law (though some do make the time to enjoy a quick harass or two). However, the principle is clearly seen – two conflicting ideas that create an uncomfortable tension. In Groucho's example, the pleasure of losing his mother-in-law forms a tension with the anguish of losing his car.

All the ideas we hold are interlinked to form a structure. When we acquire two ideas that contradict one another, our meaning structure does not fit together neatly, and we feel uncomfortable. We need to find a way of resolving this discomfort by enclosing both ideas within some more abstract idea. Had Groucho been an expert in feeling guilty, he could have created the idea, 'Losing my car is my punishment for being so unkind to my mother-in-law.' However, his screen character never showed the slightest sign of guilt. He would have been more likely to enclose both ideas within some version of, 'It's all part of life's rich tapestry.'

When events contradict our most dearly held ideas, instead of abandoning the ideas that have been shown to be wrong, many of us do whatever we can to hang on to our old ideas. Dearly held ideas are those that support our sense of being a person. Hence we will lie to ourselves and to others in order to hold on to them.

When Hitler killed himself, and when the USSR crumbled, people who had given their life to their leaders were faced with abandoning what was an essential part of their identities. While there are still a number of Germans who regard Hitler as a hero who was cruelly betrayed by his enemies, the majority of Germans in West Germany swiftly changed from being loyal Nazis to being democratic capitalists. This did not happen in Russia. While there was no return to Communism, the long-established belief in the necessity of a strong leader overcame the attempts to establish a Western-style democracy. There are many reasons for these two different outcomes, but some of these reasons relate to the kind of fantasies held by Hitler and by Lenin and Stalin.

Hitler's fantasies were straightforward and simple.

Those who belong to the Aryan race, i.e., the Germans, are the greatest and the best.

Everyone else is inferior and evil, the Jews most of all.

Because they are virtuous and dedicated to the Führer, Germans will conquer the world.

Many millions of people all around the world have similar fantasies, where they replace 'Aryan' with their own race/nationality/religion, and 'Jews' with some other enemy. After the war, many Germans were able to continue to believe in the first and second fantasy, and replace the third with, 'Because they are virtuous, intelligent and hard-working, Germans will make Germany the leading country in Europe.' Which is precisely what they did. The historian Tony Judt wrote, 'Germans turned the defect of their industrious obedience into a national virtue.'[15]

The fantasies of Lenin and then Stalin were much more complex. These were based on a theory drawn from their own interpretation of the writings of Karl Marx, and with their personal hatreds replacing Marx's understanding of and sympathy for the people who had to work for a living. Their theory, which was a fantasy, provided the justification for what they did, regardless of the consequences. A theory that has no evidence to support it is no more than a fantasy in a person's mind. However, if that person tries to force that theory on to the world, then the theory becomes a lie.

Stalin wanted to rid the country of peasants and create in their place huge collective farms. According to Leninist ideology, wealthy farmers, called kulaks, were enemies of the people, but, actually, the idea of kulaks was a fantasy. Some farmers were more efficient than others and did slightly better, but they were far from being wealthy. Nevertheless, Stalin said that they existed and had to be 'liquidated', and so a purge of peasants began. Some of the people carrying out this purge were opportunists, but others believed the propaganda of the Five Year Plan. 'They believed with the Bolsheviks that any miracle could be achieved by sheer human will.' That is, they believed that they could force reality to be what they wanted it to be. One of these people was Lev Kopelev, a young Communist who took part in some of the worst atrocities against the Ukrainian peasants. Kopelev and his comrades took everything the peasants had, including all their food. In the 1970s Kopelev recalled the children's screams. He said, 'It was excruciating to see and hear all this. And even worse to take part in it . . . And I persuaded myself, explained to myself, I mustn't give in to debilitating pity. We were realizing historical necessity. We were performing our revolutionary duty. We were obtaining grain for the socialist fatherland. For the Five Year Plan.'[16] The theory was deemed to be more important than real human suffering.

One important part of the Five Year Plan was to create a modern

201

industrial society. Amongst the large industrial projects planned was the White Sea Canal. People seen as enemies of the state, such as the kulaks and the bourgeoisie – what Orlando Figes called 'phantom classes' – became slave labour to build the canal. The labourers had to do everything by hand, using shovels and wheelbarrows. They worked to exhaustion in the cold. Many froze to death. Bodies that were not removed to a communal grave were thrown on to the shingle where their bones were mixed with the concrete and became part of the walls of the canal. Anatoly Mesunov, who had been a guard at the canal, wrote his memoirs in the 1980s where he said, 'I had my doubts about the Five Year Plan. I did not understand why we had to drive so many convicts to their death to finish the canal. Why did it have to be done so fast? At times it troubled me. But I justified it by the conviction that we were building something great, not just a canal, but a new society that could not have been built by voluntary means. Who would have volunteered to work on that canal? Today, I understand that it was very harsh and perhaps even cruel to build socialism in this way, but I still believe it was justified.'[17]

In saying this, Mesunov was not only denying the truth in order to hold on to his fantasy, but he was overlooking the past that showed that the White Sea Canal had proved to be a white elephant. To save time and money in building the canal, its depth was reduced from 22 feet to 12 feet (in some parts just 6 feet), making it useless for all but those boats with very shallow draughts.

By the time Mesunov was writing his memoirs it should have been clear to him that the revolution of which he had been part had not produced the splendid society it had promised. To admit this would mean that he had wasted most of his life. Such an admission would be devastating. So he continued to lie to himself by insisting that all the human suffering was a price worth paying.

When he was collecting all these stories from the early years of the USSR, Orlando Figes relied quite heavily on the website www.hrono.info, Russia's largest online history resource. On 19 June 2009, the home affairs ministry in St Petersburg blocked the website because, so officials said, it contained extracts from Hitler's diary, *Mein Kampf*. This book is not particularly hard to find. It is available in many languages and editions on the Amazon website. The real reason for the closure of the site was probably the article published on the site criticizing St Petersburg's governor, Valentina Matviyenko, for cutting the allowance given to survivors of the Nazi siege of Leningrad. Mean and nasty though this action is and the stupid lie told to defend it, there seems to be a deeper cause. Luke Harding, based in Moscow, wrote, 'The closure comes amid official attempts in Russia to rewrite some of the darkest aspects of its 20th-century history. School textbooks now portray Stalin not as a mass murderer but as a great, if flawed, national leader and an "efficient manager" who defeated the Nazis and industrialised a backward Soviet Union.'

A month later, the site was operating again under a new provider, but President Medvedev had announced in the previous May that he was setting up a new body to counter the 'falsification of history'.[18] How like Orwell's *1984* this all sounds! In that society the government had a 'memory chute' down which all inconvenient truths could be despatched.

Reality rarely accommodates itself to our ideas. Even when we have constructed our theory using scientific truths, and we have worked very hard at getting to know the bit of reality with which we want to interfere, the imposition of our ideas never turns out to be exactly what we had expected. What better example of the application of a theory based on scientific truths could there be than the Hadron Collider, and still it did not work as expected! When the application of the theory does work reasonably well, reality soon reminds us about the law of unintended consequences. When Tim Berners-Lee created the

World Wide Web, he did not see that he was creating a paradise for pornographers.

If our theory has no relationship to the truth, it becomes a lie when we try to apply it to reality. If to no one else, we are lying to ourselves.

Stalin knew that the whole country relied on the peasants to supply the food it needed. Over hundreds of years, the peasants had acquired the skills and knowledge necessary to work their own piece of land. However, peasants the world over tend to be very suspicious of their government's intentions, and therefore they are not particularly obedient. Stalin's desire to have an obedient populace overrode his knowledge that it was the peasants who fed Russia. He created the fantasy of the Five Year Plan to force the peasants off the land, and replace them with collective farms. Disaster followed.

The people who ran the collective farms were political appointees with little experience of farming, while the labourers had little interest in farming land that they did not own. The Party set targets for production, and the local officials, knowing that these targets were impossible to reach, lied about how much the farms had actually produced. These lies and the many failures in transportation of produce resulted in the widespread famine that began in 1932. Many of the deaths that followed were unregistered, but 'the best demographic estimates suggest that between 4.6 million and 8.5 million people died of starvation or disease between 1930 and 1933'.[19]

When we are determined to force our ideas on reality and repeatedly discover that reality refuses to respond as we wish, every failure is a threat to our sense of being a person. Stalin's defence against this fear was to blame his enemies. They were everywhere. As his paranoia increased, he ceased to be concerned with the future of the revolution and the welfare of his people. All that concerned him was his own safety. If he could not have his enemies assassinated, he sent them to the gulags.

It would be nice to think that, when a man becomes president of the United States, he will put the needs of the American people, of whom aspiring and successful presidents speak so much, before his own. Alas, that is rarely the case. Being president means constantly encountering cognitive dissonances and finding ways, many of these far from honest, of resolving them. The historian Barbara Tuchman, in her book *The March of Folly*, called cognitive dissonance 'an academic disguise for "Don't confuse me with the facts"'. She went on,

> Cognitive dissonance is the tendency 'to suppress, gloss over, water down or "waffle" issues which would produce conflict or "psychological pain" within an organization'. It causes alternatives to be 'deselected since even thinking about them entails conflicts'. In the relations between subordinate to superior within the government, its object is the development of policies that upset no one. It assists the ruler in wishful thinking, defined as 'an unconscious alteration in the estimation of probabilities'.

Here Tuchman was quoting from a report by Roger Hilsman, head of the State Department's Bureau of Intelligence, and Michael Forrestal of the National Security Council. They were advising President Kennedy about the likely outcome of further American involvement in Vietnam. Kennedy had already been advised by people who knew the situation well, including the economist J.K. Galbraith. They all agreed that, if the US government significantly increased its assistance to South Vietnam's operations against the Vietcong, the war would last longer and cost more in money and lives than was anticipated. Kennedy knew all this, but he ignored it, even though, he admitted privately, he saw the wisdom of the advice he had been given. But, as Tuchman said, he had a reason, 'the most enduring in the history of folly: personal advantage, in this case a second term'. Kennedy stated that he could not give up Vietnam to the Communists, and

205

asked the American people to vote for him. They elected him for a second term, but he did not see it out. He went to Dallas, and was assassinated. Meanwhile, America had begun conducting a long, costly, unwinnable war in Vietnam. Not learning from experience, America is now conducting a similar long, costly, unwinnable war in Afghanistan.

Tuchman concluded, '[Kennedy's] position was realistic, if not a profile in courage. Re-election was more than a year and a half away. To continue to invest American resources and inevitably lives in a cause in which he no longer had much faith, rather than risk his own second term, was a decision in his own interest, not the country's. Only an exceedingly rare ruler reverses that order.'[20]

Sometimes it is not possible to resolve two incompatible ideas simply by lying or denial. When one idea is a truth that cannot be denied, and the other idea a dearly held fantasy, the only way to hold on to both is to build a kind of Berlin Wall in your mind.

Peter Stothard, editor of the *Times Literary Supplement*, gave an example of such a wall. He said, 'I met some very rich oil barons in Texas, hard line creationists, people who had put George Bush in power. Trying to argue with these people was almost impossible. Their mind was completely separated. They'd read in detail the way fossils told them about oil, and they absolutely disbelieved that the Bible wasn't literally true on the way the world began in the Genesis story.'[21]

Here was this group of men whose work and wealth was based on knowing in detail about the various ages of the Earth, the history of fossils, and the formation of oil – all scientific truths – and at the same time they believed that none of this was true. They might have built a Berlin Wall between these two ideas, but, even though walls separate people, the people on one side of the wall know that there are people on the other side of the wall. These men knew they were lying to themselves. I would guess that when Stothard was with these men he was careful not to challenge them about their beliefs. People who construct walls like this are very sensitive to any challenge and likely to react badly. Holding two very different and opposing ideas and keeping a wall in place between them not only creates enormous tension but the wall prevents easy access to the multitude of ideas that a person holds. A person who does this cannot enjoy that ease of wide-ranging thought and novel connections between ideas that is the source of creativity. There can be no easy communication with other people because other people have always to be on guard lest they unwittingly say something that offends. The wives and children of these oilmen would know that only too well.

In much the same way, the men who penned the 'self-evident truth' that 'all men are created equal' must have been annoyed whenever someone pointed out to them that they owned slaves.

Chapter Thirteen

The Same Old Lies

Over the years, I have been told many stories about how the story-teller's marriage broke down. I know from my own marriage that it is a painful experience. Marriages break down for many reasons, but a common story is that, when the wife was looking after the children, the husband was unfaithful. Each time I listen to one of these stories, I cannot help thinking, 'Same old story, same old lies.'

The break-up of my marriage occurred when I was working in a government department where my boss, Bill, was a veteran of the war in the South Pacific. His outlook on life was somewhat austere. When I told Bill that my husband had been forced to admit to me that he was having an affair, Bill made just one comment. He said, 'A standing cock has no conscience.'

This statement removed from my mind any concern that it was my fault my husband was unfaithful, and allowed me to admit to myself that marriage did not suit me. In 1964 this was a radical thought at a time when marriage was still considered to be the pinnacle of every woman's existence. I decided that there are many things that are worth trying only once, and marriage was one of them.

Conscienceless cocks and their owners find it easy to lie. The same old lies that men tell women form a fairly short list that perhaps should be included in the sex education of girls. Not that they would take much notice. If their fantasies require that these lies be heard as truths, this is what girls will do. Some things can be learnt only by experience.

The Same Old Lies

A successful liar fits his lies into the framework of a fantasy that he persuades others is the truth. An example of this is given in Peter Stanford's biography of Cecil Day-Lewis. Stanford does not make this the basis of his book. He does not judge Day-Lewis, but simply describes the circumstances where he lied to his various women, and they accepted his lies. (Stanford also devotes much of his book to Day-Lewis's poetry.) They might not have always accepted his lies as being the truth, but, if they wanted him to be part of their life, they had to accept that this was what they got. All of this depended on the presentation of himself that Day-Lewis had constructed.

Cecil Day-Lewis was a famous poet in the 1930s, along with W.H. Auden and Stephen Spender. He joined the Communist Party in 1936, when it was fashionable to do so, but he did this without conviction, which was fortunate because his poetry was far too self-centred to be acceptable to the Party. He became very well known in literary circles, and in 1951 he was elected Professor of Poetry at Oxford University. There was some media interest when, in 1951, he was divorced for adultery. In those days, divorce was still scandalous. He then married the young actress Jill Balcon, who had been named in the divorce, but his earlier liaisons, which were of the kind which would now feature in the tabloids, were then considered to be a private matter. By the time he died in 1972 his exploits had paled in comparison to the exploits of the then headline fodder. When I read his biography, I was reminded of the lives of many of my contemporaries. Day-Lewis was a man of his time.

He was born in 1904. His mother died of cancer when he was just four. The only clear memory he had of her was being taken to her bedroom to say a final goodbye. His father dealt with his own grief by refusing to mention his wife in conversation and he refused to allow pictures of her around the house. No doubt he assumed, as many adults do, that children forget. This is a comforting lie that adults tell themselves. If they thought about it truthfully, they would know that they had many memories of their childhood. I have met people who deny remembering their childhood, yet in conversation they can reminisce quite extensively about this period in their life. This loss of memory occurs when some fact or emotion emerges that conflicts with the picture the person wants to have of himself.

In the household where Day-Lewis was a child, there was a whole herd of elephants that had to be ignored. There was the woman who must not be mentioned, the father's grief, and the child's grief and confusion. Not noticing this herd of elephants would have ensured that there were endless complications in communications and endless pretences and lies. Day-Lewis was not being presented with an image of a family where people were open and honest with one another. Relatives and friends, no matter how truthful and honest they were in their own lives, would have been drawn into the deceit and lies present in the Day-Lewis home.

Every family has its own family style in relating to one another. As a child grows up, he has a choice of rebelling against his family style or of merely adapting his family's style to the circumstances of his own life. Day-Lewis chose the second, and created a way of living that depended on lies and deceit. He kept his truth for his poetry.

Day-Lewis's father seemed not to know that a child needs to form a bond with his mother so that he can take within himself a representation of his mother. Psychologists call this representation an internal object. Children who are deprived of the opportunity to form any internal objects, as happens to young children separated from their parents during a war or conflict, find it difficult to form relationships. Once the internal object representing the mother is secure, the child can tolerate separation from her. The absence of an internal object leaves a hole, an emptiness that is real to the person in the same way as the pain of a broken heart is as real as the pain of angina.

210

The Same Old Lies

When his mother died, Day-Lewis had within himself four years' store of memories of his mother. However, the majority of these memories were in auditory, tactile, kinaesthetic and olfactory images, while the visual images were those that a baby or a toddler creates of himself in relation to giants, the most important of whom is his mother. These images could not easily be translated into words, although they might for the rest of his life inhabit his dreams. Like all four-year-olds, his task was to blend these images into the word-laden images he was able to create as his language skills increased and his mother gradually turned into a human-sized being. However his mother's death cut this process short. His father should have tried to continue this process by talking to his son about his mother, looking at photographs of her, and weaving her into their everyday life. He should have said things like, 'Your mummy loved flowers', 'She was always singing', and, most importantly, 'Your mummy thought you were the most wonderful boy in the world. She loved you very much.' But he did not, and Day-Lewis was left with an aching void that he had to fill in some way. His education at Sherborne provided very little that he needed to assist the process of creating a sustaining internal object, and so, as a young man, he tried to fill the void the way a small boy would. He looked for and found another mummy.

His new mummy, whom he first met when he was eighteen, was a young woman called Mary King. Her fantasy of what her future would be was the one that all well brought up girls were supposed to have. She would meet and marry the most wonderful man, and she would spend her life looking after him. Unfortunately, her upbringing had also undermined her self-confidence by teaching her to blame herself for whatever went wrong.

Every childhood has its own traumas, and no one emerges from childhood a neatly fashioned, well-functioning person. Most of us spend years trying to fit together the fragments of our self and repair the damage to our self-confidence that our upbringing

211

and education have inflicted. We can be in our forties, or even older, before we get it more or less right. However, some people take a short cut. Often they have within them such a huge well of sadness and unwept tears as well as a storm of unexpressed rage that they fear to look inward lest they be overwhelmed by a lifetime of buried emotions. As a result they do not want to undertake the hard, painful work of assessing their childhood with an adult eye. Instead they fashion a presentation of themselves that is both a defensive shield and a means of negotiating a way through the world that is to their advantage as they see it. This is what Day-Lewis did.

He created the character of the poet who was very appealing to women but shared his intimacies with men, particularly fellow writers. He took himself very seriously as a writer. He saw himself as being sensitive and physically delicate, and in need of looking after. Stanford wrote, 'His emotional needs, as he perceived them, were simple. "In my younger days, a mother figure was all I wanted," he was to write, and Mary took to tending to his every need. He soon developed a series of minor illnesses which necessitated bed-rest and her constant ministrations.'[1]

People who create a presentation of themselves not so much live their life as enact a role. They can feel that there is nothing inside them, and that they are a role without an actor. They cannot bear to be alone. To feel that they exist, they can create emotional dramas to make them the centre of attention. If they are writers or artists, they can use these dramas in their work. They need an audience to applaud their role, and they need the person closest to them to have the solid centre they lack. Mary supplied both the audience and the solid centre, but, after they were married, Mary made a huge mistake. She got pregnant. Did she not realize that her husband had to be her only child? Day-Lewis reacted with all the anger and venom of an only child presented with a usurper. He did what men like him always do in this situation. He had an affair. This was with Alison, the wife of a friend. He was a poet, so he wrote a poem about his affair, and how terrible it was that Mary's pregnancy had deprived him of being at the centre of her world. He knew that Mary would read the poem. She usually did read his work.

One subtle way of lying is to use a word or phrase that has two distinct meanings, but not make clear which meaning it is that you are using. The word 'sensitive' can be used in this way. In 'an artist must be sensitive to his feelings and to his surroundings', 'sensitive' means 'aware of'. In 'he is very sensitive' it means 'easily upset'. In a sleight of word, writers and artists can claim that their sensitivity is the source of their creativity and that, because they are so sensitive, they are easily upset. Day-Lewis told Mary, as he seems to have told all his women, that he was so sensitive he could not cope with any kind of confrontation. If she upset him, he would not be able to write, and the world would be deprived of his art. This was most effective in shutting Mary up.

There was another lie that he must have used on Mary when she was distressed by his infidelity. In his novel *The Friendly Tree* the principal character, modelled on Day-Lewis, has an affair with Evelyn (Alison), but returns to Anna (Mary) and says to her, 'You are my beloved, my counterpart, you are where I am at home forever.'[2] This is the ancient lie where a man tells each of his women that she has something special about her which he treasures, and that she is the most important of all his women.

If a lie works, why stop using it? When interviewed on *Desert Island Discs*, Jill Balcon said that Day-Lewis always told her that she 'never bored him'.[3]

When in 1938 Day-Lewis and Mary moved to Brimclose, their new home in Devon, Mary hoped that this would be a new start in their relationship. However, Day-Lewis soon met Billie Currell, the wife of a neighbour. This was a very public affair, especially when, in 1940, Billie gave birth to Day-Lewis's son. Mary suffered in silence. 'Day-Lewis's remorse came, eventually, in his poetry, but his words were as much an elegy for his love for Billie, now fading fast, as they were an acknowledgement of his unspecified deceit.'[4]

Why did Mary endure this public humiliation? There was a practical consideration. Day-Lewis did not earn enough to support two households. Divorce would not only be publicly shaming but it would be an admission that she had failed to be a good wife. It would mean giving up her fantasy of their life together, which must have included the stories she had been telling herself of how, one day, her husband would realize her true worth, beg her forgiveness, and stay with her, scorning all other women, for the rest of their lives together.

Instead, the war broke out, and Day-Lewis moved to London to work in the Ministry of Information. There he lived with the writer Rosamond Lehmann to whom he said, 'You have pushed out the boundaries of my life in so many directions, I feel a new man – reborn, reborn.'[5] Work at the Ministry was not onerous, but too much work was his excuse for his infrequent visits home. On those few occasions when Mary came to London, he would arrange for them to stay at a friend's flat. He explained that his digs were too squalid for her to stay there. Nevertheless, whenever he was ill, he returned to Brimclose so Mary could look after him.

In London Day-Lewis and Lehmann became a well-known literary couple, always to be seen in the best circles, but he refused to divorce Mary and marry Lehmann, despite her pleas. Natasha Spender commented, 'Both of them could give the impression that they were playing out some intense literary drama.'[6] If writers do not engage in literary dramas, what will they have to write about?

Then he fell in love with Jill Balcon. He decided to divorce Mary and marry Jill. This is the final act of this same old story. The man realizes that he needs a strong young woman to look after him in his old age. He cannot go back to any of his previous lovers because they all have one great fault. They know him too well. He needs someone young enough to impress. Many ex-wives are pleased when a young woman takes over their job. They can no longer tolerate the man's nonsense, but they do not want him to be neglected and alone.

However, old habits die hard. Balcon soon found that Day-Lewis was unfaithful to her. One of these women, Elizabeth Jane Howard, rejected him before he rejected her, and this offended him greatly. She wrote, 'Cecil always had to be in a romantic clinch. That drove him to write his best poetry. The rest was marking time or practising. And when the romance was under attack – from Rosamond, from their friends, from Jill's family – in one way he thrived. Like many poets he thrived on anxiety of one kind or other.'[7]

Lehmann never forgave Day-Lewis for his betrayal of her, but Mary saw him on family occasions and sometimes lunched with him. The same old story can seem to end well when only the adults are considered. But what of the children? Mary's sons Nicholas and Sean as adults led successful lives. They were circumspect when they talked to their father's biographer, but the biography was not about them. They did not need to say how they felt about the way their parents lied to them. They were told by neither their mother nor their father that the marriage was in difficulties. The first the boys knew was when they were told just before the divorce reached the courts.

If parents lie consistently about just one thing, say, the reality of Santa Claus, the child can be deceived. But, if they lie about something that affects every part of the children's life, the children know that something is wrong, even if they do not know what it is. Mary would have had to lie to them almost daily with statements such as, 'Daddy's had to go to visit a friend', 'No, Daddy didn't bang the door. The wind blew it shut as he was going out', 'I'm not crying, I've got something in my eye.' Knowing that something is wrong and not knowing what it is is very unsettling, even frightening.

When children discover that their parents lie, their trust in them is undermined. Children will cheerfully lie for their parents if they feel their cause is just, but they often resent having to cover up for their parents' lies, especially when their parents are lying to them and they do not know why. When friends' fathers are home every night and do all the things children want their fathers to do, it is hard to find a convincing lie to explain your father's absence, while an unconvincing lie lowers your status in the eyes of your friends. When children work out that their parents are lying to one another, the children feel that they are on a battlefield where they have to take sides. The pattern of their life develops accordingly. They deplore the lies of the parent they see as the enemy, while excusing the lies of the parent they support. Unable to express the anger they feel with both their parents, they transfer their anger to all adults. Like Holden Caulfield in *Catcher in the Rye*, they see other people as phonies. No wonder this book is so popular with the young.

The way Day-Lewis lived his life is an example of moral hazard. This term has been used quite frequently recently in reports about the economic crisis. It comes from the insurance industry where it had been noticed that, when a building's value dropped below the value for which it was insured, there was an increased likelihood that it would burn down. The basic idea of moral hazard is, 'It doesn't matter what I do. My insurance company will bail me out.'

In Day-Lewis's life, Mary was the person who bailed him out. It did not matter what he did, Mary would always take him in and look after him. Married men who know that, if they are unfaithful, their wife will throw them out are likely to think carefully before they put their marriage at risk. As much as they might be attracted to other women, they might value more their home comforts and the pleasure their children give them.

Teenagers with indulgent, rich parents can say to themselves, 'It doesn't matter what I do, my parents will bail me out.' They might put themselves at risk driving fast or using drugs, but they do not have to take the risks of competing in examinations or in a job, and perhaps losing. However, if it does not matter what you do, nothing is worth doing.

Then there is the Great Insurer, God; depending, of course, on how you see God. Some people talk about their God in terms of trust. They trust that God in His wisdom knows what is best for them. They hope that their God will look after them in the way they want to be looked after, but they do not assume that He always will. They might remember a line from Oscar Wilde's play *The Ideal Husband*, 'When the gods want to punish us, they answer our prayers.' A God like this rarely acts like an indulgent parent or a well-funded insurance company. However, there are many people who do regard their God as the ultimate in insurance cover. Believing in God is the premium you pay, and for that you get cover to do whatever you like. You can persecute and murder those who do not share your beliefs, invade their country and lay waste their land, because you are God's chosen people and He is on your side. The full extent of the lies and cruelties of George Bush and his fellow neo-cons in their conduct of the War on Terror are gradually coming to light, but they still justify what they did in terms of their God. Because America is their God's chosen country, anything they did in defence of America was acceptable to their God.

Meanwhile, the American taxpayers were in the process of becoming the insurance company that protected Wall Street.

When in 2008 the investment bank Bear Stearns was on the point of collapse, Hank Paulson, US Treasury Secretary and Tim Geithner, chief of the New York Federal Reserve, engineered the takeover of Bear Stearns by JPMorgan. To do this the US government had to underwrite $30 billion worth of bad debts acquired by the bank, and with JPMorgan find a way of avoiding the rules that stipulated that the government should never bail out investment banks. This bailout raised the question of moral hazard.

Provided the commercial banks behaved sensibly, the government should protect them because they were an essential part of the machinery of the country's economy, but the investment banks were casinos where all the players took risks. Risk-taking justified the bank's profits and the bankers' bonuses. Unfortunately, this clear distinction no longer existed. After the crash of 1929, the Glass Steagall Act was passed to separate the two kinds of bank, but in 1999 President Clinton repealed the Act. Mergers between the two kinds of banks soon followed. Thus it was that JPMorgan could act like a big brother taking care of a younger brother who had strayed, but it was their rich dad, the American taxpayer, who provided the cash needed to do this.

Paulson wanted to make this a once only and never again event. Then Lehman Brothers failed. To avoid being charged again with moral hazard, Paulson decided not to save it. But then came the American International Group, AIG. Not only had its subsidiaries been lending to subprime homeowners who were now falling into arrears, but it had been providing risky homeowners with insurance against default. Moreover, AIG did business with almost every financial institution in the world. It really was too big to fail, and so the government agreed to bail it out with an $85 billion loan in return for it effectively passing into government hands. Moral hazard was back, but also something that was unthinkable to most Americans – state capitalism.

Meanwhile, some of the British banks were in trouble. For over ten years the bankers had been basking in the praise and adulation of the chancellor, now prime minister, Gordon Brown. Bankers had made the most of moral hazard. Had they been right to do so? Some of them had to spend an anxious weekend until they found that the government, using taxpayers' money, would look after them. Sir Fred Goodwin took his undeserved rewards and scampered off to his villa in the south of France where the *News of the World* discovered him.

Moral hazard is based on a lie, 'It doesn't matter what I do.'

Everything we do has consequences, and to deny this is a very stupid lie. The consequences might mean that we suffer for what we have done, or we might not, but other people suffer. We are responsible for what we do. In July 2009 the UN Food and Agriculture organization reported that one billion people around the world suffered from hunger. This figure had increased by 100 million as a result of the global recession.[8]

Chapter Fourteen

Denying What Is There

One way of saying that a person is lying without actually using the word is to use the psychological term 'in denial', as in, 'He's in denial.' The term comes from psychoanalysis where the process of denying certain truths about yourself is considered to be unconscious. Here psychoanalysts distinguish between the lies we tell ourselves and the lies we tell to other people that are called denials. Thus, when he was brought before the court at The Hague, Charles Taylor, the former Liberian president, denied he was guilty of the charges brought against him. He said that he could not possibly be guilty of crimes such as murder, allowing hundreds of women to be forced to be sex slaves, enslaving diamond miners, and cutting off limbs and inflicting other mutilations. He had, he said, a great 'love for humanity'.[1] Like Linus of *Peanuts*, he might have loved humanity but it was people he could not stand.

In the months before the American invasion of Iraq in 2003, the writer and translator Eliot Weinberger began collecting the comments and statements made by the major figures in the war. When American troops entered Baghdad, the joyous reception by the Iraqis that Dick Cheney expected did not eventuate. Instead riots and lootings broke out. The National Museum was emptied of its treasures, and the National Library burnt down. Donald Rumsfeld, one of the architects of the war, should have anticipated this and sent troops to protect these places. Instead he said, 'The images you are seeing on television you are seeing over, and over, and over, and it's the same picture of some person walking out of some building with a vase, and you see it twenty times, and you think: "My goodness, were there that many vases? Is it possible there were that many vases in the whole country?"'[2] This is a very popular form of denial, claiming that the media got it wrong. This was a constant Rumsfeld theme, 'I am not to blame for anything that goes wrong.'

Television can leave indelible images in our mind. One that will never be erased from my mind is that of a river on which the bodies of hundreds of black people are floating. These people were victims of the genocide in Rwanda in 1994 committed by the Hutu against their former neighbours and friends, the Tutsis. There was an old story that the Tutsis originally came from Ethiopia. Their murderers threw their bodies in the river so they could float back to where they came from. It would have had to be a very long and powerful river for that to be able to happen.

When Chris McGreal visited Rwanda in 1994, he talked to the nuns in the village of Kibuya where the Hutu leader and governor of the province, Clément Kayishema, had ordered the priest to walk away while he led the massacre. Those Tutsis who survived the hail of bullets and explosions were hacked or clubbed to death. The nuns knew the killers. They were teachers, civil servants, farmers, the neighbours of those they were killing. McGreal went to the church to see the evidence of the massacre but had to leave soon after in case he was arrested by Kayishema.

When he returned to the village a few weeks later, the hastily buried bodies were being exposed by the rain washing away the dirt. The church had been scrubbed clean, but the smell of blood was still strong. There was a new Hutu priest who made no mention of the massacre. McGreal spoke to several of the Hutu worshippers. He wrote, 'Some of the worshippers denied there had been a massacre; a woman who said it was a lie refused to look at a foot sticking out of the ground beside her.'[3]

Many people have a great ability not to see what is in front of them when what is there does not fit with what they want to

221

see. Anorexic girls close to starvation can look in a mirror and see a fat girl who needs to diet. Families who wish to see themselves as well adjusted and happy will refuse to see that an adult in the family is very unhappy, or that a child is struggling with a problem and needs help. I was born into such a family. By the time I was seven the untreated lung disease I had had since early childhood had developed to the stage where I was unable to get enough oxygen, and, accordingly, when I was active, I would suddenly be overtaken by intense tiredness. My mother explained this with, 'Dorothy is lazy.' When I was twenty-seven, six weeks before my son was due to be born, I developed early signs of toxaemia. My doctor considered this to be a result of my working too hard, and sent me to hospital to rest. When I told my mother this, she said, 'That's not true. You never work hard.'

When you are the person whose true state is being denied, no matter what you do, those who deny you will simply fit whatever you do into their way of seeing you. You cannot escape from the situation unless someone sees your plight and helps you. Some members of my extended family and some of my teachers must have been aware of what was happening to me, but they did what most adults do. They sided with the parents. They might have talked amongst themselves and deplored my plight, but not one of them did anything to help me. None of them acknowledged to me that she or he was aware that I was struggling with a problem, let alone did so without criticizing me and urging me to work harder, as my teachers always did when I did well in an exam. Such an acknowledgement, even without any practical help, would have strengthened me because I would know that someone saw me as a person and not merely as a thing of little value.

When children are struggling with a problem arising from their situation at home or at school, they rarely behave in ways that adults want them to behave. Few adults are truthful enough to acknowledge that they are in some way implicated in what is

222

happening. Rather they locate the cause of the child's bad behaviour within the child. The school is not at fault for not providing the kind of education this child needs. It is the child's fault for not fitting into the school system, and he must be expelled. Many teachers deplore the limitations of the education they provide, but they can do no other because of the rules imposed on them by politicians mindful only of money and their need to be re-elected. The parents are not at fault because their child has a mental disorder such as Attention Deficit Hyperactive Disorder or Bipolar Disorder. Neither of these disorders had been invented by psychiatrists when I worked with children who were called disturbed. No physical cause of these disorders has been found to exist, though some psychiatrists claim that they have. Pharmaceutical companies make a good deal of money marketing drugs that are supposed to cure these disorders, though all these drugs do is sedate the child.[4] The parents' task is to make sure that their child takes the prescribed drugs that affect the child's developing brain in ways that scientists do not understand. The parents do what the psychiatrists and the psychologists tell them to do because they believe that the experts know best. Psychiatrists and psychologists are not at fault for practising the kind of psychiatry or psychology they have been taught. To be truthful about the limitations of their profession would arouse the ire of those colleagues who profit from the system. All of them would acknowledge that most of their patients' problems arise from aspects of society everyone would deplore, such as poverty, racism, unemployment and loneliness, but it is the government's job to deal with those.

Thus children struggle, and learn that adults lie. This is the example that adults set children, and most children decide that, if this is what being an adult means, when they grow up they will lie too. And this they do.

Children are not the only ones who need to have their situation acknowledged by others. This happens when you are the object

223

of someone's paranoia. Whatever you might do to escape from this position or to prove that you are not a threat to the person who sees you as their enemy is interpreted by the paranoid person as revealing how dangerous you are. Anything you might do to protect yourself from attack is interpreted in a similar way. Like the eight-year-old boy who claimed that the boy he was bopping on the head had forced him to do it, your persecutor claims that you are forcing him to do whatever he does in assaulting you.

This kind of thinking in people who stalk celebrities is seen by police and psychiatrists as evidence of a disordered mind. Yet, when the same kind of thinking was revealed in statements by Israeli leaders about their invasion of Gaza in December 2008, little was said by other countries' leaders who profess to have deep concern for the welfare of all people in the world. Every news bulletin at that time included Israeli spokespeople saying, 'We had no choice', and, 'The Palestinians made us do it.' Ehud Barak, Minister of Defence, said, 'Israel is at war against Hamas. We have nothing against the Palestinian people', while Israeli tanks demolished Palestinian homes, farms and businesses, and Palestinian hospitals were full of the dead, dying and injured, all as a result of the Israeli bombs and bullets. Hamas had indeed been firing rockets into southern Israel, but to us onlookers by virtue of our television screens the Israeli response seemed to be hugely disproportionate to the injuries they had suffered.

The statement 'We had no choice' is a lie used by those people who know that they have a choice but are determined to do what they want to do while at the same time absolving themselves of all responsibility for what they do. The Israeli leaders did not want to talk to Palestinians and treat them as fellow human beings. They knew, but denied that they knew, that, if they wanted Israel to be safe, they had to find a way of living peacefully side by side with the Palestinians. The only other alternative is to kill all the Palestinians, and even Hitler, well organized as he was, was not successful in his final solution. Israelis have been told this often by experienced people like Gerry Adams, once an IRA leader and implacable enemy of the Ulster Unionists who are now his colleagues in the Northern Ireland Assembly. The only way to end a conflict is for both sides to sit down and talk to one another.

Every religion has had a leader who has summed up the essence of that religion in one short statement. Rabbi Hillel said, 'What is hateful to you do not do to your neighbour; that is the whole of the Torah, while the rest is commentary thereof.' Jesus said much the same, and the history of Christianity shows how little attention most Christians have paid to what he said.

Many Israelis do try to follow Rabbi Hillel's teaching. They deplore the policy of their government where the homes of Palestinians are destroyed in Gaza, in the West Bank, and in Israel itself. The Israeli Committee Against House Demolitions (ICAHD) took a group of academics, health workers, trade unionists and non-governmental organizations from outside Israel to see what was happening in the West Bank. Amongst the group was Kristyan Benedict, Amnesty UK Campaign Manager. Part of Benedict's diary about the visit was published in *Amnesty Magazine*. He told how in Hebron 'we visit Hashem Al Azzeh and his family who live immediately below the house of Baruch Marzel. We have to climb a hill and through some rough shrubs, as Marzel has blocked the entrance to Hashem's house – a sort of mini-occupation. Hashem's house is covered in racist graffiti, and his garden full of garbage which the Marzel family throw each day.' The Hebron souq is covered with metal mesh, 'scattered on top with bricks, metal bars, assorted rubbish and an abundance of little white plastic bags glistening in the midday sun . . . The little white bags often contain urine – considered more effective now that bricks and bars cannot get through the mesh.'[5]

All of such Israeli actions, of which Rabbi Hillel would certainly disapprove, are based on the lie, 'I am superior to other people.' Avi Shlaim, Professor of International Relations at the

University of Oxford, was born in Baghdad to Jewish parents. In his account of the historical context to Israel's invasion of Gaza he wrote,

Israel's propaganda machine persistently purveyed the notion that the Palestinians are terrorists, that they reject coexistence with the Jewish state, that their nationalism is little more than anti-Semitism, that Hamas is just a bunch of religious fanatics and that Islam is incompatible with democracy. But the simple truth is that the Palestinian people are a normal people with normal aspirations. They are no better nor worse than any other national group. What they aspire to, above all, is a piece of land to call their own on which to live in freedom and dignity.[6]

The Jews who died in the Holocaust and those who survived bequeathed to their descendants the right to the moral high ground when it comes to matters of freedom and dignity. Their suffering showed us all what can happen if we fail to see and to value our common humanity. Yet, by their actions, Israeli leaders have thrown this extraordinary inheritance away.

While this terrible turmoil continues in the Middle East, all around the world there are people who deny that the Holocaust ever happened. It is not surprising that some Arab leaders deny the Holocaust. If we have enemies, we have to be blind to their suffering. If we actually recognized their suffering, we would be recognizing that they are human like ourselves. This would arouse our sympathy, even our empathy. We would have to find a way of resolving our differences other than by fighting. Of course, we could see our enemy's suffering and harden our hearts by claiming that they deserve to suffer, but this is such a mean and nasty lie. Did those children maimed and killed in Gaza, or Hiroshima, or Chechnya, or Belfast, or Darfur, or Afghanistan deserve to suffer? If we insist that our enemies deserved all the suffering we have inflicted on them we have to create a whole mesh of lies to keep the first lie in place. It is easier to stay with one monstrous lie, that our enemies do not suffer because they are not human like ourselves.

Why is it that there are people who seemingly have no reason to see Israel as their enemy and who have access to the huge volume of documentation concerning the Holocaust yet deny that it happened or, if it did, it was not as bad as the records show? They argue, it seems, that killing, say, 100,000 people is not as bad as killing a million. They do not understand that it is not the number but the killing that is wrong. We have no right to kill one another, even if the person we kill is a murderer. Killing someone in order to show that killing is wrong is just plain stupid.

It may be that Holocaust deniers are part of that large group of people who blame everything on that powerful force called 'they'. 'They' line their own pockets and lie to you. 'They' are not to be trusted. It may also be that amongst the Holocaust deniers are people who always take a contrary view because such a view gets them noticed. Other, deeper reasons lie in the person's life history.

I have never met Lady Renouf, but, when I discovered that she was born at The Entrance, which is not far from Newcastle where I was born in 1930, I could see how she might have gone from being Miss Newcastle and Hunter Valley, and the Radio 2HD Beach Girl to being an active supporter of Holocaust deniers such as the historian David Irving, Bishop Richard Williamson, and the Australian academic Frederick Thöben. I could also see how she could have gone from being Michèle Suzanne Mainwaring to Countess Griaznoff and on to Lady Renouf.

In 1946, when Renouf was born, The Entrance was a small fishing village where Tuggerah Lake empties into the ocean. Newcastle was a coal and steel town. Both places were bounded by magnificent beaches to the east and wild bushland to the west. Between 1930 and 1946 both places changed very little. Newcastle was, and still is, one of the best places in the world to raise a

227

family. It is a town of ordinary Australians. If you come from there, you can boast of many things but being grand is not one of them. Novocastrians, as they liked to call themselves, tended to be a smidgen self-satisfied. Attitudes there do not change quickly. Now the wharves and warehouses that lined the river close to the city centre have been pulled down and the ships go further up the river to huge mechanized wharves. A park and paths along the river have taken their place. I stayed in the delightful hotel that stands close to the river, and was surprised to find that the hotel restaurant, which was excellent, and a nearby group of restaurants facing the river were virtually empty on a warm summer evening. I remarked on this to the waiter who, so he told me, had been born and educated in Newcastle, had left to travel but come back to work. He said that it was the visitors to Newcastle who ate out. He explained, 'Newcastle people don't eat out. They say, "Why should we eat out when we can eat at home?"' My parents had said exactly the same.

Most of the children born in Newcastle want to stay there. However, if you cannot fit comfortably into your family and you comfort yourself with fantasies of people and places far away from Newcastle, you make plans to leave. This is not always easy. When I was at high school I was worried that Newcastle would get a university before I could escape to Sydney University. I did so, but Renouf was not so lucky. She made it only as far as Newcastle Technical College where she studied art. In those days Newcastle people were not particularly interested in art. In 1945 a Sydney ophthalmologist, Dr Roland Pope, left his entire art collection and library to the city, on condition that the council built a gallery and library to display his gifts, but it took the council twelve years to do so.

Renouf probably dreamed of success as an artist, but such dreams can be dangerous. Australian society does not tolerate 'tall poppies', that is, people who are noticeably different. Tall poppies have to be cut down. Outstanding sports men and women are highly valued, but only if they show that, when they are not winning medals, they are Australian like all Australians. Like Nicole Kidman, you can be famous when you are already famous, but the passage from being a child who is aware of his or her potential talent through the hard work of learning how to use that talent, to public recognition is very difficult. This is why many talented Australians go overseas to work. People like this need public recognition against which to measure the value of their work, but for some having an audience is as essential as food and water. Germaine Greer, Clive James and Barry Humphries were able to find the audiences that they needed and that appreciated them in England. However, their work is solidly based on their outstanding ability, Greer as a scholar, James as a writer, and Humphries as an actor. Like them, Renouf needed an audience, but her only outstanding talent was her beauty. In England the competition in this field was immense.

I would guess that Renouf had not fitted easily into her family. Once she had managed to get to London and create connections to society, she ceased to be very specific about her family back in Australia, particularly her father, Arthur Mainwaring, from whom she was estranged. This oversight led to her second husband, Sir Francis Renouf, going through a much-publicized divorce.

Every divorced woman has to find a new role which those around her recognize and respect. Renouf had been involved in a good deal of charity work, but now she made her cause the right of Holocaust deniers to argue their case openly, and to engage in debate with those who believed that the Holocaust actually happened.

However, her interest in this seemed to be more than just charitable. When interviewed by Peter Wilson, he reported that she told him that, 'Jews follow a religion that is dishonest, inhumane, supremacist, hate-fuelled, predatory and treacherous.' She described how the Jews controlled everything. This sounds like the anti-Semitism that was prevalent in Australia when I was a child, and would have still been around when Renouf was a child. Wilson wrote that she had stressed that it is the Jews' 'own selfish behaviour which has provoked anti-Semitism over the centuries, making them responsible for their own persecution'. She claimed that 'Hitler had no choice but to put Jews into concentration camps because international Zionist leaders had "declared economic war on Germany in 1933 to try to destroy Germany".' Like Ehud Barak who attacks Hamas but not the Palestinians, Renouf assured Wilson that, while she criticized Judaism, she had nothing against the Jews. She said, 'Jews who know me like me.' Wilson knew that Renouf was mistaken in this.

When I was an educational psychologist in Sydney, part of my job was to get children who had been patients in a children's psychiatric ward back into school. In various psychiatric hospitals in England, part of my work was to present a psychological appraisal of a patient at a case conference, and to introduce ward activities as part of a therapeutic programme for different patients. In all of these situations there would be staff who were hostile to me and who would if they could disrupt or prevent all I wanted to do for a patient. The common theme of all my work was to try to understand how the patient saw himself and his world. I was being opposed by those people who were envious of these patients. They were saying to themselves, 'Why should anyone try to understand them? Nobody ever tried to understand me.' This is the cry of the hurt child whose plight has never been acknowledged by those who should have cared for that child.

Perhaps Renouf envied survivors of the Holocaust who were now the recipients of much attention. I do not know. However, it does seem that her denial of the Holocaust was a lie she told herself in order to defend her fragile sense of being a person. This has to be an absolute defence. She dare not acknowledge anything that might question it. Before the interview ended, Wilson summarized all the places and circumstances where the Jews were murdered, and the approximate numbers in each place.

These numbers added up to about six million, a figure that Renouf disputes. Wilson wrote, 'Renouf listens politely but after I had cited these figures she seems not to have heard me.'[7]

Facts make no difference to those who deny in order to protect their sense of being a person.

Most of us have no direct connection with the Holocaust and so can dismiss Holocaust deniers as people with a bizarre hobby, but we cannot dismiss climate change deniers in the same way. Climate change matters – or should matter – to all of us. Writing in the *New Scientist*, George Marshall said,

It is now 44 years since Lyndon Johnson's scientific advisory council warned that our greenhouse gas emissions could generate 'marked changes in climate'. That's 44 years of research costing, by one estimate, $3 billion per year, symposia, conferences, documentaries, articles and now 80 million references on the internet. Despite all this information, opinion polls over the years have shown that 40 per cent of people in the UK and over 50 per cent in the USA resolutely refuse to accept that our emissions are changing the climate. Scarcely 10 per cent of Britons regard climate change as a major problem.[8]

Johnson's advisory council spoke only of what could happen. Now climate change is happening. As the Arctic ice melts at an increasing rate, creating access to the vast mineral and oil deposits there, companies are preparing to plunder these deposits and, as a by-product, increase the rate of global warming. In Zambia the annual flooding of the Zambezi River is occurring earlier, destroying crops usually harvested before the floods arrive and forcing the villagers to flee with what few possessions they have. Two-thirds of Egypt's rapidly growing population live in the Nile Delta that provides 60 per cent of the country's food. In 2007 the Intergovernmental Panel on Climate Change stated that the

Egyptian Delta is one of the top three areas most vulnerable to a rise in sea levels. Already significant areas are being affected by increased water levels, while large areas of farming land have lost or are losing their fertility because of salt water. To the south, the Nile, whose annual inundations used to clean the water channels, has itself become polluted from industrial and domestic waste. Thus many Egyptians lack a reliable supply of drinking water. Any plans to remedy this rapidly worsening situation are defeated by government mismanagement and corruption.[9] On the border between India and Bangladesh the Indian government is building a very strong 2,050-mile fence to prevent what it calls 'illegal immigrants and cross-border insurgents' from crossing into India. The border is patrolled by the Border Security Force (BSF) who shoot anyone who happens to stray into the wide strip of land on either side of the fence. Bangladesh is a small country but with a population of 150 million. Much of the land is low lying and already some of that has been swallowed up by the rising sea levels caused by global warming. Caught between the rising seas and the fence, will Bangladeshis stay there to drown or starve, or become a million-strong group of insurgents that the Indian government fear? Will they risk their lives, just as thousands of Africans are doing to get to Europe?

Meanwhile, as the seas warm, hurricanes along the American Atlantic coast increase in numbers and intensity, threatening more Katrinas. Three major glaciers in Washington state and Alaska have thinned and shrunk dramatically. This has been shown clearly by the records that have been kept of the glaciers since 1957.[10] The home page of the Australian Bureau of Meteorology states,

Australia and the globe are experiencing rapid climate change. Since the middle of the twentieth century, Australian temperatures have, on average, risen by about 1 °C with an increase in the frequency of heatwaves and a decrease in the numbers of frosts and cold days. Rainfall patterns have also changed –

232

the northwest has seen an increase in rainfall over the last 50 years while much of eastern Australia and the far southwest have experienced a decline.[11]

In Britain the increasing number of insurance claims for damage caused by flash floods and storms, often in places with little or no records of such claims, is likely to increase building insurance premiums, while in areas where floods occur many houses no longer qualify for insurance cover.[12]

Why do people deny that the climate is changing? Anthony, a commentator on George Marshall's blog, gave a succinct answer, 'Denial is our adaption strategy. It is so much easier than doing anything.'[13] Marshall gave a slightly longer answer. He wrote, '[Climate change deniers] describe climate change as a global problem (but not a local one) as a future one (not for their own lifetimes) and absolve themselves from all responsibility for either causing the problem or solving it.'[14]

As I write, many countries are being affected by a pandemic of swine flu. By now most people have worked out how likely they are to catch this infection, and what they can do to prevent this. Since what happens is so much a matter of luck, they comfort themselves with the thought that the pandemic, sooner or later, will come to an end. None of this way of thinking applies to climate change. It is worldwide, and has different effects in different places. It is impossible to predict with reasonable probability what will happen where you live. Even if climate change did come to an end in your lifetime, you will not be able to return to your old way of life. Everything will have changed, but no one knows how. This is the ultimate in uncertainty. No wonder people cannot bear to think about it.

Even more difficult is the fact that we have to think about climate change in a completely different way from any disaster we have had to think about in the past. It seems that what leads people to deny that the world's climate is changing is their

233

inability to create a new way of understanding the world. They had found one way of understanding the world that served them well and they see no reason to change. In her report on the conference organized by the Heartland Institute in the USA, Australian journalist Miranda Devine quoted Václav Claus, president of the Czech Republic, who used the language of the Cold War. He claimed that environmentalism had replaced socialism as the totalitarian threat to freedom in the twenty-first century. He said, 'Environmentalists do not want to reveal their true plans and ambitions: to stop economic development and return mankind centuries back.'[15] George Marshall quoted the motoring journalist Jeremy Clarkson as saying, 'Everything we've been told for the past five years by the government, Al Gore, Channel 4 News and hippies everywhere is a big bucket of nonsense.'[16] In his many media appearances Clarkson appears to be a man, unable to entertain any new ideas other than those relating to cars. A willingness to explore and accept new ideas is a direct measure of a person's self-confidence. Some people make a great show of being self-confident, but this presentation of oneself aims at hiding considerable uncertainty about themselves.

When James Delingpole of the *Spectator* interviewed Ian Plimer, Australian scientist and climate change denier, he wrote, 'He's sitting in my garden drinking tea on exactly the kind of day the likes of George Monbiot would probably ban. A warm, sunny one.'

George Monbiot, who knows more about climate change than most of us could ever know, rather likes warm, sunny days. He is a kayaker, fisherman, canoeist and gardener. What Delingpole wanted to do here was to remind his readers of Margaret Thatcher's great disdain for what she called 'the nanny state' where everything that might harm us is banned. She believed that people should be strong and independent, and not rely on the state to look after them the way nannies look after children. It is ironic that, in the last years of her life, Margaret Thatcher

234

is dependent on a team of nannies. As a frail, old woman with dementia, she requires continuous care. When she does appear in public, her nannies see that she is as beautifully dressed as she always was when she was prime minister, and her minders see that she does not make the kind of mistakes that old, frail women with a failing memory are likely to make. If only all the women like her were so well cared for!

In every country there is a class of people who have sufficient wealth, education and the right connections to protect themselves from whatever disaster might occur. Only the most thoughtful members of this class understand that climate change is the one disaster from which they cannot protect themselves and their descendants. If too little is done to stop it, people with sufficient means might move to those parts of the world least affected by the multitude of changes that global warming is bringing or will bring. However, these places will be under constant threat from the millions of people forced to flee from rising seas, or encroaching desert, or endless drought, or floods, or heat impossible for humans to bear. If we let this happen, no one will be safe.

Rather than contemplate what they might do to prevent this terrible scenario becoming the fate of their descendants, many people who lead comfortable lives fall back on their old ways of thinking. They blame climate change alarmism on the usual suspects – the left-wingers, the sandal wearers, the do-gooders. In addition, according to Ian Plimer, there are 'vested interests' like President Obama, who plans to use global warming as 'an excuse for greater taxation, regulation and protectionism'. In addition there are 'charitable bodies like Greenpeace which depend for their funding on public anxiety' and environmental correspondents who 'need constantly to talk up the threat to justify their jobs'.[17]

When I arrived in England in 1968 the English seemed to be unfamiliar with the word 'rubbish' used as a verb, as in, 'Plimer rubbishes the work of scientists who study climate change.' 'Rubbish' as a verb is useful in conversation. It is shorter than the correct word 'denigrate', and it can be said with more emphasis. I like to think that I played a small part in introducing it to the English who now use it. It also helps them to understand those Australians who take great pleasure in rubbishing people, organizations, and especially politicians. Indeed, Australian politicians specialize in rubbishing one another. Some Australians rubbish enthusiastically with great humour, but others, particularly those who fall into the category of grumpy old men, do it grumpily and quite without humour.

The first scientists who became interested in the possibility of climate change attracted little attention other than criticism from their colleagues who were building their reputations on researching well-respected theories. Soon the climate change scientists were producing interesting results that challenged old theories. This unsettled their conventional colleagues who dismissed their work as being poorly researched. Then the climate change scientists began attracting the attention of respected scientists and science writers. Even worse, they got grants for further research. Their conventional colleagues were faced with a choice. They could abandon the research on which they had built their reputations, or continue to rubbish all research that suggested that climate change was a real phenomenon. To do the first meant tolerating the unpleasant effects of changing the ideas that formed an essential part of their sense of being a person. Those scientists who were more attached to the idea of searching for scientific truth than their own pet theories made the change. Those who could not tolerate the uncertainty of changing their ideas did not. Some went on working quietly as they had always done, but others who needed an audience to survive as a person found their audience by becoming climate change deniers.

I would guess that, if I suggested to Ian Plimer that he denied climate change in order to preserve his sense of being a person, he would assure me that his personal feelings have nothing to do with his work. He is entirely objective.

Something not at all objective is to try to imagine your own death. None of us can do this. When we picture our own funeral, we do so as an onlooker. Some people try to control their own funeral by arranging it before they die. When relatives have to arrange the funeral of a family member, they say to one another, 'What would he have liked?', just in case the deceased is somewhere where he can see his funeral and approve or disapprove. Even more difficult is imagining the end of our species, ourselves among them. Instead, we see in our mind's eye a scene constructed from our favourite survival film. This scene takes for granted that we have survived and are ready to go forth and multiply. Yet, we know that many cities have flourished, only to disappear and be forgotten. We know that millions of species have appeared on this planet, only to become extinct. The only thing that assures us of our survival is our vanity.

Chapter Fifteen

Hypocrites All

Whatever the disaster, some people will see it as a chance for personal gain. Some people have jumped on the climate change bandwagon because they see it as the way to make money. They pretend to be greener than a host of George Monbiots. There is now a word for this – greenwash. It is an example of that most popular form of lying, hypocrisy.

The word 'hypocrisy' comes from the Greek *hypokrisis* meaning the playing of a part. We hope that our audience will believe our lie. We might know that we are pretending, but sometimes we lie to ourselves and tell ourselves that what we pretend is true. Such is our need to think well of ourselves.

A movement that starts as a protest will, if successful, become an arena where hypocrites can flourish. The Women's Movement begun in the 1970s, much to the derision of most men, changed the way men speak publicly about women. Racism became a key issue, and now even members of the British National Party are careful about what they say in public. The words 'gay', 'homosexual', and 'lesbian', once never uttered in polite company, are now part of our language. However, none of this means that sexism and racism are no more. Hypocrisy, like evil, flourishes like the green bay tree.

'Green' was the word chosen by those people concerned about the welfare of the planet to speak about all the things we might do to look after our planet. As soon as the word became trendy, those who wanted to appear as if they were doing the right thing but not actually do it insisted that they were green. However, the greens themselves are a canny lot. They drew attention to what these people were doing and called it 'greenwash'. 'Greenwash' is now in the Concise Oxford Dictionary where it is defined as, 'Disinformation disseminated by an organisation so as to present an environmentally responsible public image.'

Thus it was that 'Aerosols became "ozone friendly"; petrol became "green"; and nuclear power would solve "climate change".'[1] Industries that were not at all green but did not want to change set their public relations and advertising managers the task of presenting the industry as being green. However, consumers are not as stupid as some company executives like to think they are. The Advertising Standards Agency (ASA) soon found that complaints about environmental or green claims had hugely increased. The communications firm Futerra released a Greenwash Guide to help people identify examples of greenwash lying. If such lying proves to be successful in bamboozling the public, firms that use it will have little incentive to become more green.[2]

Then there are the Responsible Business Awards, presented in July 2009 by Prince Charles in the gardens of Clarence House, an occasion of much mutual self-congratulation. The Procter and Gamble Responsible Marketing and Innovation Award went to Thames Water for its campaign to promote the serving of tap water in restaurants, hotels and bars. Certainly drinking clean tap water is a more planet-friendly thing to do rather than drinking bottled water, but is not water the sole product of Thames Water? The more tap water is drunk in London, the more money Thames Water makes.

Some things go beyond the mere hypocrisy of certain kinds of public relations and advertising. Wealthy and powerful companies who can see little profit in becoming green have been paying large sums of money to 'think tanks, researchers, and media figures to produce and promote phony science purporting to debunk global warming', wrote Josh Harkinson in *Mother*

Jones. ExxonMobil was one of these. The company vowed to change its ways, but privately it went on giving financial support to organizations that denied climate change.[3] The Shell Nigeria website states that one of the ways that Shell Nigeria is managing 'major environmental challenges' is by 'sustained environmental monitoring of our operations and activities'.[4] Shell is the largest oil firm operating in the Niger Delta, and is responsible for much of the destruction of the land of the Ogoni people through its extensive oil spillages. The Movement for the Survival of the Ogoni People, led by the writer Ken Saro-Wiwa, tried to persuade Shell employees to acknowledge what they were doing, but without success. Instead, Nigeria's military government persecuted the Movement. Shell has always denied that they were involved in this and in the execution of Saro-Wiwa and eight of his colleagues. Relatives of the hanged men brought a lawsuit alleging Shell's complicity in human rights abuses in Nigeria, but it took thirteen years for Shell to agree to a settlement. Shell denied all liability. They were not responsible for what had happened. The families agreed on a settlement because they knew that, even if they went to court and won the case, Shell would appeal and drag out the proceedings for many years to come. Shell official Malcolm Brinded gave a splendid example of greenwash. He said, 'While we were prepared to go to court to clear our name, we believe the right way forward is to focus on the future of the Ogoni people, which is important for the peace and stability of the region.'[5] Like totalitarian governments, greenwash speak drains our language of all meaning.

Many hypocrites rely on the fact that the media's attention span rivals that of the legendary goldfish. There is nothing world leaders seem to like better than lining up for a photograph after having announced that they have pledged billions to a good cause, such as helping poor countries deal with climate change. Then, when the journalists and photographers have departed, these leaders renege on their promises. John Vidal reported that 'developing

240

countries have received less than 10% of the money promised by rich countries to help them adapt to global warming . . . The world's richest countries have together pledged nearly $18bn, but less than $900m has been disbursed.'[6]

Hypocrisy is built into the democratic political system. Dictators do not have to be hypocrites because they control the media. No one dare point out publicly the discrepancy between what dictators say and what they do. However, they are aware of the importance of having a good media image. Putin when he was president always showed himself to be tough and strong, but his successor Medvedev wants to appear more warm and friendly, more of a cuddly Russian bear. However, as he said, 'We should be able to give a firm response when circumstances call for it.'[7]

When on 12 May 2008, a huge earthquake devastated a large area in Sichuan province of China, the president Hu Jintao visited the earthquake zone where he, dressed in trousers and a white, open-necked shirt, comforted the victims in a way reminiscent of Tony Blair in his role as prime-minister-but-ordinary-chap-who-is-sensitive-and-caring. One striking feature of the earthquake was that, while many of the old buildings survived virtually intact, most of the newer school buildings collapsed, leaving 5,335 students dead or missing, and injuring 546 children. It was clear that the companies who had built these schools were to blame for this unnecessary destruction. One year on, the parents who wanted to see these companies punished were themselves being persecuted. Ignoring all this, Hu Jintao attended the ceremony to mourn the dead.[8]

Shanghai World Expo was expected to have as its chief exhibit the new eco-city of Dongtan. Tony Blair when prime minister and the Chinese president Hu Jintao signed the deal to build Dongtan. It was to be built by eco-architect and eco-engineers from the master plan drawn up by Peter Head of the consulting engineers Arup. However, virtually nothing has been built. Head explained to *Guardian* journalist Fred Pearce, 'China does everything by the rules handed down from the top. There is a rule for everything. The width of roads, everything. That is how they have developed so fast, by being prescriptive. We wanted to change the rules in Dongtan, to do everything different. But when it comes to it, China cannot deliver that.'[9]

Meanwhile, in London, barely a day goes past when the preparations for the London Olympics in 2012 are not criticized. When on 27 July 2009, Lord Coe announced that the building work was proceeding on time, Channel 4 News reported this, but made the theme of their story, 'What will happen to the Olympic site when the games are over?' They interviewed some Londoners who, not knowing what would happen, expected the worst. This constant and sometimes unfair criticism is the price politicians have to pay for living in a democracy. To survive they have to be masters of hypocrisy. No matter what is happening, everything is fine. Parties face one another across the political chamber and argue. If the party in power holds a certain opinion, the opposition party must hold the opposite view. Individual party members are required to present themselves as sharing the opinions of their party. To do otherwise would put their careers at risk.

Politicians must also profess to hold opinions that significant numbers of voters hold. Apparently most British politicians are passionately interested in football, while all American politicians are devout believers in God. Yet my impression of all politicians is that what matters most to them is getting re-elected. However, these are minor matters compared to the degree of political hypocrisy that arises when reality conflicts with voters' prejudices.

One particular reality that cannot be ignored is that a significant number of adults prefer to have sexual relationships with members of their own gender. However, there are a significant number of Americans who see homosexuality as being dangerous, even evil. When gay pressure groups made discrimination against

242

gays and lesbians in the army a political issue, army chiefs and President Clinton agreed on a policy called Don't Ask, Don't Tell. Don't ask anyone if he is a homosexual, and, if you are, don't tell. Reveal that you are homosexual and the army will sack you, despite the fact that the army is hard pressed to find replacements for the troops in Iraq and Afghanistan. Consequently, many homosexual men and women in the army had to pretend they were something they were not. This is not just a matter of pretending to your mother that you are what she wants you to be. Soldiers live in close proximity to one another, and they talk about sex all the time. After ten years of sexual abstinence, Dan Choi could pretend no longer. When he fell in love for the first time he knew that he could not lie about his boyfriend. Choi is a graduate of West Point, has served in Iraq, and is fluent in Arabic and Korean. From the beginning of the War on Terror, American forces have lacked fluent speakers of foreign languages, especially Arabic. Yet, when Choi spoke publicly about his homosexuality, his colleagues praised him and the army sacked him. Choi said that staying in the closet 'traumatizes people in a way . . . I'm taught the honour code at West Point: do not lie. Units are based on the honour code. But "Don't Ask, Don't Tell" says you have to lie. It forces people to lie, to hide. Hiding and lying aren't army values.'[10]

Hypocrisy often presents itself as sentimentality. In the climate change debate, we frequently hear that sentimental tosh, 'Children are our future.' Some people care about some children, but, if all adults cared about all children, we would have already created a worldwide society where all children are adequately fed and educated. They would live in decent homes and have good health care. No child would be caught up in a war or conflict. There would be no debate about climate change because, if the climate is changing, children are the ones who suffer first and most. If it is not changing, reducing emissions, reducing pollution, and planting trees would benefit all children.

243

Claiming to care about all children is an almost universal hypocrisy.

Sentimentality ignores unpleasant reality. Thus it was that at the funeral of Ken Lay, 'Kenny Boy' as George W. Bush called him, George Bush senior and his wife Barbara gathered with Lay's family and friends to hear the Reverend Bill Lawson of the Wheeler Avenue Baptist Church, Houston, deliver the eulogy. Here Lawson compared Lay favourably to John F. Kennedy, Martin Luther King, Jesus Christ and James Byrd, a black man brutally lynched, tied to the back of a truck, and dragged over dirt roads until his body split in two. What had happened to Lay, said Lawson, was a virtual lynching. Writing about this, Andrew Sullivan said, 'In this version of Christianity what matters is not so much what you do – but what's in your heart.'[11] Kenneth Lay was chief executive and chairman of Enron, the world's largest energy trading firm. Enron went bankrupt in 2001, leaving $1.8bn in debts and putting 4,000 people out of work. The bankruptcy was a result of fraud. Lay's colleague Jeffrey Skilling was found guilty on nineteen counts of fraud and conspiracy, and Lay on six counts of fraud and conspiracy. Throughout the trial, Lay, a committed Christian, insisted he was innocent. He took no responsibility for all the employees and shareholders who had lost their jobs, pensions and savings. While he was waiting to be sentenced, Lay died of a heart attack in his home at Aspen, Colorado.

I wonder how much concern the Reverend Lawson and his congregation at Lay's funeral have now for all those people who were lied to by Lay and his fellow conspirators.

Being lied to can have serious consequences.

Chapter Sixteen

Being Lied To

We all know what it is to be lied to. It happens to all of us every day. Whether we are lied to by organizations or individuals, it does not help us and often harms us.

In the business world, every company is required to publish an annual report. The bigger the company, the bigger and glossier the report. The copy that goes to shareholders is likely to be full of eye-catching pictures and worthy sentiments. In many reports the pictures and the sentiments are there to make the report look attractive to the reader. Pages of nothing but numbers can seem boring. However, in some reports the worthy sentiments are full of weasel words and empty language, all there to hide the fact that the report is largely a lie.

The Royal Bank of Scotland's accounts for 2007 were signed off on 27 February 2008. In the company report readers were assured that, 'RBS is a responsible company. We carry out rigorous research so that we can be confident we know the issues that are most important to our stakeholders and we take practical steps to respond to what they tell us.'[1] The stakeholders did not know that RBS was in the process of acquiring a massive amount of risky investments and debt. It is unlikely that RBS's stakeholders wanted the bank to be on the verge of collapse and have to be rescued by the British government, so we could conclude that this statement is a lie. It is a lie that British taxpayers will be paying for for decades to come.

At the turn of this century RBS was greatly admired around the world. In 2003 the Harvard Business School made it one of their case studies with the title 'The Royal Bank of Scotland: Masters of Integration'. Under the guidance of Sir Fred Goodwin, RBS had become in terms of its assets the biggest company in the world. It had grown big by takeovers.

When company executives and financial journalists who want to be taken seriously write about takeovers and other business transactions, they do not talk about the people involved, except to bestow some judicious praise on those whom it might be profitable to praise. Reading these reports you would think that takeovers did it all themselves, with no human beings involved. Similarly, if you read academic reports of psychological experiments you would think that the experiment did itself. There is no mention of the cock-ups and make-dos and the arguments that actually occurred. To write about those things would be gossip, and it is universally acknowledged that men do not gossip.

Those of us unfamiliar with high finance are likely to assume that the firm that takes over and the firm that is taken over profit from the deal. That is not necessarily the case. The price of a share depends on what buyers think are the firm's prospects. They will pay more for a share in a firm that they think is going to do well than they would pay for a share of a firm they think is likely to do badly. In the mid to late 1990s mergers and takeovers were all the rage. However, as we all should know, it is never wise to follow a fashion just because other people are following it. In 2002 the professional advice and research firm KPMG published a report that showed that most of the 500 biggest takeovers in the last years of the 1990s had reduced the share price of the companies concerned. The BBC report on this concluded with, 'But global merger and acquisition activity has now slumped to a 10 year low, with business leaders gripped by a new mood of caution.'[2] Sir Fred Goodwin was not one of these.

Very few women work in high finance running large companies. Most of the people in these positions are young men on the make. Perhaps we should feel sorry for young men on the make. They are driven by forces inside them that they do not understand. Indeed, they know nothing of what goes on inside them, and they dare not look. All they know is that they have to compete with other young men and win. Only thus can they prove that they are strong and brave, a man all men admire. If they lose, the worst that could possibly happen will happen. They will be nothing, a nobody, less than the dust, and all men will despise them. They know this is an absolute truth, a law of the universe, unquestionable and unquestioned. Do not tell them that they are wrong because they will despise you.

Young men on the make are a nuisance to society. Britain used to deal with this problem by sending them to fight and die in the many wars needed to maintain the Empire, while America sent theirs out West. Now the Empire is no more and the West is won. Modern armies need clever machines more than they need thousands of young men. The only place to which many of these young men could go was to the City or to Wall Street. Some young men on the make get older and wiser, and some just get older and see no reason to change their ideas. When they compete, they are rarely competing for the benefit of their firm. In firms that provide company cars for some of their staff, most of the women entitled to a car are pleased to get a good, reliable car that takes them from A to B, whereas amongst the men the competition is fierce to get the one car that all of them covet. It is the same with takeovers.

While Goodwin and his team were building up their many banking and insurance interests, the team at Barclays Bank were also busy swallowing up banks and building societies. When the Barclays team went after the Dutch bank ABN Amro, Goodwin seems to have reacted like the sales rep who saw the firm's newest Toyota Corolla slipping from his grasp. He formed a consortium with two European banks and fought off Barclays with a bid of 71 billion euros. The need to win seems to have blinded Goodwin to the fact that this price was far too high. Two weeks after RBS's corporate report for 2007 was published, RBS announced that it was issuing shares in order to raise £12 billion to cover its losses from the acquisition of ABN Amro. This move did not plug the hole in RBS's balance sheet.

The question was, where was the hole in the said balance sheet? Company reports can be very far from transparent, and financial journalists have to search for what might be hidden. The *Daily Telegraph* reported that, in RBS's 2006 report, Goodwin had written, 'Sound control of risk is fundamental to the Group's business . . . Central to this is our long-standing aversion to sub-prime lending, wherever we do business.'[3] Yet, a year later, in the 2008 report is, 'The Group has a leading position in structuring, distributing and trading asset-backed securities (ABS). These activities include buying mortgage-backed securities, including securities backed by US sub-prime mortgages, and repackaging them into collateralised debt obligations (CDOs) for subsequent sale to investors.' In fact, £5.1 billion worth of CDOs. John Lanchester, in his article 'It's Finished', asked, 'Might the weasel word be "include" – meaning, there's more of this stuff but we're not discussing it here?'[4]

Would a chief executive officer of the prestigious RBS deliberately exclude important information from his bank's yearly report? Would a large pharmaceutical company deliberately exclude certain important data from a research report? Regrettably, the answer is yes. It is very easily done. When more than one pharmaceutical company develops and markets a drug for a particular illness, it is likely that these drugs, that are marketed under different names, are not particularly different. This means that the company has to produce research which shows that the company's drug is considerably better than that of the company's competitors. Suppose the drug in question is one for depression. A research drug trial is conducted where one group of depressed people take the company's drug, and another group of depressed people take a competitor's drug. Suppose the first group shows a lifting of depression earlier and more markedly than the second group within the first six weeks. Fine, but people usually take an anti-depressive drug for three or four months. It is not like an antibiotic where you have to finish the course, but most people, and their doctors, prefer to make sure that they are back to their old selves and not likely to relapse the moment they finish taking the drug. However, many drug trials are run for no more than about six weeks. Drug companies will say that this is because trials are so expensive, but it might equally be that the drug showing a quick response had an amphetamine-like effect that lifts the person's spirits for a few weeks but then he plunges down again into the same old misery. To the drug company it seems a pity to waste all that research and development money. Why not report that the first six weeks were excellent, and leave it at that?

Depressed people supposedly cured by a drug often get depressed again, but a bank like RBS is not supposed to go broke. Yet RBS would have done so had not the British government, over the weekend of 11–12 October 2008, not given RBS £20 billion. In February 2009 a preliminary statement of the bank's annual results showed that RBS had lost £24 billion, the largest loss in British corporate history. More government money was needed. The bank received an additional £25 billion.

All this money was given on a variety of terms and conditions, so it is impossible to say just how much money the British taxpayer gave to RBS. This was not the only bank that the taxpayer bailed out with similar sums. However, as Lanchester wrote, 'The consequences of the bank's unravelling will be with us for a long time, in the most basic way: we will be paying for it. Not metaphorically but literally: instead of schools and medicines and roads and libraries, huge chunks of public money will go into RBS's balance sheet.'[5] Goodwin might be enjoying his pension but the consequences of his monstrous lies will be felt for many years to come by people ill-equipped to deal with them.

American taxpayers are no better off than the British, while no country has proved immune to the toxicity of the assets held by the banks. No one knows which banks are solvent. 'Toxic assets' or, as they call them in America, 'troubled assets' are assets that cannot be valued. We have all seen pictures of the streets of boarded-up houses in cities like Detroit. These houses might have no more value than the houses in New Orleans destroyed by the hurricane, or it might be that some will be bought at a good price because the land the houses are on is needed for a new Wal-Mart. Both the British and the American governments have bought a substantial interest in some of these banks, but both governments are very reluctant to take the banks over and nationalize them. There are several reasons for this, but the reason that will weigh heaviest for politicians is that, if the government nationalizes the banks, whichever party is in power will be blamed by the voters for whatever goes wrong in their financial management for the rest of their lives.

As suddenly as the financial meltdown of the banks appeared in the news, so just as suddenly did it disappear. In the UK people forgot the wickedness of the bankers. They had become incensed about the outrageous expenses claimed by members of parliament. Compared to politicians in a great many countries, British politicians were quite modest in what they took from the taxpayer. However, the bankers had destroyed the once considerable trust people had in them, and now the politicians demolished what was left of that trust. When swine flu arrived, there was a massive amount of publicity given to it, most of which was supplied by the government. Some of us wondered whether this was the government conniving with the media to stop us watching what the government was doing, or not doing, about the world financial crisis. Could we rely on the media to tell us what we need to know? There is a short answer to this. No, we can't.

We can never be absolutely certain about anything, although many people kid themselves that they can. However, our difficulties in forming reasonably accurate guesses are compounded by the fact that so many people lie to us, a great many of them in the media.

We all know that the media lie to us, just as we know that politicians lie to us. However, while we know why politicians lie to us – to get into power and stay in power – the reasons that the media lie are many and complex. Those who own the media or are employees of state-owned media might be simply passing on the lies of the politicians, or they might have their own reasons to lie. They need readers, listeners, viewers, and so they tailor their reports to suit what they see as their audience's tastes. Financial considerations are far more important than the truth. The BBC, which can afford to be much more truthful than many other media, is constantly criticized by politicians and interest groups such as certain Jewish lobbyists who claim that the BBC favours the Palestinian cause. Meanwhile, in Australia the ABC continues to be full of Commie ratbags and the like, or so some politicians would have us believe. Both the BBC and the ABC are always under threat where they are most vulnerable, their finances.

The multitude of ways in which the media fail to tell the truth if not set out deliberately to lie, are examined in two excellent books, Nick Davies' *Flat Earth News*[6] and David Slater's *The Media We Deserve*.[7] To those of us in search of truth David Slater gave some useful advice. 'It always requires far more application to be a considered sceptic than an automatic cynic.'[8] An automatic cynic has a set of cynical beliefs that he applies without thinking. A considered sceptic has an open but inquiring mind. Of whatever he is told he inquires, 'Why is this person or organization telling me this?' It may be that the person or organization has your interests at heart, or it may be that there is some benefit to your believing what you are told, but the benefit is not yours.

Being a considered sceptic is not an infallible method of identifying all liars. If you suspect that an organization is lying to you, you might not have the necessary information about the organization to ask the right questions, and the organization is not going to supply what you need. If you suspect that an individual is lying to you, you can ask the person, 'Why are you telling me this?' and get another lie as an answer. Face to face, it is very difficult to tell whether the person is lying.

Some people pride themselves on being very good at knowing when they are lied to. In his extensive research on lying, Paul Ekman has shown that this belief is more a matter of vanity than accuracy. However, if the liar and the person being lied to come from the same background, the person's chances of spotting that he is being lied to are increased. A friend told me that her husband was very good at identifying a lie. She said, 'As an accountant, my husband is highly numerate. I have watched him review pages and pages of accounts, all densely compressed data in numeric form. He can see the pattern in the numbers and can see when the pattern is out – he suddenly plonks his finger down in the middle of page 15 or whatever – an indication that some massaging or fudging has taken place.'

Identifying a lie in pages of numbers is a very special skill. Another friend who knew his boss extremely well told me that his boss, who had made a fortune in real estate, always knew when he was being lied to when he was doing a deal. However, in his personal life he was hopeless at spotting a lie. In our personal life we might want to believe the lies that we are being told.

Bernard Madoff, whose fraud was the largest ever committed by a single person, knew what lies his clients wanted to be told. One of the people taken in by his lies was Stephen Greenspan, a psychologist, who tried to recoup some of his losses by writing a book about gullibility with himself as one of his subjects.[9] He also wrote an article for *eSkeptic* where he set out his theory of gullibility. He said that his problem was located in his personality. He wrote,

I happen to be a highly trusting person who also doesn't like to say 'no' (such as to a sales person who has given me an hour or two of his time). The need to be a nice guy who always says 'yes' is, unfortunately, not usually a good basis for making a decision that could jeopardize one's financial security. In my own case, trust and niceness were accompanied by an occasional tendency to risk-taking and impulsive decision-making, personality traits that can get one into trouble.[10]

Nobody has a personality or a collection of personality traits. 'Personality' and 'personality traits' are no more than some of the abstract nouns that psychologists love. Greenspan could have said, 'I don't introspect much. I prefer to act, and sometimes I act without much thought. It's very important to me to be liked, so when someone is nice to me, I'm likely to agree to do what they want.' Madoff has been described as being a very nice man and so, apparently, were his salesmen. Greenspan was the ideal target for their fraud.

When Ekman looked for overt signs of lying, he found very few. He said, 'I strongly suspect that there are people who believe their own lies. If you believe your lie strongly enough, you're not going to show signs of lying.'[11] Polygraphs reveal emotions, not lies. A truthful person can be feeling intense emotion. However, Ekman has found that the lies that are hardest to keep hidden are those told when a person is faced with 'the threat of a loss or punishment [that] to the liar is severe: loss of job, loss of reputation, loss of spouse, loss of freedom'.[12] These are the lies that we hope will save us from the immediate threat of annihilation as a person. When annihilation is some steps removed, as in when we tell a white lie, we can calmly and imperceptively lie.

Recognizing that we are being lied to is an important skill. Reading the emotion on a person's face is a universal skill, and most of us are good at it. Why aren't we just as skilful at seeing that the person we are talking to is lying to us? Ekman answered this question by drawing on his thirty years' experience working in a Stone Age, preliterate village in Papua New Guinea. Perhaps the reason lay in our evolutionary history. In the village where he lived there was little privacy. The houses had no doors, and everyone saw everyone else every day. Ekman wrote,

> Lies would be most often betrayed by the target or someone observing actions that contradicted the lie, or by other physical evidence. Adultery was an activity that lying often attempted to conceal in the small village where I lived. Such lies were not uncovered by reading the betrayer's demeanour when proclaiming fidelity, but by stumbling over him or her in the bush.[13]

There are many skills that our Stone Age ancestors did not need but which we do. In a society where privacy is readily available, it is easier to lie and get away with it. Hence being able to identify a liar is very important.

The third explanation Ekman gives for our lack of ability is that we value trust. Often it seems better to accept what we are told by those we trust and depend on than to challenge their truthfulness. Ekman passed quite quickly over his second reason. Parents, he said, do not teach their children to identify a liar because 'their privacy may often require that they mislead their children about just what they are doing, when they are doing it, and why they are doing it. While sexual activity is one obvious focus of such lies, there may well be other activities that parents want to conceal from their children.'[14] Indeed there are.

Parents who have failed to instil into their children that they are to be seen and not heard are frequently in danger of being embarrassed by their children. Parents who have vowed always to tell their children the truth spend most of their waking hours in a state of embarrassment. On a crowded bus try explaining to your seven-year-old what a dildo is. Such situations have been turned into a successful television series called *Outnumbered*, with Hugh Dennis and Claire Skinner as the parents, while Tyger Drew-Honey plays Jake, the eleven-year-old, Daniel Roche plays Ben who is seven, and Ramona Marquez is Karen who is five. For each episode, the writers Andy Hamilton and Guy Jenkin outline the story and provide a script for the adults, but what the children say is largely improvised by the children. They constantly interrogate their parents, or criticize them, or comment on what their parents say and do, while Ben employs his mastery of fantasy to confuse and worry his parents.

Outnumbered shows very clearly why, down the centuries, adults have used their power to silence children. What silences the children most effectively are the parents' lies, especially those lies about the nature of the world. Children rely on their parents to describe to them how the world operates. Most parents abuse their children's ignorance by telling them lies in order to frighten them into obedience. Some parents do not do this, but, compared to all the parents in the world, they are in a minority. Tragically, most adults fail to see that they have been lied to, and so they do to their children what has been done to them.

In a debate at the Hay-on-Wye Literary Festival in 2007 the geneticist Steve Jones talked about the difficulties he had in teaching Muslim students. He said, 'To a man and a woman, there are parts of science they will not accept. That means that, in their early lives, they have been told deliberate lies by people who, I am sure, know they are deliberate lies. I don't care how charming they are, I don't care how pleasant they are, these people are evil. What is true for imams is, more or less, true for bishops.'[15] This started a series of letters to the *Guardian*. Lizzi Collinge wrote to ask if the professor could give 'the scientific definition of evil'. Steve Jones replied, 'How about "telling lies to children"; the universal habit of all religions through the ages.' Ian Flintoff then wrote to complain that there would be no more, '"once upon a time there was a little girl called Red

Riding Hood". What a cold, dull, flat and colourless world of the imagination poor Steve [Jones] and his buddies must inhabit. Give me the gods, the spirits, the myths and Father Christmas any time.' Barry Cole made clear the fundamental error in Flintoff's letter. He wrote, 'Shame he can't distinguish little lies and tongue-in-cheek games from dangerously institutionalised mythologies. So far as I know, no one has conducted a crusade to protect the honour of Little Red Riding Hood and no warring wolfian factions have tried to wipe each other out.'[16] If clerics called their holy books fantasies and mythologies what they teach would not be called lies, but nothing infuriates a religious person more than to be told that these stories are fantasies. They insist that all their beliefs are absolutely true.

However, believing that a fantasy is true leads to some very unhappy consequences.

When Lytton Strachey wrote about Cardinal Manning, whose life spanned the nineteenth century, he told a story from Manning's early childhood, lived 'in an atmosphere of evangelical piety' about which Manning had written:

> One day the little boy came in from the farmyard, and his mother asked him if he had seen the peacock. 'I said yes, and the nurse said no, and my mother made me kneel down and beg God to forgive me for not speaking the truth.' At the age of four the child was told by a cousin of the age of six that, 'God had a book in which He wrote down everything we did wrong. This so terrified me for days that I remember being found by my mother sitting under a kind of writing table in great fear. I never forgot this at any time in my life,' the Cardinal tells us, 'and it has been a great grace to me.'[17]

From then on Manning lived a pious life. He was ordained into the Anglican Church and appointed a curate in a country parish. He married the rector's daughter and, when his father-in-law died, became the rector. When his wife died of tuberculosis he was, at first, inconsolable, but her death freed him to convert to Catholicism. Later in life, when he had become the most powerful Catholic in England, he called his wife's death one of 'God's special mercies'. He never spoke of his wife, and he destroyed every record of her. When he was told that her grave was falling into ruin, he said, 'It is best so. Let it be. Time effaces all things.'[18]

Being frightened of God does not necessarily make us kind.

When Joe Bageant stayed in his hometown of Winchester, Virginia, he noticed that, on his way to the tavern where he drank with his friends, he passed two Pentecostal churches, the Second Chance Church, and the Institute for the Study of Creation Science. He wrote that this Institute was 'a uniquely American form of ignorance. With about half of all Americans ranging from the minimally literate to the functionally illiterate, truth falls before the scythe of rumor and the lust for spectacle. These Americans have eyes, which is to say a camera to shoot around them, but they have no intellectual software to edit or make sense of it all.'[19] The USA had had an excellent education system, especially in the 1960s when Bageant, a working-class boy, could take advantage of it, but since then it had fallen into decay. This is just another of the things that President Obama has to fix.

Bageant was brought up as a Southern Baptist, and so can write about fundamentalist Christianity from the inside. He left the church, but his younger brother is a Baptist pastor. American fundamentalists make up 25 per cent of Americans entitled to vote. Consequently, what they believe is important to many more people than just themselves. Like all Protestants, they have created endless variations, not just on the basic Calvinist doctrine of an individual's immediate and direct relationship with God, but also on the fundamentalist End Time Theology. This is based on the final chapter of the New Testament, the Book of Revelation. They regard this book as God's plan for the apocalypse which brings the world to an end. Fundamentalists believe that the only way to avoid a most horrible fate is to accept Jesus as your personal saviour. The conflicts in the Middle East are part of God's plan, so anyone who wants to bring peace there is trying to thwart God's plan, and must be a tool of Satan. To those who belong to the Rapturist cult of End Time believers, there is no need to do anything about climate change because, once they are all raptured into heaven and the rest of us dead or in hell, the planet will not be needed.

Bageant's parents belonged to the Rapturist cult. He told how, when he was in third grade, he arrived home from school and found the house empty. He wrote,

With increasing panic, I went through every room and then ran round the outside of the house sobbing, in the grip of the most horrific loneliness and terror. I believed with all my heart that the Rapture had come and that all my family had been taken up into heaven, leaving me alone on earth to face God's terrible wrath. As it turned out, they were at a neighbor's house scarcely three hundred yards down the road and returned in a few minutes. But it took me hours to calm down. I dreamed about it for years afterwards.[20]

Bageant found that many people raised in fundamentalist families had had similar experiences. He also found that the rapture remains very real. He wrote,

Even those who escape fundamentalism agree its marks are permanent. We may no longer believe in being raptured up, but the grim fundamentalist architecture of the soul stands in the background of our days. An apocalyptic starkness remains somewhere inside us, one that tinges all our feelings and thoughts of higher matters. Especially about death, oh beautiful and terrible death, for naked eternity is more real to us than those born into secular humanism.[21]

Being Lied To

The Irish writer John McGahern said of his Catholic child-hood, 'The world to come, hell and heaven and purgatory and limbo, were closer and more real than America or Australia and talked about daily as our future reality. The saints alone went straight to heaven. In purgatory, we would have to be purified in a flame to a whiteness like that of snow before we could join the saints in the blessedness of heaven.'[22]

Thirty years ago I met a young woman who was working in a charity in which I was involved. She described herself to me as 'a practising Christian'. One day she said to me, 'You're the freest person I've ever met.' I was astounded. I was a single mother with a teenage son, and in charge of a department of clinical psychology. I had no financial resources whatsoever. I supported my son and myself on my very modest salary. I felt far from free. Then I real-ized that what this young woman meant were not the practical constraints of my life. What she was talking about were 'oughts'. I decided for myself what I ought to do, and the 'oughts' I chose were related directly to the situation I was in and the people to whom I owed a duty of care. She, on the other hand, was totally bound by the rules of her religion, presiding over which was a God who saw everything she did, and made his disapproval known, if not now, then in the future. Her degree of self-confidence was related directly to her God's opinion of her.

For us to be able to cope with the uncertainty of our lives we have to have considerable confidence in ourselves. To have confidence in ourselves we have to feel that we are not totally helpless in the face of the forces that govern this world. Any religion that teaches that we are in the hands of God, or Allah, or some great mystical Power undermines whatever shred of self-confidence we can muster. Lacking self-confidence, we become dependent and obedient. No wonder Steve Jones calls the lies that are taught to children evil!

When we are small children, what we are told about the world by our parents and teachers becomes the framework of how we

259

see ourselves and our world. We can think that the world is the way our framework presents it until we visit a country very different from our own. Then we find ourselves shaken by the discovery that we cannot understand why certain things happen, and we cannot predict how quite ordinary things will turn out. Remembering these kinds of experiences, imagine that you are a school child again and you discover that everything you have been told by your parents, your teachers and your government proves not to be true. This is what happened to German children born between 1925 and 1940. Imagine being the child of one of those people closest to Hitler. You would have lived a life of great privilege, knowing that your father was a very important man. Then suddenly everything changed. Your privileged life vanished, and you learned that your father had committed the most vile and despicable crimes.

In 1959 Norbert Lebert wrote a series of articles, published in the magazine *Zeitbild*, about his visits to the children of high-ranking Nazis. Forty years later his son Stephan read these articles and decided to follow up those of the children who were still alive. His book *My Father's Keeper*[23] draws on his father's articles and his own conversations with some of the children. This book and Dan Bar-On's book *Legacy of Silence* show how children try to deal in many different ways with their parents' lies, but none of them successful.

Hans Frank was the Nazi governor-general of Poland where, amongst other duties, he was responsible for Auschwitz. When he was arrested by an American patrol he willingly handed over his diaries. He seemed to believe that these would show the Americans what an important person he was. These were used at his trial to convict him. A typical entry was 19 January 1940: 'I have received an order to ransack the conquered eastern territories ruthlessly, to transform their economic, social, cultural and political structures into a pile of smoking ruins.' Another on 12 January 1944 was 'We began here with three and a half million Jews; of these we now have only a few labour companies left, all the rest – let us say – emigrated.'[24] When Frank was hanged he left behind his wife and five children.

In his interview with Stephan Lebert, Niklas, the youngest of Frank's children, told him how his sister Brigitte had been obsessed with the idea of not living past the age of forty-six, the age her father was when he died. She fulfilled this prophecy by killing herself. His brother Michael, 'a proper Adonis', had refused to hear any criticism of his father. Politically he was very far to the right. He started drinking, not alcohol, but milk, ten litres a day. He grew enormously fat, and died when he was fifty-three. Whenever Niklas and his elder brother Norman were together, they talked about their father. Norman had many good memories of his father as well as bad. Niklas said, 'Norman suffers more than I do.'[25] What Niklas felt was enormous, all-consuming rage.

In the mid-1980s Niklas wrote a series of articles about his father for *Stern* magazine. These were later turned into a book. These articles and book shocked most Germans. Niklas described how on every 16 October, the day his father was hanged, he masturbated over a photograph of his father. He described his father as having no mitigating qualities. He was 'cowardly, corrupt, sexually stimulated by power, brutish, pampered and soft'.[26] Niklas was also raging against himself because he saw in himself many of his father's attributes.

The Germans were united in their opinion of Niklas. He was a disgrace. No matter what a father had done, a son should not criticize him. In the years following her husband's death, Brigitte Frank had received many letters from her fellow Germans, telling her how much they respected and admired her husband. Niklas found that by telling the truth he was very much alone.

When events reveal that a parent has lied, and that he is not the admirable person he had pretended to be, the child is forced to make a choice. To recognize and accept the truth the child has to discard many of the ideas that had been part of his identity, and to create new ideas out of his very limited experience. If the adults around him are not prepared to help him and assure him of his own value, untainted by the deeds of his parent, he might not be able to find within himself ideas that are both true and able to inspire courage and optimism. The alternative to facing and accepting the truth is to deny the truth, lie to himself and create a fantasy to sustain himself and the life he lives. Niklas Frank chose the first alternative and Gudrun Himmler, Heinrich Himmler's oldest child, the second.

Gudrun gave only one interview, and that to Norbert Lebert. After that she never even responded to a request for an interview. She was thirty when she met Lebert. Much later he told his son Stephan that he had felt sorry for her because she was 'so skinny and transparent'. She had been fifteen when the war ended and her father committed suicide after being arrested. She idolized her father, and told Lebert, 'I look on it as my life's work to show him to the world in a different light. Today my father is branded as the greatest mass murderer of all time. I want to revise that image. At least to get the facts straight about what he thought and why he acted as he did.'[27]

The surname Himmler made it difficult for Gudrun to get a job but she refused to change it until she married and became Frau Bierwitz. She never wrote the book she wanted to write where she cleared her father's name, but she devoted herself to the organization Stille Hilfe that had directly after the war helped many Nazis to leave the country or to establish themselves in post-war Germany. Maintained by the donations from about a thousand supporters, by the late 1990s Stille Hilfe was looking after elderly Nazis. Gudrun's special concern was Anton Malloth, a close friend of her father. Malloth had been a camp guard at Theresienstadt, a concentration camp which had supplied slave labour and where, amongst others, 80,000 Czech Jews had died. Of the 15,000 children in the camp, 93 survived. At the end of the war Malloth escaped being captured. In 1948 he was sentenced *in absentia* by a Czech court for his part in the hundreds of killings in Theresienstadt. He continued to evade prosecution until he was eighty-eight, when he was convicted in a Munich court of beating and kicking a Jewish inmate to death and for attempting to murder another prisoner. At his trial, the judge said that Malloth had committed these crimes because he hated Jews and political prisoners, and because he enjoyed having arbitrary power of life and death. In prison he was found to have cancer. He was released to a nursing home near Munich but died ten days later.[28] Gudrun lived in Munich.

How should we feel about people like Gudrun who suffer in childhood and then go on to behave in ways of which we disapprove? As I write, the British media are much concerned about the cruel death of a small boy who died at the hands of his mother, Tracy Connelly, and her boyfriend Steven Barker. Tracy herself had a hideous childhood where she was sexually abused by her father and the members of a paedophile ring which he ran. Her mother, a drug addict, did not protect her. Tracy was sent by the Social Services to a school away from her home, but she was not provided with a steady, long-term relationship with a caring, wise adult. No one helped her overcome the horrors of her childhood.

The media always frame such sad, terrible stories in the moral terms of who is to blame. There is no attempt to trace the network of consequences that led to the tragedy. Instead, the media and the experts invited to discuss the moral question bat accusations and defences backwards and forwards until they throw up their hands in weariness and despair, and resort to the moral answer that accuses and excuses everyone. They ask, 'Who knows what evil each of us has inside us? Who knows what each of us would do in similar circumstances?' These are rhetorical questions not requiring an answer.

Once the unknown amount of evil we are all supposed to have is mentioned, all argument is at an end. No one wants to admit that moral concepts like 'good' and 'evil' do not explain why some people are cruel while others are not.

Not all children who are sexually and physically abused go on to abuse, although they are harmed in other ways by this abuse. Not all parents who were lied to as children lie to their children, because they understood what harm their parents' lies did to them. Not all children given a religious education believe what they are told, because they see discrepancies between what their teachers say and what they do, or they cannot see the myths and legends they are told as being anything more than that. In Nazi Germany, Congo, Bosnia, and all those places where vast cruelties have been inflicted on defenceless people, there were many acts of kindness, many acts of selfless bravery. Instead of asking futile questions about good and evil, we would be better employed asking what are the events in a person's childhood that lead one child to grow up being kind to his fellow human beings, and another child to grow up wanting to destroy those whom he fails to see as fellow human beings.

This is a very difficult question to answer, not because we lack the ability to do so but because we have to look with an objective eye, not just at ourselves, but at those we expect to be able to admire. We assume that they are on our side. Take, for example, American presidents and the CIA.

Chapter Seventeen

Lying for Your Government

Anyone who is interested in why George Bush decided to invade Iraq, why so many men underwent rendition, that is, being kidnapped and placed in special prisons, including Guantanamo, and whether the British government was implicated in the torture used in these prisons, should read Tim Weiner's book *Legacy of Ashes: The History of the CIA*. In his Author's Note Weiner wrote, 'This is the first history of the CIA compiled entirely from firsthand reporting and primary documents . . . What I have written here is not the whole truth, but to the best of my ability, it is nothing but the truth.'[1]

The primary task of the CIA was to discover what America's enemies were actually doing. This was espionage, which is usually conducted by people who speak the enemy's language and know the enemy well. A secondary task for the CIA was to set up covert operations with the purpose of changing something in another country. Fidel Castro has an extraordinary record of surviving CIA covert operations. Many political leaders, especially in Central and South America, did not.

Weiner summarized what his book reveals.

The agency's triumphs have saved some blood and treasure. Its mistakes have squandered both. They have proved fatal for legions of American soldiers and foreign agents; some three thousand Americans who died in New York, Washington and Pennsylvania on 11 September 2001; and three thousand more who have died since then in Iraq and Afghanistan. The one crime of lasting consequence has been the CIA's inability to carry out its central mission: informing the president of what is happening in the world.[2]

My copy of Weiner's book is annotated with my comments and much underlining, usually where Weiner mentions the lies that the CIA told. Why did the CIA lie? Weiner explained that, for an institution to survive in Washington, the head of that institution must be able to speak directly to the president. The task of the CIA is to see how things really are. However, CIA chiefs soon learned that it was not in their interest to tell the president what he does not want to hear. Often what the president did not want to hear was the truth. We have yet to see whether Obama will be strong enough to cope with the truth.

The history of the CIA is a history of lies. It is also the history of the very peculiar people who ran the CIA. One of these was James Jesus Angleton, whose name appears in many different histories of the 1950s and 1960s, including Harold Lloyd Goodall Jr's book *A Need to Know: The Clandestine History of a CIA Family*. Goodall wrote of his family, 'We were a family who hid things from each other. We hid intangible things such as what we thought and how we felt, and then progressed to hiding tangible objects.'[3] His father hid his stash of vodka, just as he had hidden his life. By the time he was in high school Goodall had a clandestine life too. He did not tell his parents that he was not attending school but hanging out with the hippies and smoking dope. However, as his father wanted him to do, he went to college and eventually became, not surprisingly, a professor of human communications. I say 'not surprisingly' because those of us who study our fellow human beings – psychologists, anthropologists, sociologists and all the sub varieties of these professions – usually choose, out of a wide range of possibilities, to research something in ourselves and our fellow human beings that has been a problem to us.

Goodall's parents had given him his father's name but they nicknamed him Buddy. He described his father as 'the man I grew up with but never knew'. It was not until he had a son of his own that Goodall realized that he needed to learn enough about his father to be able to create a coherent story of his own life. He discovered that whatever appeared to be evidence of his father's life – photographs, employment files, personnel files – were threaded through with lies. Even the papers to do with his transfer from Veterans Administration to the position of Vice Consul of the United States in Rome in 1955, where he was to be in charge of veterans' affairs at the embassy were, to say the least, ambiguous. Neither his father nor his mother were what they seemed to be. In the embassy his father carried out the duties required of a veterans' affairs officer but for most of the time he was a CIA operative, a spy.

How much his mother Naomi knew of what her husband did Goodall never discovered. She must have known something because she had always to support his cover story. She had to be attractive, intelligent, well informed about cultural events, beautifully dressed, and always poised. In the 1950s a woman had to be poised. If you have not been a woman in the 1950s, you can have no idea how hard it was to be poised in the way 'poised' was defined then. Moreover, Naomi had to be able to have intelligent, light conversations with everyone in the embassy and their many guests, and never show any sign of boredom or disagreement. Holding her practised smile, she was not allowed to complain when, at embassy functions, a male guest peered down her cleavage or patted her bottom.

The other women at the embassy were university graduates from moneyed families. They had been visiting Europe since they were children. Naomi came from a small farm in West Virginia and her education was modest. If she had told the truth about her background, the embassy women and especially the Ambassador, Clare Boothe Luce, would have patronized her even more. At their first meeting Luce had reprimanded her for calling her son by his nickname. She was to call him Harold.

To survive in this situation she had to tweak her story. Her family were 'in agriculture', while her nursing training was spoken of as if she had been a college student. She could not mention her first brief marriage and sudden widowhood, or how she had suffered 70-degree burns when her dressing gown caught fire. She carried all this off extremely well, but she came to hate herself as the confidence she had had in who she was vanished. She lived in fear of being exposed as a fraud. Nevertheless, she willingly sacrificed herself for her husband and her country.

Even at home she could not relax. The houses and apartments used by embassy staff had listening devices already installed. If Naomi and her husband wished to speak privately they had to go into the bathroom and turn on the taps. The CIA's station chief in Rome was Angleton, a paranoid man who needed to be in control. He needed to know what his staff were saying and doing.

Increasingly Naomi felt the strain of living a lie. Moreover, she loved her husband and she knew enough to know that he was often in danger. When they were transferred to London which, with Berlin, was the centre of the Cold War CIA operations, Naomi started taking what her son described as the white pill that got her through the night and the yellow pill that got her through the day. Barbiturates and amphetamines. Along with alcohol, these were the drugs of choice of the Cold War, as they had been of the Second World War. Naomi did not have to buy them from a dealer. They were willingly prescribed by doctors.

These drugs are addictive, dangerously so, though psychiatrists would not admit this until the evidence was so great it could no longer be denied. One day in 1971 when I was in the staff dining room at the clinic where I worked, I remarked that barbiturates and amphetamines changed very markedly the people who took them. I had seen this in friends in the 1940s and 1950s. A psychiatrist sitting at the same table crushingly reprimanded me: these drugs were harmless. They did not change the people who took them. Psychiatrists went on writing prescriptions for barbiturates until the benzodiazepines came along. The patients who took these drugs soon found that they were addictive. If they tried to stop taking the drug, they suffered terribly. Instead of recognizing withdrawal symptoms, psychiatrists said that this was the underlying illness, that illness for which no physical causes has ever been found. So the patients resumed taking the drug. It took over ten years for psychiatrists to admit that benzodiazepines were addictive. The SSRI antidepressants such as Prozac and Seroxat were developed in the late 1980s, but even today few psychiatrists will admit they are addictive, although they do warn patients that they should not stop taking the drug abruptly but taper it off very slowly.

Why did psychiatrists not tell the truth about these drugs? Because, when they looked at their patients, they saw the symptoms of a mental illness. They did not see a person. They did not see the intense mental distress people feel when they are struggling to hold themselves together when their life and their world have fallen apart. They could not question, much less relinquish, their way of seeing things. Similarly, the men who ran the CIA could see only what they expected to see, and not what was actually there.

Angleton believed that he was always right. He became increasingly convinced that the Soviet Union had a master plot to deceive the American government. He considered himself to be a close friend of the MI5 officer who had trained him, Kim Philby. They worked together. Weiner wrote, 'His friendship with Angleton was sealed with the cold kiss of gin and the warm embrace of whisky. He was an extraordinary drinker, knocking back a fifth a day, and Angleton was well on his way to becoming one of the CIA's champion alcoholics. A title held against stiff competition.'[4] In 1949 Angleton was involved in organizing covert operations where agents were dropped into Albania. He gave the co-ordinates of each drop to Philby. Although every drop failed, Angleton went on to organize these drops for four years. About two hundred agents died. Angleton was promoted to chief of counterintelligence.

In his memoir *My Silent War* Philby described Angleton as a man who was easy to dupe. So is anyone who never entertains any doubt that their way of seeing things is absolutely true. This certainty provides the person who wishes to dupe with a solid basis on which to build a strategy for duping. Such a solid basis is not available with a person who doubts and questions. When in 1951 the British double agents Guy Burgess and Donald Maclean defected to the Soviet Union to avoid being arrested, a number of people in MI5 and the CIA knew that there had to be a third man, and that this man was Philby. One of these was Goodall's father. Suddenly, without any warning, his diplomatic immunity was withdrawn, and he was sent to a much lesser post in Cheyenne, Wyoming. Angleton was determined to destroy any person who might suggest that he, Angleton, was wrong. As in Rome and London, Goodall senior's cover story was that he was working in veterans' affairs, but now his home was only a few miles from the largest American nuclear site, Warren Air Force Base. Here was a centre for surveillance, not just of America's enemies, but of those Americans whom the government considered to be its enemies, that is, Americans who expressed any kind of dissent. Having spent his adult life, first as an Air Force officer and then in the CIA, protecting his country, he was now to spy on its citizens.

In Wyoming the frameworks that had sustained Goodall's parents no longer existed. Naomi could not get a steady supply of barbiturates and amphetamines, and the result was catastrophic. Apart from the terrible physical effects of the withdrawal of these drugs, the presentation of herself that had given a structure to her day-to-day life was no longer appropriate. She could not immediately resurrect the dormant strengths of her true self. The way she fell apart was dramatic and terrible. Her husband did what he had always done, work all day and in the evening drink, only now he drank to get very, very drunk.

Goodall coped as best he could. He liked being in Cheyenne where he could be an ordinary American boy. Moreover, the framework he had acquired in Rome worked well in Cheyenne. He knew how to be good. He wrote, 'My job in my family was to be a good boy. I was expected to be a good student, to obey my parents, to always be presentable, never to be disagreeable, and to involve myself in sports.'[5] He was, he said, typical of those children whose parents had classified jobs they could not talk about. They all had pressed clothes, military haircuts, and shined shoes. They were polite, and tried never to do anything that might result in something negative being put in their parents' file. They learned to 'keep our feelings to ourselves and our mouths shut'.[6]

He did not change in this as he got older. He never spoke about his parents to his friends or family. He became very skilled at being politely silent and at deflecting the conversation away from difficult topics. If asked about his home life, he answered, 'Fine.'

He described how, when he and the other boys – sons of embassy staff or of the military or defence contractors – played together, they always played war games. He remembered these war games when he watched pictures of the conflicts in Iraq or Afghanistan or Israel and Palestine. He knew how children during a war acquire the logic and language of war. He said, 'I am not surprised that there are thousands of otherwise reasonable adolescents who, often uneducated and unemployed and surrounded by religious hatred, volunteer for the radical Islamic jihad and then become terrorists and suicide bombers.'[7] One war breeds another war, and the men to fight it.

271

Weiner told the story of how, in September 1949, over Alaska, an air force crew found traces of radioactivity in the atmosphere. This discovery was still being analysed when 'the CIA confidently declared that the Soviet Union would not produce an atomic bomb for at least another four years. Three days later, Truman told the world that Stalin had the bomb.'[8]

The CIA's knowledge of what was happening inside the Soviet Union did not improve over the years of the Cold War. They needed agents on the ground who spoke the language and knew that country. They could not find or train such people. Instead, they resorted to spy planes that saw little of importance and created their own disasters. When Stalin died in 1953 the CIA knew nothing of the people who might take his place, nor of the kind of problems they would face. They told the president that Stalin had a plan for world domination when in fact, as Nikita Khrushchev later said, he was afraid of war. The Soviet Union had not recovered from their war against Germany. They had poured money into building nuclear bombs because they were afraid that America might use their nuclear arsenal against them, but this depleted what little they had to provide the bare necessities of Russian life. Like Saddam Hussein fifty years later, Stalin did not want his enemies to know how weak he was.

Eisenhower feared that the demands of the military for very expensive fleets of ships and planes and other military hardware to fight the Cold War would cost the Treasury far more than it could afford. He decided that he would base his strategy on nuclear bombs and covert operations. Therefore, the American government built more and bigger bombs, and assumed that the Soviet Union was doing the same. The CIA's estimates of the Soviets' military strength were based not on intelligence but on politics and guesswork. From 1957 onwards, the CIA advised Eisenhower that the Soviets were building intercontinental ballistic missiles (ICBMs) much faster than the United States was doing. In 1960 they told him that the Soviets would have five hundred ICBMs by 1961. The American Strategic Command prepared a first strike plan where they would use more than three thousand ICBMs against the Soviet Union, and we would be in the midst of a nuclear war. The truth was that the Soviets did not have five hundred ICBMs. They had four.[9]

America need not have built a huge nuclear arsenal, while the CIA's many covert operations into other countries cost money and lives and achieved nothing, except instil in those people who had suffered these operations a lasting hatred for America. At the end of his presidency Dwight Eisenhower read the thick stack of reports that he had commissioned about the CIA and concluded that he was leaving his successor, John Kennedy, 'a legacy of ashes'.

It was on this basis of the legacy of ashes that the sorry story of the Cold War was played out in the thirty years that followed, when finally the Soviet Union split apart, not for military reasons but economic. When the Cold War did come to an end, the American government had to consider what to do, not only with their own nuclear weapons but with Russia's, because Russia could not afford to deal with them themselves. The American government set aside $4.4 billion for 'atomic energy defense environmental restoration and waste management activities' and another $112 million 'to provide repositories for the disposal of high-level radioactive waste and spent nuclear fuel'.[10] The US also budgeted for $475.5 million for their 'Co-operative Threat Reduction' programme for Russian nuclear weapons.[11] They called all this 'The Costs of Victory'.

During the Cold War the whole world lived under the threat of Mutually Assured Destruction or MAD, and mad it was. If one side dropped a nuclear bomb on the other, the other would respond in kind. Cities would be destroyed and a cloud of radiation would spread around the world. By the early 1980s CND and other peace groups were gathering huge support. It seemed to me that the kernel of the problem was the way we always had

273

enemies, real or imagined. I wrote a book where I asked whether we could live without enemies.[12] Whenever I had the opportunity at a conference, I asked the men who were so knowledgeable about the size of bombs and the damage they could do whether we could live without enemies. The answer was always 'No.' I found that these men were always irritated by my asking. They did not want to consider what people actually did. They were concerned with important abstract matters. And so today, in many of the discussions about climate change, abstractions abound. If the effects of climate change on people are mentioned, they are likely to be spoken about in very general terms, as if all people are the same. Only thinkers like George Monbiot can see that it is the degree of civilization that we have reached that allows many of us to approach the best of what we can be. We do not have to fight for our existence. We can be caring, humane, generous. As our civilization collapses, as it will if climate change is not halted and reversed, we will be too busy fighting for our existence to care for anyone else other than our own. As Monbiot says, the psychopaths will take over. At present there are many psychopaths in power, but, in countries where the law is valued and upheld, psychopaths are kept in check. With climate change will come disasters the like of which we have not seen before, and against which we have no defences. The rule of law prevails only in stable states, and, in a world whose climate and its effects are unpredictable, there can be no stable states.

The final section of Weiner's book, about the CIA under presidents Clinton and George W. Bush, makes very sad reading for all of us who are left with the tragic chaos of Iraq and Afghanistan, and the consequences of this. The CIA had no knowledge of what Saddam Hussein was doing. All they had were the lies told by certain Iraqi expatriates who were looking after their own interests. Bush and Cheney were determined to invade Iraq, and they had persuaded the easily persuaded Tony Blair to join them. The CIA told them what they wanted to hear, that Saddam Hussein had weapons of mass destruction. The CIA lied. Should we now believe what the CIA says about the use of torture, and what the British government says about not being complicit in that torture?

Goodall's book is about the lies of silence. He was 'left to grieve for all that had been lost in those empty spaces and the long silences between us'.[13] Towards the end of his autobiography, Barack Obama wrote of the silences in his father's family. He had discovered the story of his father's life, and of his father and grandfather. He saw, and knew himself, the confusion that a black man suffers when he lives in a country controlled by white people. Sitting beside his father's grave, he said to him,

> There was no shame in your confusion. Just as there had been no shame in your father's before you. There was only shame in the silence the fear had produced. It was the silence that betrayed us. If it weren't for that silence, your grandfather might have told your father that he could never escape himself, or re-create himself alone. Your father might have taught those same lessons to you. And you, the son, might have taught your father that this new world that was beckoning all of you involved more than just railroads and indoor toilets and irrigation ditches and gramophones . . . You might have told him that that these instruments carried with them a dangerous power, that they demanded a different way of seeing the world. That this power could be absorbed only alongside a faith born out of hardship, a faith that wasn't new, that wasn't black or white or Christian or Muslim but that pulsed in the heart of the first African village and the first Kansas homestead – a faith in other people. That silence killed your faith.[14]

The journalist Sathnam Sanghera had a very different background from that of Goodall and of Obama, yet he came to the same conclusion in his memoir *The Boy with the Topknot: A*

Memoir of Love, Secrets and Lies that won the Mind Book of the Year Award in 2009. Well educated though he was, Sanghera was in his mid-twenties before he discovered that the father he had lived with all his life, who had taken him to and from school every day, had, for all that time, been diagnosed as schizophrenic. His parents were Sikhs from rural Punjab. Theirs had been an arranged marriage, and no one had explained to his mother why her husband behaved in such bizarre and sometimes brutal ways. She was a very brave woman. She never learned to speak English, but she lived for her family and her religion. She did not know that in London her younger son did not lead the life of a good Sikh boy. Sanghera kept his London life separate from his family life in Wolverhampton, so it was with considerable reluctance that he set to work to discover his parents' history.

He uncovered a story that went back to his great-grandfather. He concluded that,

> Maybe, if my great-grandfather's (possible) mental illness had been discussed and acknowledged within the family, then maybe, when my father started showing signs of psychosis, he would have got the kind of treatment he needed sooner, and maybe my mother would have been spared the violent attacks she endured, and maybe she wouldn't have been blamed for the illness, and maybe the family would have made more effort to ensure my father stopped drinking, which might have meant that he had fewer relapses, and wouldn't have throttled that poor schoolgirl, and, maybe, if these things had been understood and acknowledged, then maybe my sister would have been made aware of her illness sooner and maybe she wouldn't have stopped taking her medication and ended up in hospital. Put it another way: sometimes it's better to talk about difficult subjects rather than conceal them beneath a web of secrets and lies.[15]

Discovering this meant that he had to tell his mother the truth about his life. I won't tell you what happened when he did because I don't want to spoil this wonderful book for you.

We lie in order to prevent our sense of being a person falling apart. If we acknowledge to ourselves that we are lying, if we assess the situation truthfully, and construct our lies carefully and for as short a time as possible, we have a chance of getting away with what we are doing, and not causing too much damage to ourselves and other people. However, situations where we can do this are rare, because everything we do is linked one way or another to everything else that we do. We might lie to save another person from harm, an act that has no benefit to ourselves, but, at the same time, we have protected ourselves from the pain we feel when we see another person suffering. The best we can do is to be truthful with ourselves, and not tell ourselves that we are being truthful when in fact we are lying. One lie that most people tell themselves and insist that it is the truth is that they are better than some other group of people.

Children have to be taught this lie by adults. Left to themselves, they would recognize from their earliest encounters with other children that all people are much the same. We each have our individual appearance and personal idiosyncrasies, and our individual way of seeing things, but, as a species, we are very much alike. We do terrible damage to ourselves and other people when we lie to ourselves and other people and say that we are superior to other people. The monstrous horror of Nazi Germany was built on this lie.

Chapter Eighteen

Never Say You're Sorry

Robert Jay Lifton wrote that, when he interviewed Nazi doctors and they discussed Auschwitz, 'They seemed to me to be like messengers from another planet.'[1] Yet they were not from another planet. They were ordinary human beings who had taken the lie 'I am superior' to its furthest extremes. Whatever religious, political, class, race or gender beliefs you may hold, if you see yourself as being superior to another group of people, and you tell yourself that your superiority entitles you to deal as you wish with your inferiors, then all that will stop you from behaving like the doctors at Auschwitz are the circumstances in which you find yourself.

Josef Mengele, the Angel of Death, was the second son of a well-to-do industrialist. His family was described as 'strict Catholic'. On official forms he described himself as a Catholic or, in the preferred Nazi terminology, 'a believer in God'. He was a good student and seemed headed for an academic career. However, he joined the SA in 1934, joined the Party in 1937, and applied for membership of the SS. Lifton said of him that he 'would have become under other conditions a relatively ordinary physician-professor'.[2]

Like the Klamroths and the Himmlers, the Mengeles would have subscribed to the belief in Aryan supremacy well before Hitler arrived on the scene. However, one lie always needs others to support it. Hitler had not just talked about the inferiority of the Jews that merited their death. He incorporated this lie into a mystical imperative that loyal Nazis, and especially doctors, had to carry

278

out. This meant that, when a Jew arrived at Auschwitz or the other camps, he or she was already dead. Therefore, it was not a crime or a sin to send Jews to the gas chambers or to use them for experimentation before killing them. Moreover, the killing itself was a healing. Jews were killed in order to heal the Nordic race. The Nazi doctor, said Lifton, saw himself as a healer with the special powers of a shaman, a priest. Albert Speer told Lifton about the extraordinary experience he had when, for the first time, he heard Hitler speak. What he described was 'a classical experience of transcendence, an ecstatic state of feeling outside oneself and swept up by a larger force that could connect one or reconnect one with ultimate spiritual principles'.[3] From this Speer concluded that he belonged to Hitler and would one day share his omnipotence and power. Many thousands of slave labourers died in the armament factories that Speer organized. Throughout history a great many people have used a transcendental experience to justify the cruelty they inflicted on other people.

Lifton described how each Nazi doctor divided himself into two selves, the Auschwitz self and the home self, the husband, the father, the music lover. This kind of splitting is a common defence used by people who doubt their own value, and seek to hide themselves behind a role. As Sathnam Sanghera had found, dividing himself between a home self and a London self meant that he was not at ease in either place. To be at ease with himself he had to be one whole person.

Lifton called the doctors' splitting of themselves 'doubling', which comes from the fantasy that somewhere there is another version of ourselves. This concept reflects the way the Nazi doctors needed to create an impermeable wall between the home self and the Auschwitz self. No hint of what the home self must have known, that killing people is wrong, must leak through to the Auschwitz self. Neither should there be any hint of concern for other people. These doctors did not want to be reminded of

279

the emotions of sympathy and empathy. To maintain the wall between the two selves, the Auschwitz self had to become numb, what Lifton called 'psychic numbing'.

Psychic numbing was not peculiar to Nazi doctors. It is a common way of lying to yourself. You tell yourself that you do not feel the emotions you see as a weakness. Earlier I told the story of the three-year-old girl who defended herself against the pain of her mother's beatings by declaring that it did not hurt (page 73). From the way the mother told the story, it is clear that she was psychically numb. A mother who was not would have been overcome with guilt and remorse.

Remorse is a very uncomfortable emotion. Many of us are kind and caring, not because we are particularly virtuous, but because we do not want to feel remorseful. On the other hand, many tell themselves and others that they have nothing to feel remorseful about. Perhaps the most popular song sung at funerals and karaoke nights is Frank Sinatra's 'My Way'. As if doing something your way exonerates you from the necessity of feeling remorse for your mistakes. Whenever someone in government or business has to appear to apologize for having inflicted injury on other people, out comes the PR lie, 'lessons have been learnt'. As if learning something from a disaster exonerates you from having caused a disaster, especially when what had been learnt is rapidly forgotten.

Central to the structure of ideas we know as our sense of being a person is our life story. Like all stories, it has a beginning, a middle and an end. Nothing is more threatening than discovering that our life story is not what we thought it was, that our future is not going to be what we planned it to be, that our present is different from what we thought it was, and that much of the past we have constructed is a lie. Remorse requires us to recognize that our past is not what we want it to be. However, recognizing the harm we have done brings to mind all the regrets we have buried, the painful matters of being unloved, betrayed, and rejected. We try to construct a past we can live with. If we cannot bring ourselves to accept our mistakes, failures and losses, we lie to ourselves and to others about our past. The lies we tell in order to avoid remorse come in many forms, from the nearest we can get to 'I'm sorry', to the blatant, 'I'm not to blame.'

Robert McNamara, Secretary of Defense for John Kennedy and then Lyndon Johnson, had much to be sorry for. In his book *In Retrospect: The Tragedy and Lessons of Vietnam* and his film *The Fog of War: Eleven Lessons from the Life of Robert S. McNamara*, he got very close to saying, 'I'm sorry', but each time he did, he turned away. The historian Marilyn Young pointed out how one sentence from *In Retrospect* is often quoted, 'We were wrong, terribly wrong', but, 'If you read the whole paragraph, what it says is, "We weren't wrong in our values and intentions; we were wrong in our judgements and capabilities."' This is a longer version of Tony Blair's 'I did what I believed was right.' Hitler, Pol Pot and Bin Laden all did what they believed was right. Young went on, 'The book, as a whole, is an excuse. It's a struggle. He almost comes to terms, and then he runs away from coming to terms. And he does the same, I think, in *The Fog of War*. And he did the same thing for the whole of the rest of his life; an approach to what he is responsible for, and then a bouncing off, too awful to face.'[4]

McNamara is chiefly remembered for his part in the Vietnam War. He was largely responsible for the escalation of American intervention in Vietnam and for the conduct of the war almost to its end when he realized that, for all the bombs they dropped on Vietnam, they could not defeat the Vietcong. In that war at least three million Vietnamese, around one million Cambodians and Laotians, and 58,000 American soldiers died. The herbicide Agent Orange, used to strip the leaves off trees and expose the Vietcong soldiers, killed some 400,000 Vietnamese and caused millions of cases of cancer and other illnesses, and birth defects in unborn babies. Members of the American military who handled

Agent Orange suffered as the Vietnamese did.[5] These were not the only terrible events with which McNamara was associated. He was also associated with some terrible events in the last years of the Second World War.

The war in the Pacific against Japan was fought island by island. By 1945 American forces had reached Guam and the Marianas in the north Pacific. The American bombers had to make a long flight to reach the Japanese mainland, and the Japanese defences proved to be much better than the Americans had expected. The B-29s flew at altitudes between 25,000 and 30,000 feet, altitudes that the Japanese fighter planes could not reach. However, at those altitudes, not only were there ferocious winds, but, curiously, a powerful stream of air never encountered before. This we now call the jet stream. The B-29 crews could bomb from that height, but with very poor accuracy.

The man in charge, General Curtis LeMay, realized that he needed a new strategy. McNamara, in the Air Force and working as a systems analyst, was one of the people who advised LeMay. A group of American manufacturers had created a jellied form of gasoline that would stick to anything and start extremely hot fires. It was called napalm. In Japan the buildings were made of wood. LeMay decided to have the B-29s stripped of everything that was not needed for the bombers to go in loaded with napalm, and at 10,000 feet. On 9 March 1945, 334 B-29s took off from Guam. 'The target area was 3 by 5 miles, containing a large industrial complex. However, each square mile held over 100,000 civilians. The bombs fell, and within thirty minutes the resulting fires were out of control, driven by 40 mph winds. Tokyo, hit by strings of incendiaries, became a holocaust. Water boiled in the canals after the temperature reached over 1800 degrees F. For three hours the B-29s kept coming.' Some 84,000 Japanese were killed and 4,100 injured. The Japanese called it 'slaughter bombing'.

More and more cities fell victim to such bombing. When

Kobe was to be bombed, not enough napalm bombs were available, so magnesium thermite bombs were used. These bombs burn with an intensity of 2,300 °F.[6]

Much has been said about the atomic bombs used on Hiroshima and Nagasaki, but many people born after the war might not know about the firebombing, which destroyed much of the Japanese defences and brought most Japanese close to starvation. President Truman decided to use the atomic bombs to bring the war to an end more quickly and save American lives. In the film *The Fog of War* McNamara told how, 'LeMay said that if we'd lost the war we'd have all been prosecuted as war criminals, and I think he was right. He, and I'd say I, were behaving as war criminals. What makes it immoral if you lose but not if you win?' He did not attempt to answer this question.

The first lesson in the film is 'Empathize with Your Enemy.' Here McNamara said, 'In the Cuban missile crisis we put ourselves in the skin of the Soviets. In the case of Vietnam, we didn't know them well enough to empathize.'[7] The Cuban missile crisis brought America within a hair's breadth of a nuclear war. Kennedy was faced with a choice of using force to stop Khrushchev from installing nuclear missiles in Cuba, or negotiating with Khrushchev. Despite being urged by his military advisers to invade Cuba, Kennedy made the effort to look at the situation from Khrushchev's point of view, and, with that, devise a response that was firm but not requiring Khrushchev to lose face if he withdrew the missiles. The missiles were withdrawn and the crisis passed.

McNamara's statement about not knowing the Vietnamese was very economical with the truth. McNamara and the two presidents he worked for, Kennedy and Johnson, did not know the Vietnamese because they did not try to know them, and they did not try because knowing what the Vietnamese were actually like would have ruined their theory.

Vietnam had been a colony of the French who saw it as a cash cow to be milked for the benefit of the French. When Japan was defeated, the French wished to re-establish their colonial rule, while the Vietnamese wanted to be independent. The French, like the British and the Americans, regarded the inhabitants of the countries of Indochina as inferior beings. In American slang, they were 'slope-eyes' and 'gooks'. When China turned Communist, the colonial powers, including America, created the domino theory that was useless at predicting what would happen but it did terrify those who held it. This theory predicted that, like a row of dominoes, Vietnam, Laos, Cambodia, Malaysia, and all the way south to Indonesia would fall under Communist China's rule. The colonial powers' lack of understanding of the people of Indochina underpinned this theory. Tuchman wrote, 'Because Orientals on the whole looked alike to Western eyes, they were expected to act alike and perform with the uniformity of dominoes.'[8]

America went into Vietnam to stop the dominoes falling. The Vietnamese saw the Americans as just another colonial power in a long line of invaders. For all its history, armies from the East and from the West have tramped across Vietnam and harassed its people. The Vietnamese wanted to be independent and so fought the Americans. McNamara said that they did not understand the Vietnamese. Why did they not understand? America did not lack excellent libraries, and knowledgeable historians and political commentators. McNamara did not know about Vietnamese nationalism because he did not want to know.

McNamara was sacked by Johnson because he told Johnson something Johnson did not want to hear. McNamara had realized that the ferocious bombing of North Vietnam by the American Air Force was not defeating the Vietnamese. This was hard for McNamara to admit. When I was in Hanoi not long after the country was beginning to be opened to tourists, I was taken on a trip in a small boat that was made out of oil drums beaten flat and then bolted together. My guide told me that the Americans could not believe that they were being beaten by people physically much smaller than them and whose equipment was largely recycled from whatever scraps and pieces could be found. He did not speak of 'the Vietnam War'. To the Vietnamese, it was the American War.

The historian Howard Zinn pointed out that McNamara advocated pulling out of Vietnam, not because the war was wrong, but because they were losing. After McNamara left the government, he did not talk publicly about the war. He did not dissent from government policy. Zinn said, 'Once you enter the machinery of the government, once you enter the house of empire, you are lost. You are going to be silenced. You may feel anguish, and you may feel torn, and you may weep, and so on, but you are not going to speak out.'[9]

History repeats itself because people do not learn from history. They prefer the safety of the same old lies. Bush and Cheney did not know how the Afghans and the Iraqis saw their situation, and they did not want to know because this information would show them that the situation was not what they wanted it to be. Tony Blair once said, very complacently, that he wished he had studied history. Before deciding to join Bush and Cheney, he did not consult the British historians of Iraq or Afghanistan, even though the history of Britain has long been entwined with both these countries. And so, Bush, Cheney and Blair repeated the mistakes of the Vietnam War, and added a few mistakes of their own. All the members of Blair's cabinet behaved as Zinn said they would, except two, Clare Short and Robin Cook. Short dithered before deciding to resign, but Cook knew that the course for him was clear. In his resignation speech, he said, 'Neither the international community nor the British public is persuaded that there is an urgent and compelling reason for this military action in Iraq . . . Why is it that we should take military action to disarm a military capacity that has been there for 20 years, and which we helped to create?'[10] Robin Cook knew his history.

The Australian Federal Supreme Court judge Marcus Einfeld

excused his crimes with, 'I don't think I'm the slightest bit dishonest. I just made a mistake.'

In Sydney on 8 January 2006, Einfeld's Lexus sedan was captured on a speed camera doing 60kph in a 50kph zone in the suburb of Mosman. No driver in Sydney would have thought badly of Einfeld for exceeding the speed limit in this way. On Sydney streets the speed limits change frequently, and there are speed cameras, so it often feels, every few metres. Unkind people say that speeding fines provide NSW police with a significant part of their revenue.

Einfeld faced a fixed fine of $A77 and the loss of three demerit points, bringing him close to when he would lose his licence. In court on 7 August, Einfeld explained that he had lent his car to an American friend, Professor Teresa Brennan. She, alas, could not corroborate this as she had died not long after returning to America. The magistrate dismissed the case. Overseas visitors do not have to pay speeding fines, so this should have been the end of the matter. No one would have been surprised by Einfeld's explanation. Australians are famous for their hospitality, especially in the way they lend their cars to overseas visitors who, apparently, come from countries where there are no speed limits.

Then some pesky journalist found that Teresa Brennan had died in 2003. When confronted with this, Einfeld said that it was another American academic by the same name who had borrowed his car. She too had died not long after she had returned to America. However, mobile phone records showed that Einfeld was actually in the Mosman area on the day of the offence. Einfeld admitted that he was, but said he was driving his mother's Corolla. Security footage at the car park of his mother's apartment showed that the car did not leave its garage that day.

Einfeld was a highly respected man. He was an Officer of the Order of Australia as well as one of the hundred Australian National Living Treasures. However, he did have a record of avoiding traffic fines. On 29 March 2008, Einfeld was arrested and charged with thirteen offences. When Supreme Court judge Bruce James sentenced Einfeld, he explained that the sentence was for 'deliberate, premeditated perjury' and 'planned criminal activity'. He sentenced Einfeld to three years in full-time custody, two years of it non-parole for perjury and attempting to pervert the course of justice.

A few days before the sentencing, Einfeld was interviewed on ABC Television's *Four Corners*. Here he said,

> I don't think I'm the slightest bit dishonest. I just made a mistake and it was a fatal mistake, it was a very serious mistake, a very serious error of judgement. I'm desperately sorry for what I did. I'm sorry to my family, my elderly mother and my children. I'm sorry to the public at large because they've been my audience over the years. I lied. I can't say it simpler than that. I told a lie, which was a disgraceful thing to do and for which I have been paying ever since. I'm being as frank as is humanly possible. I think Australian people are pretty good at forgiving people who come clean.[11]

Australians are not particularly forgiving of people who lie until they are forced to tell the truth, but they do feel quite tenderly towards someone who provides them with a good laugh.

Einfeld also provided Australians with a question to discuss. Why wouldn't he pay the $A77 fine? He might have got some demerit points, but, if he could not drive for about six months, he could afford a chauffeur. The general consensus was that Einfeld saw himself as being so important that he was above the law.

He would not have been the first Australian to believe this of himself. A few years before, two Sydney radio presenters showed very clearly that they believed that they could do no wrong. These were Alan Jones on 2GB and John Laws on 2UE. They were very influential. Their many listeners formed their opinions according to what Jones and Laws said. Politicians, including the then prime minister John Howard, paid court to them. The two men expected and received great respect. Except from the people on *Media Watch*.

Media Watch was a weekly programme on ABC Television. Its brief was to comment on the peculiarities and biases of the media. In 2009 *Media Watch* celebrated its twentieth anniversary with a programme about its history. In this the audience was reminded how they had enjoyed *Media Watch*'s reports on the dyslexic *Illawarra Mercury* that sometimes even managed to misspell its own name. There was the investigative journalism on commercial news channels that might claim that the journalist was in one European city when the footage accompanying his report showed that he was in another. And then, most famous of all, was Cash for Comments.

John Laws had no time for Australian banks. Neither did many Australians who felt that they only had to walk through the front door of their bank for the bank to charge them for that privilege. Laws kept up a constant barrage of criticism. For instance, on 24 November 1997, he said, 'So here's how it works – the bank makes 2.2 billion dollars profit, the bank closes branches, the bank loses two and a half thousand staff. And then they do it all over again.' Months went by, and then suddenly his criticism of banks ceased. Instead, on 1 March 1999, listeners heard, 'You know we do forget sometimes when we criticize them, that banks are made up of people. So there you are, see, banks make very big profits, but are they unreasonable about it? Maybe not when you know the whole story.'

What had happened? *Media Watch* had friends in all kinds of places who would secretly slip them useful documents. Thus the presenter Richard Ackland was given a document that showed that Laws' change of opinion was underpinned by a million-dollar contract with the Australian Bankers' Association to promote the banks. What followed became known as the Cash for Comments. Both Laws and Jones were found to praise on air those who paid them to do so. The scandal did not end Laws' career, far from it. He finally retired in 2007.

Media Watch asked Laws for an interview for their anniversary programme. He agreed to do so, provided what he said was not edited. Here is a slightly abridged version of what he said.

Well, I mean the cash for comment thing disappeared, as well it should, having proved absolutely nothing except that people like me and Alan Jones actually got paid for working which might come as a bit of a surprise to people at the ABC. As far as *Media Watch* itself was concerned, I don't think it ever did any good ever. It was destructive. It is very easy to be destructive and difficult to be constructive. We spent our time doing our best to entertain people. *Media Watch* seemed to spend its time doing its best to denigrate people. And as for someone like, was it, Richard Ackland, that pompous would be lawyer, what gives him the right to sit in judgement on people like me who has entertained people all over Australia for 50 years? Where is Richard Ackland now, what contribution has he made to television and radio? I think it was rather a shame that they even thought of doing a programme like *Media Watch*. It wasn't new. I did a similar one in about 1970 for Channel Nine but it was a funny one where people would send in mistakes in newspapers like the queen pissed over the bridge rather than passed over the bridge and we'd have fun with it, but *Media Watch* was vicious and I think unfounded.[12]

Not a lot of remorse there, is there?

Lynndie England was given a great deal of advice about whether she should feel remorse. Some people said she should, many said she should not. Lynndie had become famous, or infamous, when the photograph her lover, Charles Grainer, had taken of her holding on a leash a naked Iraqi prisoner crawling out of his cell in Abu Ghraib was flashed around the world. No doubt

289

that photograph inspired a number of Muslim young men to join al-Qaeda or a similar group. Equally, there can be no doubt that Donald Rumsfeld and the CIA were involved in the cruelties committed at Abu Ghraib, but it was only a small group of soldiers who were punished. Grainer was sentenced to ten years in prison, and Lynndie to three.

When Lynndie went to prison she was pregnant with Grainer's child. Released after serving half of her sentence, she and her son Carter went to live with her parents in a trailer park in Fort Ashby, West Virginia. Her parents had divorced over her father's infidelity but got together again, though not very amicably. Lynndie and Carter shared a single bed in her parents' trailer. Lynndie was on medication for depression.[13]

On 30 May 2009, Lynndie agreed to be interviewed on BBC Radio 4 *Saturday Live*. The interviewer asked her, 'Did you think of them [the prisoners] as individuals?' She replied, 'I didn't think of them individually. These are the enemy. These are the bad guys. They did worse things to us.' She added, 'Everyone has to go through life with a bit of humiliation.'

When the interviewer asked her whether she accepted that what she had done was wrong, she replied that she was obeying orders. The next question surprised her. 'If ever you met any of these men, what would you say to them?' She replied, 'Nobody's ever asked me that question before. I'd say it wasn't personal.'

Lynndie knew what it was to be humiliated. When she had been interviewed by the *Guardian* journalist Emma Brockes, she told her that her mother had once hit her so hard with a table tennis bat that it broke, but this was how parents in West Virginia treated their children. Lynndie said, 'I mean, yeah, we were brought up right. If we were out of line, we were spanked. We got privileges taken away. We had to do chores, dishes. Mow the grass.'[14] Army training involves humiliation. Grainer had humiliated her in gross sexual ways. She seems to have told herself that all this humiliation was not important, especially if the person humiliating you also protected you. However, no matter what we tell ourselves, we always know when we are being humiliated and we resent it. How can you not know when humiliation is such a threat to our sense of being a person?

What would have happened to her if she had said to herself, 'What I did was wrong'?

Depression is a defence where we try to hold ourselves together and stop ourselves from falling apart. Depression serves a purpose. It gives us a space where we can consider the ways we have interpreted certain events in our life and identify where we have lied to ourselves. We then have to confront the truths that we had been denying. Many people manage to do this, but they do so with the help of patient friends, or a wise therapist, or simply because they have confidence in their own strength and good sense. Lynndie had none of these advantages. All she had were antidepressant drugs. These do not cure depression. What they do is numb the pain. They do not remove the awareness that you are poised on the edge of a precipice down which you can easily fall.

Lynndie knew that, in humiliating the Iraqi prisoners, she was harming them. But to admit this to herself meant that she would suffer the fate that she feared the most, that she would fall apart. There was no one there who could tell her that this happens to all of us when ideas central to our sense of being a person have been shown to be wrong; no one who could tell her that, even though we feel that we are falling apart, it is only some of our ideas. Our sense of being a person is there, and it is complaining, 'Oh, it's terrible. I'm falling apart.' Even as our sense of being a person is complaining, it is busy putting itself together again.

To become, like Winston in *1984*, a nothing, the events that shatter our ideas also destroy the confidence we had in ourselves. Perhaps Lynndie will find, as many women have found, that, even though she has lost her confidence in herself, she values something that she has produced, her child, and for his sake she will refuse to become a nothing.

291

At the end of the Radio 4 interview, Edward Stourton, a journalist who has covered a great many conflicts, said, 'In every conflict I have found the inability to grasp the humanity of the people on the other side.' Perhaps this will prove to be the fatal flaw that prevents us from dealing effectively with the dangers that lie ahead.

Chapter Nineteen

Some Hard Truths

Uncertainty and aloneness are part of our human condition, just as breathing is. We might deny that this is so, but we would be lying. We all know what I mean by uncertainty and aloneness. We all know how easy it is to misjudge the height of a step and stumble; mistake a stranger who looks like a friend for that friend; struggle to distinguish a dream from a real event; retrieve a memory of something that turns out not to have happened; predict with certainty an event that never eventuates; be mystified by a visual image that alternates between a vase and the profiles of two people. We all know how we can be with a group of friends and, in the midst of their company, we suddenly feel alone. Friends they may be, but they live in a world very different from our own. We might not feel lonely in our own world but enjoy being an observer or knowing that we are different from other people, or we might feel sad because those we are closest to do not know who we are.

Neuroscientists can now explain why such uncertainty and aloneness exists. We can find this to be intellectually interesting, and be reassured that we are not basically different from other people. However, such knowledge does not tell us how we can cope, hour by hour, day by day, with such uncertainty and aloneness.

We have a choice. We can accept uncertainty and aloneness as part of our existence, just as we accept that every day we have to find sufficient food and water for our survival. Or we can be so frightened of feeling uncertain, so terrified of being alone, that we try to find ways of denying our fear. However, our fear exists, so denying it is a lie. Whichever way we use to deny the hard truth of our uncertainty and aloneness, it is destructive.

There are substances that, if ingested, dull our awareness of our fear. They also have a deleterious effect on our body and our life. For all those stories about Uncle Bob who lived to ninety and smoked sixty cigarettes a day, the truth is that nicotine ages and kills. Living is difficult when you cannot breathe properly. Being addicted to a drug means that you are no longer free. Something else has taken over your life. In the 1970s cannabis was the drug chosen by those who wanted to appear to be sophisticated and cool (if you really were you would not need to take a drug), and now it is cocaine. Cocaine is 'expensive, energizing, esteem-boosting, inclining its users to delusions of grandeur and paranoia in equal measure'. Alcohol is always popular, and it will combine with cocaine 'in the liver to produce coco-ethanol, a whole new buzz which stays active for twice as long as cocaine'.[1] Reality, as T.S. Eliot said, is too much for human beings to bear, or at least, not all the time. We all need a break from it. Sleep does not always provide such a respite, because reality can follow us into our dreams. If politicians cared about the welfare of people, and not merely about the prejudices of their voters, they would realize that all of us need something that will, for a small part of the day, take the edge off our fear of uncertainty and aloneness, and the stress of daily life, be it alcohol, a drug, or coffee and cream cakes. However, some of us need help in resisting the temptation to over-indulge. Prohibition serves only to make what is banned desirable, but high prices and a lack of advertising help all but the most heavily addicted to be more moderate in our desire to have some relief from reality.

Sex is popular because the excitement masks the fear and provides closeness without commitment. Happiness from good sex can last for quite a while, but sex without enjoyment, especially when enjoyment is a pretence, or when the sex is coerced or worse, will serve only to heighten awareness of uncertainty and aloneness. The lie that men have been telling for thousands of years, that they cannot control their sex drive (a standing cock might have no conscience but that does not preclude it from having good sense and foresight), has caused immeasurable pain and cruelty. The truth is that many men use their sex drive to deal with their fear. They dare not recognize their fear of uncertainty and aloneness, much less admit it to others. However, the best sex is sex between equals. While those women and men, girls and boys who work as prostitutes might be as brave as they can be about what they do, no one would choose to work as a prostitute if there were economically much better alternatives available. There are some women, and some men, who choose to prostitute themselves not for economic reasons but as an expression of their self-hatred. The issue that needs to be addressed here is the source of that self-hatred. Most politicians are men, and, because they would not face up to the lie men tell about their need for sex, they will do nothing effective about the cruelties involved in prostitution and pornography.

Vast numbers of people try to reassure themselves that they are safe from the fear of uncertainty and aloneness because they believe in some religious or political creed that promises complete security and, eventually, complete happiness. How wonderful it would be if that were possible, but it is not. For us to perceive anything we have to be able to perceive its opposite. To perceive light, there has to be darkness; to know we are alive we have to know death; to recognize that we are happy, we have to know what it is to be sad. Moreover, every event has fortunate and unfortunate consequences. If we love, we can suffer loss: if we refuse to love, we are lonely. The more freedom we have, the less security. Perfect security is the security of the prison. Perfect happiness in heaven or paradise would be possible only if you forgot that you were ever alive, but then you would not know that you were happy.

The way we are constructed physiologically means that we cannot be certain about anything. Everything we know is a guess. It is possible to develop a degree of certainty by testing the evidence in the world around us. However, no matter how good the evidence might be, we can express it only as a probability. Some of our ideas have a high degree of probability of being true, while other ideas have none. When other people give us information, what we receive is not the information the sender intended, but our interpretation of the other person's message. The Bible might be God's message to us, but what we receive when we read the Bible is not God's message but our own individual interpretation of that message. There are as many interpretations of God's word as there are people who have heard His words. If we had always understood this, there would have been no religious wars. We might also be a great deal more careful in making sure that we understand what the person talking to us actually means.

When our ideas are supported by evidence, we can regard them as truths. Ideas unsupported by evidence are fantasies. Our truths are probable truths, not absolute truths. Our physiological makeup prevents us from ever being absolutely sure that any truth is an absolute truth. Many people claim that they are in possession of an absolute truth, but the means by which they acquired this absolute truth is a fantasy. Just saying, 'God told me' does not make a fantasy a truth. Saying, 'I hope this is God's word', or 'I believe that this is God's word' is true if you are reporting yourself truthfully, but this does not make your hope or your belief a universal truth. If your hope or belief gives you comfort and courage, then that is your way of dealing with uncertainty and aloneness, but, if you have gone beyond your personal truth and are trying to force on to other people your fantasy that your personal truth is an absolute truth, you are inflicting on others the harm that we all suffer when other people try to force their ideas on to us. If you get angry with those people who do not accept what you say, you inadvertently reveal a great deal about yourself.

We can become angry with people who refuse to accept the solid evidence for theories concerning climate change or evolution, but this is the anger of failing to suffer fools gladly. As children we were all recipients of this kind of anger from our teachers, and as adults we recognize it in others and ourselves. This anger is very different from the anger shown by devotees of a particular religious or political creed when someone disagrees with them. No matter how charming and friendly they are, once you reveal yourself as not sharing their creed and, indeed, being critical of it, the anger directed at you might be no more than a certain frostiness, but you are left in no doubt about the devotees' displeasure. Only the circumstances you are in protect you from a more violent response from them. The discussion you are involved in might be very intellectual, but the devotees feel that what you have said is a grave threat to their sense of being a person. The primitive pride, whose function it is to protect our sense of being a person, reacts to this threat with anger.

Primitive pride often manifests itself as vanity. Some little vanities, such as priding ourselves on the quality of our spaghetti bolognaise or our ability to look good no matter how limited our wardrobe, help maintain our self-confidence and thus are very useful. But other vanities go beyond these modest ones and become delusional. Scientists like Steve Jones and Richard Dawkins and experts like David Attenborough are much abused by those who wish to see human beings as totally separate from and infinitely superior to the rest of the living world. Similarly, psychologists like me, who explain what we do in terms of how we create ideas and what we do with those ideas, are either ignored or attacked by those who want to see themselves as the centre around which the universe revolves. Ideas such as the universe is indifferent to our existence, or that religious or political creeds are attempts to deny our inherent uncertainty and aloneness, are seen as abhorrent. When the truth does not flatter their vanity, most people lie. This might involve lying to others, but it always involves lying to ourselves.

If you must lie to others, do it knowing that you are lying, and be aware that there will be unintended and unimagined consequences. Never lie to yourself. If you do, you will not be able to escape the terrible consequences. Lying to yourself does not obliterate the truth you do not want to recognize. Lying to yourself means trying to hide from yourself something you already know. For instance, consciously you might tell yourself, 'My father was a good man. He wanted only the best for me', but unconsciously you know that your father was often unjust and sometimes cruel. Your anger and resentment might be hidden, but when some situation reminds you unconsciously of how much you feared your father, you can find yourself directing anger and resentment at someone who might have irritated you but who did not deserve the fierceness of your response. You will not be able to understand why you did this, but you are left having to deal with the consequences of what you have done. If you do not understand where this torrent of anger originated, how can you repair your relationship with, say, your partner or your boss or your child?

Sometimes the lie you are telling yourself and the truth that you know but do not wish to acknowledge set up such a conflict within you that you feel yourself falling apart. So great is your fear that you resort to one of the desperate defences that psychiatrists call mental illness – schizophrenia, mania, obsessions and compulsions, agoraphobia, and the most popular desperate defence, depression. To be able to give up such a desperate defence you have to recognize your truth, terrible though it may be, and abandon your lie.[2]

People often say that they did something, followed by, 'I don't know why.' Whenever I hear this I hope that what the person meant was, 'I know why but I'm not going to tell you.' If they

298

really do not know why they did certain things, they are in trouble. Even when we act quickly, seemingly spontaneously, we need to be able to think back over what we did and know the reasons why. Our unconscious thinking is infinitely faster than our conscious thinking. Unconsciously we see connections and draw conclusions in a fraction of a second. However, we are able to reflect consciously and truthfully on an unconscious train of thought. When people say they cannot do this, they mean they are too frightened to do this. They are scared to look within themselves because they are afraid of what they will find.

Hidden truths always seem much bigger than the same truths brought forth into the clear light of day. As many people have discovered, the clear light of day is provided by yourself in the conversation you have with what Edmund Gosse called the 'companion and confidant in myself'. Talking these matters over with another person can be illuminating, but it is not essential if you strive to be truthful with yourself. Another person can be helpful in asking good questions and finding alternative interpretations, but, if you practise being truthful with yourself, you will find that such questions and alternative interpretations will come readily to your mind. By recognizing your own truths, no matter how painful and saddening these might be, you make yourself into a whole person who is much better able to deal with whatever life throws at you. Have you noticed that the word 'integrity' means both 'wholeness' and 'honesty'?

This process of discovering your own truths can be greatly impeded by the plethora of 'oughts' in your head. If you have been brought up to be obedient, you can find it hard to distinguish between what you think and what you ought to think. Moreover, when you inspect yourself, you do it as a cold, critical judge who expects the worst of you and not as a friend who is on your side. Hilary Mantel was brought up as a Catholic and, even though she had rejected Catholicism when she was twelve, she was left with a strong sense of guilt. She told an interviewer,

'You grow up believing that you're wrong and bad. And for me, because I took what I was told *really* seriously, it bred a very intense habit of introspection and self-examination and a terrible severity with myself. So that nothing was ever good enough. It's like installing a policeman, and one, moreover, who keeps changing the law.'[3]

If you have been brought up to be obedient in the way Jenni Murray was, you might, like her, still experience the fleeting fear that your mother knows what you are thinking, or the God you were taught to worship knows what is going on in the privacy of your own mind. Just as many of those who lived under Nazi or Communist rule felt that the Party knew what they were thinking, many North Koreans and Muslims educated in fundamentalist madrassas would feel that their Dear Leader or Allah is privy to their thoughts. The purpose of forcing people to be obedient is to prevent them from being able to speak truthfully to themselves.

It is impossible for anyone to know what you are thinking unless you disclose your thoughts. Neuroscientists might put your head in a scanner, and then claim that, because a particular part of your brain lights up, you were engaged in mathematical reasoning. You might have been reciting the two times table to yourself, but you can tell the neuroscientist that you were engaged in finding a new and better solution of Fermat's last theorem. Other people might try to guess what you are thinking but they cannot know. To believe that some supernatural force knows what you are thinking is to believe that a fantasy is true.

In any system where those in power want to force their subjects to be obedient, punishment alone will not achieve their aim. Punishment either frightens people into obedience or makes the recipients rebellious. If the rebellious give a lead, the obedient might follow. Knowing this, leaders of repressive states like Hitler and Stalin become increasingly paranoid, fearing enemies everywhere. Successful authoritarian systems achieve the required level of obedience by those in authority telling their subjects the most destructive lie. This is, 'You are too weak, too ignorant, too unacceptable to be able to look after yourself. You cannot survive without God/Allah/the Party to look after you. If you are not obedient, you will not be looked after and you will perish.'

Being told that you have been born in sin, or have to reach a certain level of goodness to be saved, or that you are infinitely less important than the Party destroys your self-confidence. Moreover, this lie prevents you from being able to grasp the hard truth that the only person who will look after you is yourself. A few people will look after you now and then, but you are the only person who will look after you consistently and all the time. To survive the inherent uncertainty and aloneness of your existence you need to acknowledge the responsibility you have for yourself. Until you take responsibility for yourself, you remain a child.

Reviewing the television documentary *Terror in Mumbai* about the terrorist attack on 26 November 2008, Sam Wollaston told how the young men, little more than boys, who assaulted the grand hotel, the Taj Palace, were astounded by its opulence. The conversations they were having over the phone with their commander were taped by the Indian secret service. One boy told his commander, 'There are computers here with 30-inch screens. It's amazing. The window is huge.' Their commander said, 'Throw some grenades, my brother, there's no harm in throwing a few grenades. How hard can it be to throw a grenade? For your mission to end successfully, you must be killed. God is waiting for you in heaven.'[4] All the boys died except one, but he is not likely to see places like the Taj Palace ever again.

You might be asking yourself, shouldn't children be brought up to be obedient? How can we have a society if people won't obey the law?

It depends not just on what you mean by 'obedient' but what you mean by 'child'. When babies are born they are simply there

301

being themselves, but we have our own ideas about what it is to be a baby. Some of us see children as being in essence good, and others see babies as being in essence bad. If we see children as being in essence good, in educating them we want to bring out all the wonderful potential in each child. If we see children as in essence bad, such as having been born in sin, or being a container for dangerous instincts, in educating them we want to control that badness.[5] As the Bible says, 'He that spareth his rod hateth his son: but he that loveth him chasteneth him betimes.'[6]

A baby is born looking for faces, especially friendly faces. When one friendly face keeps recurring, the baby forms a bond with that face. For the baby, forming a bond means trying to please the mothering person. All the mothering person has to do is to be a patient teacher who understands that the baby lives in a world very different from the mothering person's own. It is impossible to be a perfectly patient teacher, but your children will forgive you if they are certain that you are trying to do your best. This does not mean that they will not take advantage of your mistakes. After all, they do have to learn how to survive in the world, and taking advantage of other people's mistakes is an important skill to possess.

Babies are born with the ability to imitate another person, but it is nine months or so before they start to comprehend what is being said to them. Perhaps this is why children are far more impressed with what adults do than with what they say. If you are truthful, your children are likely to be truthful. If you lie, your children are likely to lie. Moreover, if you demonstrate how to think critically about what other people tell you, your children are likely to develop the skill of being a considered sceptic. The world your children will be living in will be very different from the world you know, but, whatever that world will be, the skill of sceptical inquiry will be essential for understanding that world and surviving in it.

We need to remember that many of the lies that people tell

302

are not readily apparent. What the person says may appear to be true, but it is based upon a lie about the nature of the world and our existence. When we base what we say or do on such a lie, any enterprise we undertake is doomed to failure.

One hard truth that we must always bear in mind is that we cannot force reality to be what we want it to be. You might want to build your house on a cliff where you will have a fine view of the ocean, but, if a geologist tells you that the rising sea water will soon bring down the land on which your house will stand, you would be foolish indeed to persist with your plan. Similarly, it is foolish to try to force others to believe what you want them to believe, or to do what you want them to do. If you persist in doing this, the results will not be what you want them to be. Persuasion is often effective, but only when you begin with the hard work of coming to understand how those you wish to influence see themselves and their world. Discovering how other people see themselves and their world often shows us how misguided we are in our own ideas. This, of course, is the reason why many people never want to hear the ideas of other people.

Even when you persuade people to do what you wish, you must never forget another hard truth, that everything is connected to everything else. You may choose to live in a silo and communicate only with those who are in the silo with you, but you delude yourself if you think that what you do is not connected with everything else in the world. The air we pollute mingles with the currents of air that sweep around the world. Ideas do not circulate around the world but a multitude of interpretations of ideas do. We encounter and interpret other people's ideas, and pass on our interpretations to others, who then pass on their interpretations of our interpretations. We can be greatly surprised when the interpretations of interpretations of original ideas come back to us. The millions of people in Britain who owe their health if not their lives to the National Health Service were astounded to see photographs of opponents of President Obama's health-care

303

plan carrying placards declaring that the NHS was the equivalent of Nazism.

Some people like to think that they have divided their life so that there are different sections that are unconnected with one another. There are writers who tell themselves that their writing is totally separate from their life. Some literary intellectuals would argue that the work of writers like Hemingway, Day-Lewis, Sartre and Beauvoir whose truthfulness might be questioned should be judged quite separately from their life. The fact that they lied extensively in their personal life has nothing to do with their writing. Whenever I hear this, I wonder what lies in his own life the intellectual wants to be excused. When people talk about impermeable divisions between life and work, or between different relationships, such as with colleagues or with family, they are talking about fantasies. Our interpretations of everything we have experienced are stored in our unconscious where they collide and perhaps merge to create new ideas, some of which become the basis of our artistic and creative work. Our unconscious is not divided into 'me living' and 'me writing'. We might behave differently in different situations, but we are just one person, no matter how fragmented and jumbled up we might feel ourselves to be. If this were not so, those of us who had less than happy, loving childhoods would never be able to put together what felt like fragments of ourselves into something that feels whole.

Writers often report that they knew that they were writers when they were young children and had written only a few sentences. Their urge to write was more than an ability to deal effectively with words, but this ability allowed them to express something of what it was to be alive, and, in doing so, make sense of their experience. For them writing was an important part of what it was to be alive. Writers whose need to know and to understand outstrips their vanity and their fear of uncertainty and aloneness are able to discover truths – their own individual truths and

304

universal truths about people – through their writing. They might begin by writing about themselves but then they go on to write about the whole human condition. We read them in order to discover about ourselves. Such writers do not imagine that there is a division between how they live and what they write.

Of course, none of us believes the politician who, caught being unfaithful to his wife, declares that his private life has nothing to do with his work as a politician. A man who lies to his wife will certainly lie to the public.

When we are in our teens and twenties, a fantasy that most of us enjoy is that everything important that has happened in the history of the world occurred after we were born. Everything that happened before we were born is unimportant and has no effect on what is happening now. People who argue that it is not necessary for children to study history are still harbouring that youthful fantasy. They have not recognized that the past is never past: it is always with us.

Those of us who studied the history of the British Empire might remember the futility of the many campaigns by the British to subdue the Afghan tribesmen. The campaign of 1878 to 1880 was fought in large part in Helmand Province by the Kandahar Field Force. Supplies sent to these troops were attacked and plundered by the Afghan fighters. 'The various tribes still made it abundantly clear that as little as they liked each other, they liked the British still less. [In equipment issued to the troops] the standard issue items were frequently unsuitable to the harsh conditions on the ground. The British soldiers had to improvise. The battle of Kandahar finally settled the campaign once and for all. The British really did now begin to withdraw and this time it was for good. At the end of the day, the British had spent an enormous amount of effort to achieve a situation that seemed virtually identical to that at the beginning of the war.'[7] This report is from a history of the British Empire but it could easily have been from an account of the current campaign in Afghanistan. In 1979 the

Soviet Union invaded Afghanistan. They set up a puppet government and began training an Afghan army to keep control. They
threw their huge military might against the guerrilla army of the
Mujahadeen. The number of Russian troops steadily increased,
but they were no match for their opponents, who struck when
and where they were least expected and faded into the night,
taking their dead with them. The Russians called them 'dukhy',
ghosts. Over 15,000 Soviet troops died in the war. When it became
obvious that the war was unwinnable, the Soviets withdrew.
Meanwhile, the American government, engaged in the Cold War
against Communism and lacking a knowledge of Afghan history
and therefore no foresight, was supplying arms to the Mujahadeen,
some of whose people became the Taliban.[8] Now that the illegal
arms trade is a huge international business, the Taliban do not
lack American arms with which to fight NATO forces.

The past is always with us because what is happening now is
connected to the past. However, we cannot go back to the past
in the way, when we move from place to place, we can go back
to where we began. Time, said Einstein, is a dimension we move
along. We each have our own stretch of time that we advance
along. It is seamless, but in our mind we divide it up, creating
imaginary stages. We invest these stages with a significance that
we can, if we are unwise, regard as being real.

In 1994 I wrote a book called *Time on Our Side* which was
concerned with how we feel about time passing and growing
older. I found that, whatever age they were, people did not like
the idea of growing older. At whatever age people were, they
defined 'old' as being ten years older than they were. Hence they
viewed with fear their next and rapidly approaching decade.
People in their late twenties talked to me quite seriously about
how they knew that, once they turned thirty, it was downhill all
the way. I found too that most people had fixed ideas about how
people at a certain age ought to behave.[9]

If people want to believe this nonsense, that is their choice, but I do object when these people insist on imposing their ideas on other people. When I was in my teens I found that adults felt entitled to advise me on how I ought to behave, and, when I failed to do what they advised, they proceeded to criticize me. To my horror this situation recurred when I entered my seventies. I find that many people younger than me have fixed ideas about how people over seventy ought to behave. I am often congratulated on being able to give a lecture and answer questions afterwards, something I have been doing for forty years. A journalist who was writing a piece for a women's magazine about attitudes to clothes phoned me and asked, amongst other things, what in my wardrobe were my favourite clothes. When I replied, 'My jeans', she gasped and said, 'You don't still wear jeans!' Another young woman, phoning me about something that led me in my answer to mention that I was seventy-eight, could not contain her surprise. 'But you don't sound old!' Should I take voice lessons in sounding old? And the advice I get! Do people really see me as being too old to manage my own life? I try now never to mention that I might occasionally feel tired. When I was younger I could say that, but not now, because as soon as I do, I get told that I should not work so hard. The person advising me is not saying to me, 'Do give up doing housework and shopping so you can concentrate on doing the work you love.' She (it's usually a she) is telling me to stick to the housework and shopping that I dislike and give up the fun of writing and lecturing, and meeting so many lovely people. Why do younger people behave like this? They would say that it is because they are concerned about me, but, if they looked at themselves a little more closely and truthfully, they would see that someone like me, and the many thousands of my contemporaries who live their life as I do, do not fit the fixed ideas they hold. All too often, rather than change our own ideas, we often prefer to try to force other people to change in order to fit our own unexamined ideas.

When I compare notes with my contemporaries, I find that

one thing we all agree on is that, as we get older, we become less and less inclined to suffer fools gladly and silently. This way of thinking might occasionally be apparent in this book.

Time passes, and the time each of us has is limited. This is a hard truth we have to live with. If we decide that it is an absolute rule that, at each stage of our life, there are particular ways in which we must behave, then all we have done is to create a stick with which to beat ourselves.

We cannot go back to the past. Sentimentalists will talk about some past golden age, but it requires considerable ignorance of history to believe that any such golden age ever existed. Some people see themselves as living in a golden age, but it is merely that they are fortunate enough to be able to enjoy the pleasures and advantages any age offers to a small group of people. When the golden age of the British Empire ended in the Second World War, there were many people who could not bear to recognize that their golden age had passed and the golden age of the United States was beginning. Any regular viewer of British television will have a remarkable, though biased and romanticized, knowledge of the more colourful parts of British history. This is a result of nostalgia for a past when being British was more impressive than it is now. It is likely that it will take Americans even longer to acknowledge that America's golden age is passing as power and influence moves to China and India and the countries of the Pacific Rim.

No matter how determinedly you refuse to know anything about world politics and economics, you are part of it. What you do affects what happens in politics and economics, and what happens there affects you. This is a hard truth from which none of us can escape.

In 2008 I was invited to become an honorary professor at London Metropolitan University (LMU). I could hardly say no, as the part of the university where I would be teaching was very close to where I lived. I taught one class and enjoyed it. I readily agreed to repeat this with a group of students in May 2009. The lecturer who had asked me to teach had made sure I was paid for my work. However, by the following May the university was in dire financial straits and there was no money to pay me. I agreed to work without being paid. What concerned me far more than forgoing this modest payment was what had happened after the Dalai Lama had been given an honorary degree by the university.

The LMU had inherited from its predecessor, the University of North London, strong links with Tibet and had offered scholarships to Tibetan students. However, immediately after the Dalai Lama had been given his degree in May 2008, criticism of this award by the Chinese media was so strong that two months later the vice-chancellor, Brian Roper, found it necessary to write to the Chinese Embassy in London. The contents of his letter were not disclosed, but it was confirmed that Roper had met embassy officials where, according to the university, the vice-chancellor 'expressed regret at any unhappiness that had been caused to the Chinese people by the recent award of an honorary doctorate to the Dalai Lama. It was not the university's intention to cause any such unhappiness.'[10]

Many of the universities in the developed world rely on fees from overseas students to balance their budget. At that time over 400 Chinese students were studying at LMU.[11] There were many factors involved in the state of the LMU budget, but certainly I must in future bear in mind the importance of not causing an affront to the Chinese people.

Older generations can remember a time long ago when people saved their money. If they had a mortgage, they worked hard to pay it off. Younger generations forgot all about this. They had credit cards, and, if they had a mortgage, they believed that house prices would continue to rise, and their house, which they did not completely own, would be worth more and more. Margaret Thatcher, and then Tony Blair and Gordon Brown talked endlessly about the need for economic growth, as if there were no limit to what the planet could provide for us. These delusions came to an end in September 2008. Meanwhile, the Chinese had gone on living the way they had always lived. They worked hard and they saved their money. When their government moved to a curious hybrid of Communism and capitalism, many Chinese began to earn significantly more. They could not spend their extra money. There were few goods to buy, and they needed to save for their old age. They now had money to invest, and they invested it in the USA. China was selling more goods to the USA than the USA was selling to them, so the Chinese State Reserve Bureau (SRB) put the American dollars they were earning into American securities. It came to a point where the Chinese government could not afford to sell their immense holdings in the USA because the number of American dollars they would then hold would reduce the value of the dollar, and thus destabilize the world economy. Rather than buying gold, SRB began buying copper, which was becoming an even more important metal because it is needed for the hybrid cars that are being developed. Metals are easier to store, much easier than oil, so the Chinese began buying aluminium, zinc, nickel, titanium, indium, rhodium and praseodymium.[12] Australia abounds in precious metals, and the Chinese SRB did not simply buy what was being produced but set about expanding Chinese business interests there.

The first English settlers in Australia called England their home, and their descendants continued to call it home, even if they had never set foot in that country. Now the song that Australians sing lustily wherever they roam is, 'I still call Australia home'. Tears and cheers are an essential accompaniment. When Britain joined the European Union, Australians had to find other markets for their products. They found them in Japan, India, South-East Asia and, of course, China. In 2008 Kevin Rudd, who speaks Mandarin fluently and had been a diplomat in China, became prime minister. In his book *When China Rules the World,*

310

Martin Jacques referred to Rudd as 'the first Chinese-oriented political leader to be elected in the West'.[13] The days when Australia was part of the British Empire were well and truly over.

In the Great Depression of the 1930s Australians suffered terribly because their economy was closely tied to that of Britain. The measures the British government used to deal with the financial situation caused great unemployment. When I was in Australia at the end of 2008 and the beginning of 2009, people were very anxious about what was going to happen to their economy, but, in less than six months, it was clear that there would be no recession. On 30 July 2009, Saul Eslake, chief economist of the Australian and New Zealand Bank (ANZ), made a detailed presentation to ANZ Global Market customers called 'The Global Financial Crisis and the Australian Economy'. He said, 'Australia has weathered the global downturn remarkably well', and summarized the reasons why as:

> Partly reflecting 'good luck' (Australian banks in good shape, resilient housing market, limited exposure to manufacturing exports, significant exposure to China)

> Also reflects 'good management' by both the Reserve Bank (large and timely interest rate reductions) and the Federal Government (timely and for the most part well-targeted fiscal policy measures)

Senior people at ANZ have never been in the habit of praising Australian Labor prime ministers. The times are indeed a-changing.

Everything is changing all the time. We cannot force everything to stay the same, nor can we go back to where we were. Ignoring what is true does not make it go away. Our financial systems cannot go back to where they were, and the climate is changing, no matter how much people may deny this.

What the media likes best are stories of drama and doom.

When the big banks were collapsing and Gordon Brown was striding the world stage as the economic genius and world statesman who knew how to save us from the disaster that his policies had played no small part in creating, the media brought us minute by minute accounts of events as they unfolded. This was interspersed with experts explaining what was happening. However, once the last firework had exploded, the bankers and the politicians were faced with working out what they could do to clean up the mess and prevent something similar ever happening again. The media thought that this was dull, and turned eagerly to the scandal of the MPs' expenses. The sums of money involved in the scandal were comprehensible, unlike the trillions that the bankers had lost, and meant more to all the people who were wondering how they were going to manage to live in much reduced circumstances. Nevertheless, the media made so much of this scandal that a considerable amount of the reporting on and discussions about the economic crisis were relegated to the inside pages or the financial pages.

However, we did learn that Jon Macintosh, a Mayfair hedge fund manager, had revealed a capacity for insight when he said, 'We [he and his colleagues] are like goldfish. We swim once around our bowl and when we complete the circle everything looks new.'[14] J.K. Galbraith had already shown that, throughout history, those who worked in the financial markets had no memory of earlier cycles of boom and bust, and would proceed to repeat the foolish behaviour of their predecessors. A failure to learn from experience is a mark of immaturity. The more we learn from experience, the wiser we become, provided that what we learn does not simply reinforce our prejudices and strengthen our ties with our favourite fantasies. All the people whose job in a bank, a hedge fund, or an insurance company enables them to take risks and lose their firm huge sums of money should have branded on the backs of their hands the warning from George Santayana, 'He who does not learn from history is doomed to repeat it.' However, as many critics have observed, you can take a banker to water but you cannot make him think.

Meanwhile, the British government was demonstrating what Will Hutton called the St Augustine position, 'O Lord help them be tough on the City – but not yet.'[15] Hutton pointed out that all governments needed to reform 'the entire structure of western finance – bonuses, credit rating agencies, capital adequacy requirements, banks that are too big to fail, the use of offshore tax havens, the role of derivatives – from top to bottom'. They had to change what caused the crisis, that is, 'the stranglehold of a new financial oligarchy upon public policy'.[16] This oligarchy had been given the freedom to operate very much as it wished when the British and American governments relaxed the banking regulations. As teachers have always known, if you remove all the rules governing teenagers' behaviour, you give the teenagers the power to make demands upon you that you have no power to refuse. Because the government had done nothing since the crisis to re-establish the regulations, 'the banks are exploiting the vacuum to return to business as usual'.[17] They had not abandoned 'the intellectual delusion that financial markets were efficient'.[18] Larry Elliott, economic editor of the *Guardian*, pointed out that, when in the 1970s the unions in the UK had become, in effect, more powerful than the Callaghan government, resulting in its defeat in 1979 and thus bringing the Conservatives under Margaret Thatcher to power, they were punished severely by Thatcher. Yet, as Elliott said, 'The sins of the financiers were far more heinous.'[19]

Very quickly after the financial crisis of September 2008 a number of excellent books by different authors were published, each explaining aspects of the crisis. However, books explaining why the present government has not acted quickly to regulate the banks, and why the Leader of the Opposition, David Cameron, has not disclosed his plans for dealing with the economy other than by cutting government spending are not likely to appear for several years when those who know where the bodies are buried feel free to disclose what they know. Both Brown and Cameron have formed close connections with important people in the financial world; they have made promises and given guarantees. Neither can afford to impose on the markets, the banks and the hedge funds the kind of regulation that might reduce the likelihood of another crisis comparable to the present crisis. In early September 2009, the month when the British political parties hold their annual conferences, Cameron gained media attention by talking about the size of the budget deficit and the need for spending cuts. Brown must have known that, as much as he and his ministers talked about the recession being over, the recession had merely stopped getting worse. It was not the time to talk about cuts because cuts mean job losses, but Brown foolishly did so. Cameron had intended to embarrass Brown, but he had stupidly created for himself a Janus-like position where, when he looked one way, he was the face of the warm, cuddly, caring Conservatives, and, when he looked the other way, he was the face of selfish, cold, uncaring Thatcherism. Those of us who are old enough to remember Thatcher and her spending cuts now make up the generations who exercise their vote in an election. We are also old enough to know that, in the election season, truth vanishes and fantasies prevail. Brown and Cameron will continue telling us that the recession is over, green shoots of regeneration are everywhere, and now the deficit must be reduced. They are telling these lies in the hope of cheering us up and getting us to spend the money we do not have and which we cannot borrow because the banks will not lend.

Both Ben Bernanke of the US Federal Reserve and Mervyn King, Governor of the Bank of England, have said that the recession is over, but neither has said that the US or the British economy has returned to its pre-crisis level. The only people who are celebrating are the bankers who are back to their normality of paying themselves large bonuses. On 30 September 2009, the chancellor, Alistair Darling, announced that, 'I am . . . pleased that the main banks incorporated in the UK have agreed to lead the way in implementing the agreement reached on bank remuneration at the G20, and expect them to set the standard for all other UK and international financial institutions to follow.' However, it is easy to promise something when you know that you are unlikely to be forced to fulfil your promise. An unnamed banker told the *Financial Times*, 'We are happy to comply in principle, but it is essential that it is enforced in the same way across the G20.' If this does not happen, the talent, if that is the right word, will move to the banks that have no regulations to limit bonuses. As usual, the USA wants to do what suits it best. 'The US view is that the nature of the businesses involved is so diverse that banks need to be given the flexibility to come up with the right package for each type of employee.'[20]

Meanwhile, the price of oil does not reflect a booming world economy, rather the reverse. The British pound is falling against the euro and the US dollar, while, minute by minute, my pounds are worth less and less in Australian dollars.[21] On 23 September 2009, John Cameron of TorFX reported that, 'Sterling slumped to a fresh 12-month low against the Australian Dollar, on concerns that the widening budget deficit will curtail demand for UK assets.'[22] Sales figures for the summer of 2009 show that British retail stores had a very quiet time. People do not believe the politicians who tell them that the worst is over. Instead of spending, they are saving, and paying off their debts. Those in employment fear for their jobs, while young people leaving school or university are facing the likelihood of not being able to get a job. What politicians are calling green shoots are, in fact, the effects of the money that both the American and British governments have put into their economy. These effects seem unlikely to stimulate lasting growth. The bankers, having promised the government that they will return to lending to businesses and home buyers, have, as usual, looked after their own interests and refused to lend, thus, effectively, 'making a sustainable economic recovery almost impossible'.[23]

Are the politicians ignorant of all this? Or are they telling the lies that politicians tell when they are preparing for an election? Is Brown hoping that before May 2010 and Cameron hoping that soon after May 2010 a veritable jungle of green shoots will burst out over all of the economy? The hard truth is that it takes experience, good judgement and considerable luck for a government to recognize the right moment to cease putting money into the economy and to start balancing the budget. Both Brown, who as chancellor and then prime minister presided over boom and bust, and Cameron, who has never been in office, seem to lack two of these necessary qualities. Which of them will have luck has yet to be seen.

Brown and Cameron made their promises and gave the guarantees when they believed, as many people in the financial markets believed, that the good times would go on forever. They forgot that nothing lasts forever. They must know, though they are unlikely to disclose that they know, that no prime minister or president controls the fortunes of the country he or she governs. They can influence, but they cannot control. No leader, however powerful, has ever controlled that constant variable, luck. Kevin Rudd and his colleagues made some judicious decisions, but they also had a great deal of good luck. The previous prime minister, John Howard, buddy of George Bush and the bankers, had left a budget surplus, and China did not have a recession. Whether we encounter the circumstances that will allow us to put into action our wisest ideas or our wickedest fantasies depends on chance. It is a matter of luck.

Luck or chance is beyond human control. Luck is not interested in our existence. It does not even know of our existence. Luck cannot be influenced by our degree of virtue, by the talismans we carry, or by our prayers to our gods. In fact, luck does not exist, other than as an idea in our heads. The truth is, events happen. Some events prove to be to our advantage, and some do not. We could call the events that are to our advantage 'lucky', and those that are to our disadvantage 'unlucky', but the fact that we have a word 'luck' does not necessarily mean that luck exists. We have a great many words for things that exist only in our fantasies, and we should always beware of this when we use them.

We should also be aware of the metaphors we use when we talk about our experience. Metaphors are in our heads, but their effects can be real.

For his response to the destruction of the Twin Towers George Bush chose the metaphor of war. Thus began the War on Terror, described by Naomi Klein as a 'global war fought on every level by private companies whose involvement is paid for with public money, with the unending mandate of protecting the United States homeland in perpetuity while eliminating all "evil" abroad'.[24] When in July 2005 a group of young British-born Muslim men exploded bombs on the London Underground and on a nearby bus, the British government chose the metaphor 'crime' with which to refer to these acts. While many of us might deplore some of the actions law-enforcement officers have used in arresting and bringing to court men who might have been planning to emulate the suicide bombers in London, the metaphor 'crime' has proved to be infinitely better in its results than the metaphor 'war'. Meanwhile, America's long-running war on drugs is proving to be as disastrous as the War on Terror.[25]

We cannot remove metaphors from the way we think and talk. Metaphors are an essential tool in creating meaning. We encounter something new and, to make sense of it, we look for a meaning that has some resemblance to this new thing. Probably most of us have never thought about the kind of people who work in financial markets, but, when the financial crisis forced us to do so, we tried to find words to describe these people. A simile might have sprung to mind – they are like teenagers. This simile explains so much of their behaviour, such as their short memory, their lack of foresight, and their lack of concern for others, that

317

we might change our simile into a metaphor. These people are not 'like teenagers', they are 'a bunch of teenagers'.

Referring to the people who caused such financial chaos as 'a bunch of teenagers' might be a means of expressing our anger and contempt, but, if we treat our metaphor as being an accurate and complete description of these people, that is, a full account of what is true about these people, we make a grave error. The people who caused such financial chaos might have behaved like teenagers but they are not teenagers. There is more to them than their teenage behaviour. We need to be aware of the inability of metaphors to reveal everything that is true. This applies to everything we talk about, including climate change.

The phrase 'greenhouse effect' is a metaphor developed in the 1820s by Joseph Fourier, a French physicist and governor of Egypt, to describe how the heat from the Sun warmed the planet but the heat radiated by the Earth was prevented from escaping by the atmosphere. This is similar to the way the panes of glass in a greenhouse let the heat in but do not let all of it escape. At that time scientists assumed that gases did not retain heat in the way that solids and liquids did. In May 1859, six months before Darwin published *On the Origin of Species*, John Tyndall, an Irish physicist working in London, showed that, while heat passed through oxygen and nitrogen, the main gases in the atmosphere, it could not pass through coal gas. This was at the height of the Industrial Revolution when in Britain huge volumes of coal gas were heading skywards from the multitudes of factories, offices and houses.[26] Perhaps some of the scientists who listened to Tyndall's presentation of his work at the Royal Institution wondered what the outcome of the warming of the planet would be, but most of the people there would have been sure that the beneficent God would continue to favour Britain, as her wealth and power demonstrated. How dare Darwin upset their equanimity and certainty!

A mere 150 years later, the effects of the warming of the planet were there for all to see. Tyndall's experiments did not explain everything that was involved in these changes. The metaphor of the greenhouse was far from being a complete truth. Moreover, climate change is linked with other huge problems, such as millions of people living in poverty, the world population outstripping what food the world could produce, a need for energy that could not be sustained, over-consumption and waste in developed countries, destruction of the habitats of plants and wildlife, destruction of the forests, pollution of the air and the oceans, extinction of species, water shortages, wars and conflicts, poor people suffering from curable or preventable diseases, or being forced into prostitution and slavery. These are problems that will not be solved simply by stabilizing the climate. Indeed, to solve one of these problems the other problems must be dealt with as well. There is now a multitude of conversations or, as we social scientists say, discourses about climate change and all its implications. These discourses are full of metaphors, some of which have been expanded into myths, each of which offers a way of understanding climate change.

Whenever we encounter a story that is new to us, we understand the new story in terms of a story we already know. This might be our own life story, or the story of a person we know or have heard about. Or we might resort to a myth or legend, or a story from one of the great religious books. When the new story touches our life, as the story of climate change does, the myth we choose is one that in some way reassures us. Every story involves some kind of change, and so we need to be reassured that we shall be safe, be looked after, have the power we need, and emerge triumphant. These are the needs and desires that are represented in the myths that underlie the discourses about climate change.

'Discourses' is a much nicer word than 'argument', but 'argument' is a much truer word to apply to what goes on in discussions about climate change. Sometimes the argument is about scientific results and has the theme 'I'm better informed than

319

you are', but, when the discussion is about the long-term outcomes of climate change, the people involved are arguing about the outcomes predicted by the myths they use to structure their ideas about climate change. If people are unaware that the myths they are using are more fantasy than truth, the arguments are likely to become very heated.

This was why Mike Hulme, Professor of Climate Change at East Anglia University and the first Director of the Tyndall Centre for Climate Change Research, called his book *Why We Disagree about Climate Change.*[27] He was not concerned about climate change deniers but with the different myths that people concerned about climate change use as frameworks for their thinking. In the many discourses he encountered, he identified myths that have some similarity to four biblical myths, namely, Lamenting Eden, Presaging the Apocalypse, Constructing Babel, and Celebrating Jubilee.

In the Lamenting Eden myth, climate change means the loss of the wilderness as we have known it. Such a loss not only diminishes us but something beyond us, something valuable. The Presaging the Apocalypse myth represents our understanding that, left unimpeded, climate change could mean that a stage could be reached where the climate was one to which our species could not adapt. We would disappear, just as unknown millions of species have disappeared. The Constructing Babel myth refers to the Genesis myth where, after the Flood, those who had survived said, 'Go to, let us build us a city and a tower, whose top may reach unto heaven; and let us make us a name, lest we be scattered abroad upon the face of the whole earth.'[28] The Lord came down to inspect the city and the tower, and proceeded to scatter the people all over the Earth. He removed the one language they all spoke and imposed on them dozens of different languages. All this was just the thing the Lord always did whenever He thought His supremacy was being challenged. The Greeks called such a challenge *hubris*, while in climate change discourses we call it *technological solutions*. Those who envision some huge technology that will outwit climate change have forgotten the existence of the law of unintended consequences, formerly known as the Lord. The myth Celebrating Jubilee comes from Leviticus, one of the books of the Old Testament that is particularly strong on slavery. According to Leviticus, you must not make slaves, or bondmen and bondmaids, of those who share your religious beliefs, but it is perfectly acceptable to make slaves of 'the heathen that are around you' and 'the children of the strangers that do sojourn among you'. However, every fifty years 'the trumpet of the jubilee' will sound and 'ye shall return every man unto his possession, and ye shall return every man unto his family'.[29] Whether this includes the bondmaids is not clear. Leviticus is actually far from clear, but it does seem that whether you were able to enjoy Jubilee depended on whether you had pleased the Lord. If you were good, you got your reward. This is the still very popular belief in the Just World. If you are good, you get rewarded, and, if you are bad, you get punished. In this myth climate change is our punishment for being wicked. However, if we are good and switch off electric lights and recycle our rubbish, we will get the reward we deserve. (Grown-up people know that it is sensible to consume modestly and recycle what is left over, whether or not the climate is changing. They do not require a reward, spiritual or otherwise, for doing this.)

These four myths represent some of the ideas that we might hold, not just about climate change but about ourselves. The Lamenting Eden myth has within it the belief in a Golden Age, and the longing to remain a child and be looked after. The myth of the Apocalypse represents our fear of uncertainty. So great is this fear that the many people who deny that climate change is happening, or who say that the whole thing is a government conspiracy, cannot bear to think that what lies ahead is something against which they cannot protect themselves or their children. The myth Constructing Babel is the delusion that, 'I am supremely

321

powerful and shall overcome all that threatens us.' The myth of Celebrating Jubilee takes us back to Lamenting Eden. We have erred and have been cast out of Eden, but, if we are good and work hard to show that we are good, our work and goodness will be rewarded. We shall be let back into Eden.

The way these old stories are being used in trying to interpret what climate change means to us presents us with the hard truth that, in coming to understand how our bodies, our environment, the Earth and the universe operate, we are very intelligent, but, when it comes to understanding ourselves, we are very stupid. It is not an innate stupidity but a self-imposed one, resulting from our fear of uncertainty. As I set out in the opening chapters of this book, experiencing our sense of being a person, making intelligible the world around us, and communicating with others are processes made up entirely of guesses. There is nothing about which we can be absolutely certain. Rather than understand and accept that this is our reality, we deny our uncertainty, and consequently the ways in which we act upon the world and interact with others often result in disasters, if not for ourselves then for others. If we look at climate change and all the other major issues in our world, there is nothing that we could not solve if we worked together. What stops us is our ignorance of ourselves. This wilful ignorance prevents us from finding efficient methods of co-operating with one another. This wilful ignorance prevents us from enabling not just the survival of our species but a good life for everyone.

At the heart of this wilful ignorance is the refusal to acknowledge to ourselves, much less talk about with others, what happens to us when we discover that there is a serious discrepancy between what we thought our life was and what it actually is. We all know what happens – that feeling of disintegrating, falling through infinite space, no longer existing, and the terror, the utter terror. We all know this experience. Not only has it happened to us but we have seen it happen to members of our family and to our friends. We have seen it, or the results of it, on our television screens. Robert Reich recognized it when he watched Alan Greenspan testify before the House Committee on Oversight and Government Reform.

For eighteen years Alan Greenspan dominated the American financial world. When he was Chairman of the Federal Reserve, his slightest utterance caused markets to rise or fall. A film taken on the day he retired, aged eighty in 2006, shows him walking quickly and confidently, smiling happily but modestly at the cameramen. He was never a handsome man, but photographs taken in 2007 show his face firm and healthy, with only the wrinkles that come with smiling. But then the whole edifice of American prosperity of which he had been the architect began to crumble. When in October 2008 he appeared before the House Committee the flesh of his face had fallen into deep furrows. He looked very old. Watching this, Robert Reich, academic, politician, author and long-time commentator, said, 'He looked miserably tired, contrite to the extent that he will ever be contrite, and he looked like his world, certainly his worldview, had collapsed.'

Greenspan told the House Committee, 'What happened to the bankers, yes, they knew they were involved in an underpricing of risk and at some point that correction would be made. I fear that too many of them thought they would be able to spot the actual trigger point of the crisis in time to get out.' He went on, 'I made a mistake in presuming that the self-interest of organizations, specifically banks and others, was such that they were capable of protecting their own shareholders.'

A year after the collapse of Lehman Brothers Greenspan agreed to be interviewed for the BBC Television series *The Love of Money*. Here he repeated what he had told the House Committee, that he had expected that the bankers would never put the interests of their bank and the interests of their shareholders at risk. He said, 'I was shocked into disbelief of a complete breakdown of that premise.'

Greenspan went on to talk about credit default swaps that were supposed to insure the packets of subprime mortgages that were being traded. By 2007 the CDS market had grown to a value of 62 trillion dollars. He said, 'It was potentially a very significant problem because I don't see how anybody knew what the actual nature of the contracts were that were exchanged.' If he had not understood credit default swaps, why had he not asked a banker to explain? If the banker did not understand them, surely someone who was engaged in trading them could have done so. If the bankers and the traders did not understand CDSs, was it sensible of him to allow people to buy and sell pieces of paper, the meaning of which no one understood but might relate to something that did not exist in the real world, namely, a strong probability that people who could not afford a mortgage would pay that mortgage off? Perhaps it was that Greenspan did not want to understand CDSs. He could not let himself know all this because he had adamantly and successfully opposed all the attempts by the Commodities Future Trading Commission to regulate this market. His basic principle as chief of the Federal Reserve was that free, unregulated financial markets were essential for the American economy. He assumed that those working in these markets would have as their top priority the solvency of their firm. When the crisis came, both these ideas were shown to be wrong.

Why did Greenspan not know that the ideas underpinning his worldview were wrong?

The reason we have regulations for most of the activities in buying and selling is that we cannot be trusted always to do the right thing. Not that all of us are dishonest, but we do tend to get carried away by our ideas, especially where our greed, vanity and fear are involved. Greenspan had spent the most important part of his working life with men who had power, influence and money. These were men who took great pride in their power and position. Had he not seen them behave recklessly, without regard to the welfare of others, or to the possibility of an adverse outcome? Had he not been aware of the corrupting influence of power? He presented himself as a modest person, but had he never felt the delight of having power and choosing to use it? Or, and I fear this must be the case, had he never looked inside himself and used what he found there to understand other people? Had he done so, he would have known that to trust men whose sole purpose in life is to make money always to behave honourably is as sensible as to swim with a great white shark and trust it not to eat you. Can it be true that, if Alan Greenspan had applied his intelligence to understanding himself, we would not have had this global financial crisis?

As Robert Reich could see, when Greenspan discovered that the two ideas that underpinned his whole worldview were wrong, he fell apart, as we all do in this situation. Putting ourselves back together again means assembling another set of ideas that give us our sense of being a person. For some of us this task means enduring a period of uncertainty while we search for ideas that more truthfully represent our situation. Those who do this emerge as much wiser people. However, there are many people who cannot tolerate any uncertainty. In this situation, they try to reassemble themselves using their old ideas. This assemblage will not hold together if they include in it the idea, 'The disaster was my fault.' So they discard that idea, and look around for someone else to blame.

Greenspan chose as his scapegoat all of us, the human race. When in the BBC interview he was asked about the future he said, 'The question isn't whether or not competitive markets function perfectly. They do not. Regrettably, there is nothing better. Crises will happen again but it will be different. It's human nature.' There will be future crises but, 'No two crises have anything in common except human nature.' As he sees it, we are the cause of all future crises because we are incapable of learning from experience.[30]

The reason our species has achieved so much is that we *do* learn from experience. We learn far, far more from our experience than any other species learns from its experience. We can choose not to learn, and we can learn things that are not true, but we cannot help but learn. Perhaps, if those who wish to work in the global economy were given an education where they came to understand that the fear and greed that drive the markets arise from the way we experience ourselves and our world, a global economy might evolve where everyone involved has equal rights and responsibilities. Such an economy would need rules and regulations, just as each competitive sport operates within the framework of its rules and regulations. All that stands in the way of this is our wilful ignorance of ourselves.

However, our wilful ignorance stems from our dark secret. Our first experience of falling apart comes in childhood. It so terrifies us that we resolve never to experience it again. More often than not, our first experience is associated with doing something wrong, or being blamed for doing something wrong. It occurs to us that we could avoid the punishment, and the terror, if we blamed someone else. 'It wasn't me, miss.' 'He made me do it, miss.' 'It's human nature.' Or as Winston Smith said, 'Do it to Julia! Do it to Julia! Not me! Julia! I don't care what you do to her.'

Interposing another body is our dark, shameful secret. This is why we will not talk about our fear of being annihilated as a person. Faced with the threat of annihilation as a person, we interpose another body. For many of us, the body of anyone will do.

Gitta Sereny told how she had got to know Richard Glazar, a Czech who survived Treblinka. She described him as 'one of the most honest men I have ever met'. He had been one of the 'work-Jews', *Arbeitsjuden*, whose job it was to pack up and send to Germany all the things collected from the victims. One night when Sereny and he had been talking for hours and he was tired, he told her something he probably would not have told her had he been more aware of what he was doing. In March 1943 very few transports were arriving. He said, '"The *things* were our justification for being alive. If there were no *things* to administer, why would they let us stay alive?"'

One day towards the end of March, when they had reached the lowest ebb of their morale, Kurt Franz, the deputy commander, walked into their barracks, a wide grin on his face. 'As from tomorrow,' he said, 'transports will be rolling again.' And do you know what we did? We shouted, 'Hurrah, hurrah.' It seems impossible now. Every time I think of it, I die a small death; but it's the truth. That is what we did; that is where we had got to.'

Sereny wrote, 'It was one of the most terrible truths anyone had told me.'[31]

The sad truth is that we do not use the defence of interposing another person's body only when we are in the direst of circumstances. We do it when the possibility of being annihilated as a person is not immediate but far away, barely on the horizon, or not there at all. Interposing another's body becomes a habit. We do it without thinking, and, if challenged, we justify what we have done by lying. We interpose a body when we scapegoat someone, or make use of someone. We do it when we choose to be selfish, uncaring. This happens in families, among friends and colleagues all the time. We do it when we refuse to accept responsibility for what we have done and instead blame someone else.

When, after the Berlin Wall had come down, Timothy Garton Ash went back to East Germany and interviewed some of the Stasi who had been connected with his file, he found that,

Everyone I talked to had someone else to blame. Those who worked for the state say 'it was not us, it was the Party'. Those who worked for the Party say 'it was not us, it was the Stasi'.

Come to the Stasi, and those who worked for foreign intelligence say 'it was not us, it was the others'. Talk to them, and they say 'it was not our department, it was XX'. Talk to Herr Zeiseweis from department XX and he says 'it wasn't me'.[32]

In the excuses for avoiding blame, truth plays a very little part. For more than ten years, Amnesty International has been documenting Shell's activities in the Niger Delta. In July 2009 they published their report *Petroleum, Pollution and Poverty in the Niger Delta*, and manoeuvred Shell into taking part in an online discussion in which more than 445 people took part. In this discussion, 'a company representative was forced to concede that Shell's activities had contributed to poverty and conflict in the Niger Delta'. However, we must understand that Shell's contribution to these problems was very small, tiny in fact. According to Shell, Amnesty got everything wrong. Moreover, Shell pointed out that, 'Amnesty failed to acknowledge the company's contribution to Nigeria's economy and community development in the Niger Delta.' Amnesty replied, 'Positive activity in one area does not absolve anyone of responsibility for failures in other areas. Human rights abuses cannot be offset.'[33]

Senior managers at Shell in the Niger Delta have shown that indifference to others that is an essential part of interposing a body between yourself and annihilation. Now that television news brings us pictures of this terrible indifference to others, do you not watch incredulous that people should behave in this way? When you watched the scenes of children and teachers taken hostage in their own school in Beslan in North Ossetia in 2004, did you not expect to see ambulances with doctors and nurses waiting outside the school, ready to look after the hostages when they either escaped or were released? Yet there were none. The Russian government sent soldiers but not medical care. When the people of New Orleans were crowded together, waiting to be rescued from the hurricane and the flood, did you not expect to see an endless line of coaches speeding to the scene? A few arrived, but they were refused permission to collect passengers. Did you not expect the Burmese generals to save their people from the hurricane, and the Sri Lankan army to rescue the Tamil civilians from the fighting? What we saw was the massive indifference those in power often show to those they regard as their inferiors.

We see people as inferiors because we want to interpose their bodies between us and the terror we do not understand. Yet, if we did understand this terror, we would know that it was unnecessary to feel afraid. All that has fallen apart is some of our ideas. Important ideas, certainly, but merely ideas. Our ideas are nothing but guesses. We are always free to construct new ideas, ones that are closer to the truth of our situation. We can never be absolutely sure about anything, but we can always look for the evidence to support what we think might be true. The evidence, if it exists, is there in the real world, in our own lived experience. If there is no evidence, then our idea is a fantasy. Fantasies are very important, but, if we make them the basis of a whole edifice of belief and action, tragedy for ourselves if not for others will be inevitable.

When Muntazer al-Zaidi was released from the prison where he had been sent as punishment for hurling his shoes at George Bush, he wrote an article about why he had wanted to insult Bush in this way. In it he said, 'I wanted to express my rejection of his lies, his occupation of my country, my rejection of his killing of my people. My rejection of his plundering of the wealth of my country, and destroying its infrastructure. And casting out its sons into a diaspora.[34]

Note that of all the crimes al-Zaidi wished to avenge, lies were the first. We all know why. When people lie to us, they make it so much harder for us to create ideas that had a strong possibility of being true. Lies undermine our security. The lies other people tell us and the lies we tell ourselves increase the amount of uncertainty with which we have to live. Lies destroy the trust we have in others and in ourselves, and thus increase our alone-ness. To live as easily as we can with the inherent uncertainty and aloneness of being a person, we must be truthful with ourselves and with others, no matter how difficult that may be.

We cannot agree on the existence of other Gods and heavenly places, or on who is better than who, but a truth we all seem to agree on is that we exist and so does our planet in the universe. If this is perhaps the only truth on which we can all agree, then would it not be sensible if we looked after one another and the Earth which is our home?

Notes

Preface

1 'Granola and green tea sharpen Peter Mandelson's appetite', *Guardian*, 10 August 2009.
2 Timothy Garton Ash, *The File: A Personal History*, Atlantic Books, London, 2009.
3 'On the money', *Guardian*, 31 October 2008.
4 Edward Rowe, Motor Industry Consultant, Sydney, 28 March 2009.
5 http://news.bbc.co.uk/1/hi/business/davos/7859179.stm, 30 January 2009.
6 Paul Mason, *Meltdown: The End of the Age of Greed*, Verso, London, 2009, p. 64.
7 'Another bonus for Fred the Shred . . .', *Daily Mirror*, 24 March 2009.
8 'What happened to other bankers blamed for the credit crunch?', *Guardian*, 1 October 2009.
9 Garton Ash, *op. cit.* p. 66.
10 *Ibid.* p. 195.
11 *Ibid.* p. 232.
12 www.bbc.co.uk/blogs/thereporters/markmardell/europe.html, 1 August 2009.
13 Elizabeth Pisani, *The Wisdom of Whores: Bureaucrats, Brothels and the Business of AIDS*, Granta, London, 2008, p. 309.
14 *Ibid.* p. 311.

Chapter One: How Can We Know What Is True?

1 www.naomiklein.org/articles/2008/05/chinas-all-seeing-eye
2 Chris Frith, *Making Up the Mind: How the Brain Creates Our Mental World*, Blackwell Publishing, Oxford, 2007, p. 40.
3 Marco Iacoboni, *Mirroring People: The New Science of How We Connect with Others*, Farrar, Straus and Giroux, New York, 2008, p. 92.
4 *Ibid*. p. 14.
5 *Ibid*. p. 58.
6 Frith, *op. cit*. p. 124.
7 'Shades of Meaning', *New Scientist*, 27 June 2007, p. 44.
8 Frith, *op. cit*. p. 98.
9 *Guardian Science Course: Part V Energy* in association with the Science Museum, May 2008.
10 *Leading Edge*, BBC, 12 June 2008.

Chapter Two: The Curious World We Live In

1 Howard Jacobson, 'Behold! The Jewish Jesus', *Guardian*, 9 January 2009.
2 'Who did most to knock man off his pedestal', *New Scientist*, 20/27 December 2008, p. 71.
3 *Sydney Morning Herald*, 17–18 January 2009.
4 '"He wasn't prepared for a second-class life": why injured rugby star went to Switzerland to die', *Guardian*, 18 October 2008.
5 'The man who mapped the heart', *Guardian*, 16 December 2008.
6 'In search of the God neuron', *Guardian*, 27 December 2008.
7 'Mind-reading software reveals brain images', *New Scientist*, 20 December 2008, p. 13.
8 www.nspcc.org.uk/Inform/research/statistics/child_homicide_statistics_wda48747.html

9 www.badscience.net/about-dr-ben-goldacre/
10 'Calls to scrap the "leap second" grow', *New Scientist*, 20 December 2008, p. 10.
11 K. David Harrison, *When Languages Die*, Oxford University Press, New York, 2007, p. 62.
12 Professor Brian Cox, *Horizon*, BBC Productions, 2008.
13 Harrison, *op. cit.* p. 113.
14 'High Anxieties: The Mathematics of Chaos', BBC4 TV, I-330 Films Ltd, 2008.
15 Paul Krugman, *The Return of Depression Economics and the Crisis of 2008*, Penguin Books, London, 2008, p. 54.
16 'One last chance to save mankind', *New Scientist*, 24 January 2009, pp. 30–31.

Chapter Three: Do You Know What I Mean?

1 Michael J. Reddy, 'The conduit metaphor: A case of frame conflict in our language about language' in Andrew Ortony (ed.), *Metaphor and Thought*, Cambridge University Press, Cambridge, 1979, pp. 284–324.
2 D.C. Dennett, 'Memes and the exploitation of imagination', *Journal of Aesthetics and Art Criticism*, 48 (1990), 127–35.
3 David Healy, *Mania: A Short History of Bipolar Disorder*, Johns Hopkins University Press, Baltimore, 2008, pp. xviii, 77.
4 'This artist is deeply dangerous', *Guardian*, 18 June 2008.
5 Dan Hind, *The Threat to Reason*, Verso, 2008, p. 43.

Chapter Four: Why Lying Is Necessary

1 Harold Lloyd Goodall Jr, *A Need to Know: The Clandestine History of a CIA Family*, Left Coast Press, 2006, p. 321.
2 Dorothy Rowe, *The Successful Self*, HarperCollins, London, 1988.
3 Antonio R. Damasio, *The Feeling of What Happens: Body*

and Emotion in the Making of Consciousness, Vintage, London, 2000, p. 337.

4 Frith, *op. cit.* p. 169.

5 Patricia Churchland, 'The Big Questions: Do we have free will?', *New Scientist*, 16 November 2006, p. 14.

6 'Tomorrow is a long time', *Guardian*, 16 August 2008, Suze Rotolo, *A Freewheelin' Time: A Memoir of Greenwich Village in the Sixties*, Aurum Press, London, 2008.

7 Vasudevi Reddy, *How Infants Know Minds*, Harvard University Press, Cambridge, Mass., 2008, p. 41; B. Frederickson, 'Positive emotions' in C.R. Snyder and S.J. Lopez (eds), *Handbook of Positive Psychology*, Oxford University Press, New York, 2002, pp. 120–34.

8 *Guardian Guide*, 2–8 June 2007.

9 Tobias Wolff, *This Boy's Life*, Bloomsbury, London, 1989, p. 180.

10 Tobias Wolff, *In Pharaoh's Army: Memories of a Lost War*, Bloomsbury, London, 1994, p. 207.

Chapter Five: How We Learn to Lie

1 Reddy, *op. cit.* p. 85.

2 Richard Dawkins, *The God Delusion*, Black Swan, London, 2006, p. 320.

3 Reddy, *op. cit.* p. 47.

4 *Ibid.* p. 164.

5 *Ibid.* p. 121.

6 *Ibid.* p. 217.

7 Judy Dunn, *Sisters and Brothers*, Fontana, London, 1984, p. 30.

8 Edmund Gosse, *Father and Son*, Oxford University Press, Oxford, p. 35.

9 *Ibid.* p. 37.

10 Reddy, *op. cit.* p. 219.

11 Imre Kertész, *Fatelessness*, trans. Tim Wilkinson, Vintage Books, London, 2006, p. 169.
12 Murray A. Straus, *Beating the Devil Out of Them: Corporal Punishment in American Families and its Effects on Children*, Josey-Bass Inc, San Francisco, 1994.
13 http://ebooks.adelaide.edu.au/o/orwell/george/o79n/#chapter23
14 Reddy, *op. cit.* p. 219.
15 Simon Hoggart, 'We're sorry say bankers. Well, sort of', *Guardian*, 11 February 2009.
16 Jenni Murray, *Memoirs of a Not So Dutiful Daughter*, Bantam Press, London, 2008, p. 4.
17 *Ibid.* p. 57.
18 *Ibid.* p. 52.

Chapter Six: The Danger of Being Obedient

1 Gitta Sereny, *The German Trauma: Experiences and Reflections 1938–1999*, Penguin Books, London, 2000, p. 145.
2 Katrin Himmler, *The Himmler Brothers*, trans. Michael Mitchell, Macmillan, 2007, pp. 295, 297.
3 *Ibid.* p. 167.
4 *Ibid.* p. 267.
5 Wibke Bruhns, *My Father's Country: The Story of a German Family*, trans. Shaun Whiteside, Arrow Books, London, 2009, pp. 35, 213.
6 *Ibid.* p. 37.
7 *Ibid.* p. 119.
8 *Ibid.* p. 35.
9 Albert Speer, *Inside the Third Reich*, trans. Richard and Clara Winston, Weidenfeld and Nicolson, London, 1970, p. 9.
10 Sereny, *op. cit.* p. 273.
11 Bernd Freytag Von Loringhoven, *In the Bunker with Hitler: The Last Witness Speaks*, Phoenix, London, 2007, p. 100.

12 *Ibid*. p. 48.
13 Proverbs 13:24.
14 Bruhns, *op. cit.* p. 31.
15 *Ibid*. p. 33.
16 Lytton Strachey, *Eminent Victorians*, Oxford University Press, Oxford, 2003, p. 153.
17 *Ibid*. pp. 150, 151, 152, 153.
18 Alfred Andersch, *The Father of a Murderer*, trans. Leila Vennewitz, New Directions Books, New York, 1980.
19 Himmler, *op. cit.* p. 23.
20 *Ibid*. p. 2.
21 *Ibid*. p. 16.
22 *Ibid*. p. 36.
23 Gosse, *op. cit.* p. 63.
24 Dan Bar-On, *Legacy of Silence: Encounters with Children of the Third Reich*, Harvard University Press, Cambridge, Mass., 1989, p. 28.
25 Himmler, *op. cit.* p. 39.
26 Boris Cyrulnik, *Resilience*, trans. David Macey, Penguin Books, London, 2009, p. 79.
27 *Ibid*. p. 188.

Chapter Seven: Deciding What Is True

1 'Us and them', *Guardian*, 18 April 2009.
2 Cyrulnik, *op. cit.* p. 98.
3 Krugman, *op. cit.* p. 191.
4 Clive Stafford Smith, *Bad Men: Guantanamo Bay and the Secret Prisons*, Weidenfeld and Nicolson, London, 2007, p. 189.
5 Robert Jay Lifton, *The Nazi Doctors: Medical Killing and the Psychology of Genocide*, Basic Books, New York, 2000, p. 15.
6 'Obama administration says goodbye to "war on terror"', *Guardian*, 26 March 2009.

7 John Humphrys, *Lost for Words: The Mangling and Manipulating of the English Language*, Hodder, London, 2004, p. 326.

8 Kevin Myers, *Watching the Door*, Atlantic Books, London, 2008, p. 98.

9 Gillian Tett, *Fool's Gold: How Unrestrained Greed Corrupted a Dream, Shattered Global Markets and Unleashed a Catastrophe*, Little, Brown, London, 2009, p. 35.

10 Lewis Carroll, *Alice Through the Looking Glass*, Macmillan, London, 1973, p. 220.

11 William D. Cohan, *House of Cards: How Wall Street's Gamblers Broke Capitalism*, Allen Lane, London, 2009, p. 1.

12 Don Watson, *Watson's Dictionary of Weasel Words*, Random House, Sydney, 2004, p. 1.

13 www.guardian.co.uk/politics/2009/mar/27/yesterday-in-parliament/print

14 www.dorothyrowe.com.au

Chapter Eight: How Important Is the Truth to You?

1 Nikos Petousis, *Skeptical Intelligencer*, Vol. 11, 2008, pp. 3–5.

2 Cyrulnik, *op. cit.* p. 193.

3 'Girl who ran away from home after row found dead in forest', *Guardian*, 25 September 2007.

4 http://news.bbc.co.uk/1/hi/england/hampshire/7015370.stm

5 Gosse, *op. cit.* p. 29.

6 Rory Bremner, *The Insider's Guide to Writing a Prime Ministerial Memoir*, BBC Radio 4, 18 May 2007.

7 www.pms.ac.uk/compmed

8 'The complementary medicine detective', *New Scientist*, 26 April 2008, pp. 44–5.

9 *Beyond Fear*, HarperCollins, 3rd edition, 2007, *The Successful Self*, HarperCollins, 1993, *Guide to Life*, HarperCollins,

London, 1996, *My Dearest Enemy*, *My Dangerous Friend*, Routledge, London, 2007.

10 Edzard Ernst and Simon Singh, *Trick or Treatment?: Alternative Medicine on Trial*, Bantam Press, London, 2008.

11 *The Weekend Australian* Magazine, 7–8 March 2009.

12 http://news.bbc.co.uk/1/hi/world/europe/8058224.stm

13 *Dispatches*, Channel 4, Quicksilver, 2009.

14 'Grudge between Lord Myners and Sir Fred Goodwin born at board table', *The Times*, 28 February 2009.

Chapter Nine: Fantasies Are Important

1 'Supersize lions roamed Britain', BBC News, Oxford, 1 April 2009; http://news.bbc.co.uk/1/hi/england/oxfordshire/7974948.stm

2 Seth Godin, *All Marketers Are Liars: The Power of Telling Authentic Stories in a Low-Trust World*, Penguin Books, London, 2007, p. 15.

3 Jeffrey Meyers, *Hemingway: A Biography*, Da Capo Press, New York, 1999, p. 138.

4 *Ibid.* p. 240.

5 *Ibid.* p. 47.

6 *Ibid.* opposite p. 205.

7 *Ibid.* p. 552.

8 Dorothy Rowe, *Depression: The Way Out of Your Prison*, 3rd edition, Routledge, London, 2003, pp. 57–62.

9 Meyers, *op. cit.* p. 5.

10 *Ibid.* p. 11.

11 *Ibid.* p. 5.

Chapter Ten: The Delights of Shared Fantasies

1 17 April 1980, quoted in the *Guardian*, 17 April 2009.

2 Carole Seymour-Jones, *A Dangerous Liaison*, Century, London, 2008, p. 88.

3 *Ibid.* p. 304.

4 *Ibid.* p. 87.

5 *Ibid.* p. 94.

6 Tett, *op. cit.* p. 4.

7 Seymour-Jones, *op. cit.* p. 101.

8 *Ibid.* p. 132.

9 *Ibid.* p. 211.

10 *Ibid.* p. 257.

11 Frederic Spotts, *The Shameful Peace: How French Artists and Intellectuals Survived the Nazi Occupation*, Yale University Press, New Haven and London, 2008.

12 *Ibid.* p. 3.

13 *Ibid.* p. 52.

14 Hilary Spurling, *Matisse the Master*, Hamish Hamilton, London, 2005, p. 393.

15 Spotts, *op. cit.* p. 159.

16 Spurling, *op. cit.* p. 425.

17 *Ibid.* p. 399.

18 Marcel Ophüls, *The Sorrow and the Pity*, 1969.

19 Seymour-Jones, *op. cit.* p. 275.

20 Spotts, *op. cit.* p. 57.

21 *Ibid.* p. 45.

22 Carmen Callil, *Bad Faith: A Forgotten History of Family and Fatherland*, Vintage Books, London, 2007, p. 311.

23 *Ibid.* p. 270.

24 *Ibid.* p. xxv.

25 *Ibid.* p. 138.

26 *Ibid.* p. 304.

27 *Ibid.* p. 31.

28 Spotts, *op. cit.* p. 45.

29 Frances Stoner Saunders, *Who Paid the Piper? The CIA and the Cultural Cold War*, Granta, London, 2000.

30 Seymour-Jones, *op. cit.* p. xvii.

31 *Ibid.* p. 469.

32 *Ibid*. p. 305.
33 *Ibid*. p. xii.
34 www.msnbc.msn.com/id/3080244/
35 Cyrulnik, *op. cit.* p. 211.

Chapter Eleven: Special Fantasies: Beliefs and Delusions

1 Tett, *op. cit.* p. 131.
2 www.telegraph.co.uk/news/newstopics/celebritynews/
   4347520/Sir-David-Attenborough-religious-viewers-send-
   me-hate-mail-for-not-crediting-God.html
3 Tobias Wolff, *In Pharaoh's Army*, p. 5.
4 Howard Jacobson, 'Behold! The Jewish Jesus', *Guardian*,
   9 January 2009.
5 Don Engel, 'Unfair to Atheists', *New Scientist*, 20 October
   2007, p. 27.
6 Gosse, *op. cit.* p. 21.
7 *Ibid*. p. 101.
8 *This Week Australia*, 13 March 2009.
9 Nassim Nicholas Taleb, *Fooled by Randomness: The Hidden
   Role of Chance in Life and in the Markets*, 2nd edition,
   Random House, New York, 2005, p. 156.
10 Tett, *op. cit.* pp. 65, 69.
11 Gosse, *op. cit.* pp. 88, 90, 92.
12 Bruhns, *op. cit.* p. 12.
13 *Ibid*. p. 334.
14 *The Crusades*, written by Terry Jones and Alan Ereira,
   BBC/A&E Network Co-production, MCMXCV.
15 Dorothy Rowe, *Beyond Fear*, 3rd edition, HarperCollins,
   London, pp. 616–24, www.hearing-voices.org
16 Bruhns, *op. cit.* p. 276.
17 Myers, *op. cit.* p. 57.

18 *Ibid*. p. 85.
19 *Ibid*. p. 91.
20 Speer, *op. cit*. p. 291.

Chapter Twelve: Varieties of Lies

1 *Wall Street Journal*, 28 June 2007.
2 Bar-On, *op. cit*. p. 93.
3 *Ibid*. p. 62.
4 Orlando Figes, *The Whisperers: Private Life in Stalin's Russia*, Penguin, London, 2007, p. 36.
5 *Ibid*. p. 38.
6 Gosse, *op. cit*. p. 47.
7 *Ibid*. p. 46.
8 *Ibid*. p. 255.
9 Hilary Mantel, *Giving Up the Ghost*, Harper Perennial, London, 2004, p. 21.
10 Tett, *op. cit*. p. 298.
11 Edmund L. Andrews, *Busted: Life Inside the Great Mortgage Meltdown*, W.W. Norton, New York, 2009, quoted in *Guardian* supplement, 11 July 2009.
12 Tett, *op. cit*. p. 299.
13 Simon Hoggart, 'Lies, damned lies and a vision of the future', *Guardian*, 9 October 2007.
14 Joel Cooper, *Cognitive Dissonance: Fifty Years of a Classic Theory*, Sage Publications, London, 2007, p. 7.
15 Tony Judt, *Postwar: A History of Europe Since 1945*, Pimlico, London, 2007, p. 275.
16 Figes, *op. cit*. pp. 86, 92.
17 *Ibid*. p. 111.
18 'British academics protest after Russia closes down history website', *Guardian*, 13 July 2009.
19 Figes, *op. cit*. p. 98.

20 Barbara W. Tuchman, *The March of Folly: From Troy to Vietnam*, Abacus, London, 2005, pp. 378–9.
21 Peter Stothard, *The Book Show*, ABC, 12 February 2009.

Chapter Thirteen: The Same Old Lies

1 Peter Stanford, *C. Day-Lewis: A Life*, Continuum, London, 2007, p. 84.
2 *Ibid*. p. 106.
3 *Desert Island Discs*, 19 October 2007.
4 Stanford, *op. cit.* p. 175.
5 *Ibid*. p. 191.
6 *Ibid*. p. 227.
7 *Ibid*. p. 240.
8 *Amnesty Magazine*, July/August 2009, p. 6.

Chapter Fourteen: Denying What Is There

1 'Liberian ex-leader Charles Taylor hits out at "lies and misinformation" at war crimes trial', *Guardian*, 14 July 2009.
2 Eliot Weinberger, *What I Heard about Iraq*, Verso, London, 2005, p. 25.
3 Chris McGreal, 'Out of Africa', *Guardian*, 27 March 2009.
4 Joanna Moncrief, *A Straight Talking Introduction to Psychiatric Drugs*, PCCS Books, Ross-on-Wye, 2009.
5 Kristyan Benedict, '10 Days in the West Bank', *Amnesty Magazine*, July/August 2009, pp. 26–2.
6 Avi Shlaim, 'How Israel brought Gaza to the brink of humanitarian catastrophe', *Guardian*, 7 January 2009.
7 Peter Wilson, 'Lady Michele Renouf: mistress of reinvention', *The Weekend Australian* Magazine, 14–15 February 2009.
8 George Marshall, 'Why people don't act on climate change', *New Scientist*, 25 July 2009, pp. 24–5.

9 'Nile Delta: "We are going underwater. The sea will conquer our lands"', *Guardian*, 21 August 2009.
10 www.reuters.com/article/environmentNews/ 6 August 2007.
11 www.bom.gov.au/climate/change/
12 'Global warming pushes up building insurance costs', *Guardian*, 30 July 2009.
13 http://climatedenial.org, 21 April 2009.
14 *Ibid.* 9 April 2009.
15 'Climate sceptics fight tide of alarmism', *Sydney Morning Herald*, 14–15 March 2009.
16 http://climatedenial.org, *op. cit.*; Jeremy Clarkson, 'Ignore the end of the world', *Sun*, 18 April 2008.
17 'Meet the man who has exposed the great climate change con trick', *Spectator*, 11 July 2009.

Chapter Fifteen: Hypocrites All

1 Andy Rowell, 'Greenwash goes legit', *Guardian*, 21 July 1999.
2 www.futerra.co.uk/services/greenwash-guide
3 www.motherjones.com/print/25079
4 http://www.shell.com/home/content/nigeria/society_environ-ment/dir_community_environment.html
5 http://news.bbc.co.uk/1/hi/world/africa/8090493.stm
6 *Guardian Weekly*, 2 February 2009.
7 *Guardian*, 27 July 2009.
8 http://edition.cnn.com/2009/WORLD/asiapcf/05/12/quake.anniversary/index.html
9 'Greenwash: The dream of the first eco-city was built on a fiction', *Guardian*, 23 April 2009.
10 ABC News, 13 May 2009.
11 Andrew Sullivan, 'St Ken of Enron leads Bush's new Christianity', *The Sunday Times*, 16 July 2006.

Chapter Sixteen: Being Lied To

1 John Lanchester, 'It's finished', *London Review of Books*, 28 May 2009.
2 http://news.bbc.co.uk/1/hi/business/1835621.stm
3 Lanchester, *op. cit.* p. 8.
4 *Ibid.* p. 8.
5 *Ibid.* p. 6.
6 Nick Davies, *Flat Earth News*, Chatto and Windus, London, 2008.
7 David Slater, *The Media We Deserve*, Melbourne University Press, Melbourne, 2007.
8 *Ibid.* p. 3.
9 Stephen Greenspan, *Annals of Gullibility: Why We Get Duped and How to Avoid It*, Praeger, Westport, CT, 2009.
10 Stephen Greenspan, 'Fooled by Ponzi (and Madoff): How Bernard Madoff Made Off with My Money', www.skeptic.com/eskeptic/08-12-23
11 'Wizard of deception', *New Scientist*, 15 September 2007, p. 56.
12 'The truth about lying', *Guardian*, 12 May 2009.
13 Paul Ekman, *Telling Lies: Clues to Deceit in the Marketplace, Politics, and Marriage*, W.W. Norton, New York, 2001, p. 339.
14 *Ibid.* p. 342.
15 'Scientists divided over alliance with religion', *Guardian*, 29 May 2007.
16 *Guardian* letters, 30 May, 31 May, 2 June, 6 June 2007.
17 Strachey, *op. cit.* p. 10.
18 *Ibid.* p. 13.
19 Joe Bageant, *Deer Hunting with Jesus*, Portobello Books, London, 2008, p. 184.
20 *Ibid.* p. 185.
21 *Ibid.* p. 185.
22 John McGahern, *Memoir*, Faber and Faber, London, 2005, p. 47.

23 Stephan and Norbert Lebert, *My Father's Keeper: Children of Nazi Leaders – An Intimate History of Damage and Denial*, trans. Julian Evans, Little, Brown and Company, New York, 2001.
24 *Ibid*. pp. 128, 129.
25 *Ibid*. p. 150.
26 *Ibid*. p. 141.
27 *Ibid*. p. 106.
28 Obituary, *Independent*, 19 December 2002.

Chapter Seventeen: Lying for Your Government

1 Tim Weiner, *Legacy of Ashes: The History of the CIA*, Allen Lane, London, 2007, p. xiii.
2 *Ibid*. p. x.
3 Goodall, *op. cit*. p. 333.
4 Weiner, *op. cit*. p. 46.
5 Goodall, *op. cit*. p. 219.
6 *Ibid*. p. 296.
7 *Ibid*. p. 193.
8 Weiner, *op. cit*. p. 48.
9 *Ibid*. p. 158.
10 http://usgovinfo.about.com/library/weekly/aa040900b.htm
11 http://usgovinfo.about.com/library/weekly/aa040900a.htm
12 Dorothy Rowe, *Living with the Bomb: Can We Live without Enemies?*, Routledge, London, 1985.
13 Goodall, *op. cit*. p. 9.
14 Barack Obama, *Dreams from My Father*, Canongate, Edinburgh, 2008, p. 429.
15 Sathnam Sanghera, *The Boy with the Topknot: A Memoir of Love, Secrets and Lies*, Penguin, London, 2008, p. 293.

Chapter Eighteen: Never Say You're Sorry

1 Lifton, *op. cit*. p. 446.
2 *Ibid*. p. 449.
3 *Ibid*. p. 474.
4 www.democracynow.org/2009/7/7/vietnam_war_architect_ robert_mcnamara_dies
5 www.alertnet.org/thenews/newsdesk/HAN428909.htm
6 www.b-29s-over-korea.com/firebombing/firebombimb_ intro.html
7 *The Fog of War: Eleven Lessons from the Life of Robert S. McNamara*, dir. Errol Morris, Sony Pictures Classics, 2002.
8 Tuchman, *op. cit*. p. 315.
9 www.democracynow.org, *op. cit*.
10 http://news.bbc.co.uk/1/hi/uk_politics/2859431.stm
11 www.theaustralian.news.com.au/business/story/0,28124, 25218595-17044,00.html
12 Australian Broadcasting Corporation Television, 2009.
13 'What happens in War happens', *Guardian*, 3 January 2009.
14 *Ibid*.

Chapter Nineteen: Some Hard Truths

1 Tom Feiling, *The Candy Machine: How Cocaine Took Over the World*, Penguin Books, London, 2009, pp. 2, 3.
2 Dorothy Rowe, *Beyond Fear*, 3rd edition.
3 'I accumulated an anger that would rip a roof off', *Guardian*, 12 September 2009.
4 Channel 4 *Dispatches: Terror in Mumbai*, 30 June 2009; *Guardian*, 1 July 2009.
5 Dorothy Rowe, *Wanting Everything*, HarperCollins, London, 1991, pp. 78–104.
6 Proverbs 13:24.

7 www.britishempire.co.uk / forces / armycampaigns / indian campaigns/campafghan1878.htm
8 Jonathan Steele, 'The Afghan 80s are back', *Guardian*, 1 September 2009.
9 Dorothy Rowe, *Time on Our Side*, HarperCollins, London, 1994.
10 'University apologises to China for Dalai Lama's degree', *Guardian*, 9 July 2008.
11 Martin Jacques, *When China Rules the World: The Rise of the Middle Kingdom and the End of the Western World*, Allen Lane, London, 2009, p. 317.
12 'A "Copper Standard" for the world's currency system?', *Daily Telegraph*, 15 April 2009.
13 Jacques, *op. cit.* p. 291.
14 'Return of the gravy train – did the crash really change the City at all?', *Guardian*, 24 June 2009.
15 'O Lord help them be tough on the City – but not yet', *Guardian*, 8 July 2009.
16 'The G20 has saved us, but it's failing to rein in those who caused the crisis', *Observer*, 6 September 2009.
17 *Ibid.*
18 'O Lord help them be tough on the City – but not yet', *Guardian*, 8 July 2009.
19 'If we're back to business as usual it's curtains for Labour', *Guardian*, 12 August 2009.
20 'UK banks face tougher bonus curbs than US', *Financial Times*, 1 October 2009.
21 'Pound slides back against dollar and euro', *Guardian*, 22 September 2009.
22 www.torfx.com/blog/2009/09/pound-rallies-against-dollar-as-stocks.html
23 'Jobless figures show demise of the slump may be exaggerated', *Guardian*, 21 September 2009.

24 Naomi Klein, *The Shock Doctrine*, Penguin, London, 2008, p. 12.
25 Feiling, *op. cit.*
26 'The man who discovered greenhouse gases', *New Scientist*, 13 May 2009, pp. 46–7.
27 Mike Hulme, *Why We Disagree about Climate Change: Understanding Controversy, Inaction and Opportunity*, Cambridge University Press, Cambridge, 2009.
28 Genesis 11:4.
29 Leviticus 25:44, 45, 9, 10.
30 *The Love of Money*, a Money Programme Production, BBC Productions, 2009.
31 Sereny, *op. cit.* p. 163.
32 Garton Ash, *op. cit.* p. 175.
33 *Amnesty Magazine*, September/October 2009.
34 'Why I threw the shoe', *Guardian*, 18 September 2009.

Index

ABC Television 251, 287, 288
ABN Amro 247–8
Aborigines 66–7
Abu Ghraib 79, 289–91
Adams, Gerry 225
Advertising Standards Agency
   (ASA) 239
Afghanistan 114, 185, 206, 243,
   265, 271, 274, 285, 305–6
Agent Orange 281–2
AIDS xix
Aitkenhead, Decca xii
Al Azzeh, Hashem 225
al-Qaeda 114, 290
al-Zaidi, Muntazer 329
Alançon, François d' 93
Alchemy Partners 141
alcohol 183–4, 294
aloneness 293–4, 295, 301
American Association for the
   Advancement of Science 33
American Home Mortgage 197
American International Group
   (AIG) 218
Amnesty International 328
Amnesty Magazine 225
Andersch, Alfred, *The Father of a
   Murderer* 96
Andrews, Edmund, *Busted: Life
   Inside the Great Mortgage*

Meltdown 197
anger 51, 53, 55, 99, 122, 124, 160,
   194, 212, 216, 296–7
Angleton, James Jesus 266, 269–70
anxious attachment 84, 96–7
Archimedes 129
Arnold, Thomas 95, 104
as if perception 2, 121
Ash, Timothy Garton xiii, xviii,
   327–8
Ashdown, Paddy 133
ATR Computational Laboratories
   (Kyoto) 25
Attenborough, Sir David 173, 297
Auden, W.H. 209
Auschwitz 74–5, 102, 164, 165,
   260–1, 278, 279
Australia, Australians ix, xiv, 5, 13,
   66–7, 80, 92, 120, 138–9, 154,
   183, 228–9, 232–3, 236, 251,
   286–9, 310–11
Australian Bankers' Association 288
Australian Bureau of Meteorology
   232–3
Australian bushfire 138–9
Australian and New Zealand Bank
   (ANZ) 311

babies
   and imitation 65–6, 67, 302

perception/response mechanism
67–8
and refusal to obey 69
and sense of self 61–4, 67
Bacon, Francis 43
Bageant, Joe 257–8
Balcon, Jill 209, 213, 214–15
Bangladesh 232
Bank One 172
banking and finance xii, xiv, xv,
xvi, 81–2, 117–18, 141–2, 156,
161, 172–3, 178–9, 196–8,
217–18, 245–9, 250, 288–9,
310–16, 323–5
Bar-On, Dan 102
Legacy of Silence 260
Barak, Ehud 224, 230
Barclays Bank 247
Barker, Steven 263
Bayes, Thomas 10
BBC xv, xviii, 18, 26, 28, 30, 83,
114, 115, 132, 246, 251, 290,
323, 325
Bear Stearns 117–18, 217–18
Beauvoir, Simone de 154–7, 158,
159, 161–4, 166, 168–70, 304
The Prime of Life 164
Beckham, David and Victoria 154
beliefs 122–3, 171
challenges to 16
changing 174
clinging to 138–42
definition 143
as fantasy 172–82
as ideas 177
nothing bad can happen to me
139–40
and persuasion 303
questioning 127
rationalizing 180–1

religious 124, 129–30, 131
scientific 125–6, 128
as true 173–4, 256
validity of 130–1
Benedict, Kristyan 225
Benin 14
Bernanke, Ben 314
Berners-Lee, Tim 203–4
Beslan (North Ossetia) 328
Bienenfeld, Bianca 157, 168–9
Bierley, Steve 42
Big Bang 29
bipolar disorder 23
Blair, Tony xii, 133–6, 175–6, 177,
198, 241, 274, 281, 285, 309
Bodanis, David 15
Böll, Heinrich 96
Bond, Michael 134
Bost, Jacques-Laurent 157
Bourgeois, Louise 42–3
brain-mind division 7–8
brains
and access to the physical world
8, 9–10
Bayesian 10–11, 35
computer metaphor 8–9
and creation of meaning 163
and interpreting the world 22,
35, 43–4, 47
and perception 12–16, 17
and scanning technology 24–5
(un)conscious aspects 39–41
Brando, Marlon 58
bravado lies 73–6, 79–80, 98, 280
Brennan, Teresa 286
Brinded, Malcolm 240
British Psychological Society 65
Brockes, Emma 290
Brown, Gordon 218, 309, 314, 316
Bruhns, Wibke 90, 91, 92, 94–5,

183–4
In My Father's Country 180, 181
bullying 80
Burgess, Guy 270
Bush, George W. xii, 113, 135, 171, 175, 198, 206, 217, 244, 274, 285, 316, 329
Byrd, James 244

Callaghan, James 313
Callil, Carmen 164–5, 165
Calvin, John 131
Cameron, David 313–14, 316
Cameron, John 315
Campbell, Alastair 175
Cash for Comments 288–9
Castro, Fidel 265
categories 108–10, 112, 122–6
Chain of Being 21–2
chaos theory 33–4
Charles, Prince of Wales 137, 239
Cheney, Dick xii, 79, 170–1, 220, 274, 285
children
  and anxious attachment behaviour 84, 96–7
  background superiority 87
  and child-rearing xix–xx
  claiming to care for 243–4
  and consequences of adult lies 259–64
  and deception 70–2
  and in denial lies 222–3
  deportation of 164, 165, 262
  and divorce 131
  education of 17
  effect of extreme events on 144
  as embarrassment 254–5
  and fantasy 97, 136, 150, 153
  and feeling bad 100–4
  and feeling guilty 82–6
  and feelings of rage 99–100
  and formation of inner life 195
  and lying 72–6
  and memory 209–11
  as obedient 92–5, 300–2
  and omniescence of God 193–5
  and parental (dis)agreement 70
  and parental fantasy 160–1
  and parental omniscience 71–2, 82–6, 100–1, 193, 195–6
  and physical punishment 73–4, 76, 94–105, 151, 290, 302
  and sceptical inquiry 302
  sexual abuse of 140–1, 263
  treatment of 110–11
  truth-telling 69–70, 131–3
  and war 271
China 241–2, 284, 308, 309, 310, 316
Chinese State Reserve Bureau (SRB) 310
Choi, Dan 243
Churchland, Patricia 47
CIA 166, 264, 265–75, 290
Clarkson, Jeremy 234
Claus, Václav 234
climate change xix, 18–19, 34–5, 161, 231–7, 239–40, 243–4, 258, 274, 318–21, 322
Clinton, Bill 218, 243, 274
CND 273
Coe, Sebastian 242
Cognitive Dissonance 199–207
Cohan, William D. 117
Cold War 268, 272–4, 306
Cole, Barry 256

Collinge, Lizzi 255
colour 13–14
Columbus, Christopher 173
communication
 conscious/unconscious listening
  39–40
 and imitation 66–7
 infant 63
 misunderstanding/misinterpre-
  tation 36, 37–8
 receiving 39
 unstated implications 38–9
Comoedia 162
complementary and alternative
 medicine (CAM) 134, 137
conduit metaphor 37–8
conflict *see* war and conflict
Connelly, Tracy 263
Cook, Robin 285
Cooper, Joel, *Cognitive Dissonance:
 Fifty Years of a Classical Theory*
 199
Copernicus, Nicolas 22
Court of International Justice (The
 Hague) 87, 220
Cox, Brian 28, 30, 31
Crash: How the Banks Went Bust
 (TV programme) 141
Creation Museum (Petersburg,
 Kentucky) 175
Creationists 175, 206–7
Cuba 283
Currell, Billie 213–14
Cyrulnik, Boris 104, 110, 121, 171
 Resilience 121

Daily Telegraph 248
Dalai Lama 309
Damasio, Antonio 52
Darling, Alistair 314–15

Darquier, Anne 164, 166
Darquier, Louis 164–6
Darquier, Myrtle (née Jones) 164,
 165–6
Darwin, Charles 22, 70, 175, 176,
 180
 On the Origin of Species 179,
 318
Davies, Nick, *Flat Earth News* 251
Davies of Oldham, Lord 120
Davies, Paul 22
Dawkins, Richard 107–8, 297
 The God Delusion 64–5
Day-Lewis, Cecil 209–16, 304
 The Friendly Tree 213
Day-Lewis, Nicholas 215
Day-Lewis, Sean 215
Delange, René 162
Delingpole, James 234
delusion ix, 142, 143, 182–7, 297,
 310, 321–2
Demchak, Bill 178
Dennis, Hugh 255
depression 66, 81, 111, 125, 130,
 148, 248–9, 290, 291
Descartes, René 156
Desert Island Discs (radio
 programme) 213
Devine, Miranda 234
Diagnostic and Statistical Manual
 (DSM) 127, 130–1
Dignitas 23
Dimon, Jamie 172–3
domino theory 284
Donaldson, Trooper Mark 22–3
Dongtan 241–2
Don't Ask, Don't Tell 243
Drew-Honey, Tyger 255
Dreyfus, Alfred 162
Dreyfus-le-Foyer, Henri 162

drugs 248–9, 268–9, 270, 294
Duhon, Terry 178–9
Dullin, Charles 163
Dunn, Judy 70
Dylan, Bob 49–50
   The Freewheelin' Bob Dylan 49

East Anglia University 320
Edwards, Rosemary 132
Egypt 231–2
Einfeld, Marcus 285–7
Einstein, Albert 31, 306
Eisenhower, Dwight D. 272–3, 273
Ekman, Paul 252, 253, 254
Eliot, T.S. 294
Elliott, Larry 313
emotions *see* feelings and emotions
End Time Theology 257–8
Engel, Don 175
England, Lynndie 289–91
Enron 244
Ernst, Edzard 133–4, 137
   Trick or Treatment 137
error of judgement xi, 48, 287
Escher, Sandra 182
eSkeptic 252
Eslake, Saul 311
evolutionary biologists 23
Exeter University 134
existence, making sense of 7–8
Exposition Sartre (2005) 169
extraverts 41–2, 150, 157
ExxonMobil 240

Faith Foundation xii
familial lies 210–16
fantasy 142, 296
   and about-to-happen happiness
    58
   and beliefs 124, 172–82, 256

childhood 97, 136, 150, 153
complexity of 201–3
constructing/creating 20–2, 147,
   149–50, 157–8
definition 143
as delusion 182–7
development of 143–6
as harmful 153–4
importance of 147, 329
as means of survival 149–52
as myth 171
parental 160–1
power of 167
preference for 41–2
romantic 51
and science 147
shared 153–71
and splitting of self 279–80
and truth 147–9, 152, 180–1, 300
and world domination 166, 170–1
fear and terror
   and anger 122
   and authority 92, 168, 184
   and being found out 268
   and being overwhelmed by chaos
    46, 48
   childhood 5, 74, 76, 79–80,
    94–106, 190–1, 195, 300
   and creation of meaning 163
   and falling apart/being annihi-
    lated xi, 50–1, 55, 124, 204,
    291, 298, 326
   and fantasy 186–7
   and gender 42–3, 295
   and God 90, 127, 152, 194, 195,
    256
   and looking inward 212
   and rejection/abandonment 135,
    156–7
   and sex 294–5

and silence 275
and time passing 306
and uncertainty/aloneness 304,
    321
feelings and emotions 42–3, 51–3,
    72, 158, 184, 210, 253, 280
Ferdinand II of Aragon 177
Festinger, Leon 199
Figes, Orlando 202, 203
finance *see* banking and finance
Financial Times 315
Flintoff, Ian 255–6
Forrestal, Michael 205
Four Corners (TV programme) 287
Fourier, Joseph 318
France 158–60
Frank, Brigitte 261
Frank, Hans 260–1
Frank, Michael 261
Frank, Niklas 261, 262
Frank, Norman 261
Franz, Kurt 327
Frederickson, Barbara 52–3
French National Radio 162
Freud, Sigmund 40, 62, 110–11, 170
Freytag von Loringhoven, Bernd
    93–4
Freytag von Loringhoven, Wessel
    94
Frith, Chris 8, 11, 14, 47, 121
    Making Up the Mind 121
Froelich, Paula 178
Frost, Robert 50
Futerra 239

Gaia hypothesis 34–5
Galbraith, J.K. 33, 205, 312
Galileo Galilei 22
Gallant, Jack 25
Gallimard, Gaston 163

Gardner, Dr Richard 130–1
Gaza 224–6
Geithner, Tim 217
generational differences 36, 42–3
genes 23–4
Germany, Germans xviii, 87–98,
    112, 180–1, 200, 230, 260, 262
Glass Steagall Act (1929) 218
Glazar, Richard 326–7
global warming *see* climate change
Godin, Seth, *All Marketers Are
    Liars* 146
Goebbels, Joseph 163
Goldacre, Ben, 'Bad Science' 27
Golden Age myth 27, 308
Goodall, Harold Lloyd 'Buddy', *A
    Need to Know: The Clandestine
    History a CIA Family* 45, 266–8,
    270–1, 275
Goodall, Naomi 267–8, 270–1
Goodwin, Sir Fred xii, xvi, 81–2,
    141, 218, 246, 247–9
Gore, Al 234
Gosse, Edmund 70–3, 99, 105,
    132–3, 176, 179, 193–4, 299
    Father and Son 169
Gosse, Philip 70–3, 176–7, 179–80,
    193, 195
Grainer, Charles 289–91
Grass, Günter 96
greenhouse effect 318
Greenspan, Alan 323–5
Greenspan, Stephen 252–3
greenwash 238–9
Greenwash Guide 239
Greer, Germaine 229
Group 47 96
Guantanamo 79, 113, 115
Guardian 27, 42, 154, 242, 255,
    290, 313

Guardian Online 27
guesses 48–9
guilt 68, 74, 76, 80–2, 83–6, 98,
    104, 299–300

Hadron Collider 203
Hage, Patsy 182
Ham, Ken 174–5
Hamas 224, 226, 230
Hamilton, Andy 255
hard truths
    and connectedness of things
        303–6, 308
    and discovering own truths
        299–303
    and divided life 304–5
    economic 309–16
    and history 305–6
    and interposing another's body
        326–30
    lying to oneself 298–9
    metaphors and myths 316–22
    and passing of time 306–8
    and reality 303
    uncertainty and aloneness 293–8
    and wilful ignorance 322–6
Harding, Luke 203
Harkinson, Josh, *Mother Jones*
    239–40
Harvard Business School 245–6
Hay-on-Wye Literary Festival
    (2007) 255
Hayes, John-Dylan 25
HBOS 81
Head, Peter 241
Healy, David 42
Hearing Voices Network 182
Heartland Institute (USA) 234
Hemingway, Ernest 147–9, 150–2,
    304

Hemingway, Mary 149
Hillel, Rabbi 225
Hilsman, Roger 205
Himmler, Anna 97, 98, 104
Himmler, Ernst Herman 97–8, 105
Himmler, Gebhard (Snr) 95–8, 104,
    112
Himmler, Gebhard Ludwig 88–90,
    97, 104–6
Himmler, Gudrun 262–3
Himmler, Heinrich Luitpold 88–9,
    97, 105, 162, 187, 262
Himmler, Katrin 89, 96, 97–8, 104,
    105
Hind, Dan, *The Threat to Reason* 43
Hiroshima 283
history xiii, xix, 27, 123, 155, 203,
    225, 279, 285, 305–6, 308,
    312–13
Hitler, Adolf xiii, 17, 87, 89, 91,
    93, 106, 112, 140, 158, 161,
    180, 181, 186, 200, 224, 260,
    278, 279, 300
    Mein Kampf 203
Hitler Youth 91–2
Hoggart, Simon 81, 198
Holocaust 226–31, 262–3
homosexuals 127, 183, 242–3
Hornby, Andy 81–2
Howard, Elizabeth Jane 215
Howard, John 288, 316
Hu Jintao 241
Hulme, Mike, *Why We Disagree
    about Climate Change* 320
Humphries, Barry 229
Hussein, Saddam 170, 272, 274–5
Hutton, Will 141, 313
Hutu 221
hypocrisy
    and global warming 239–40

and green movement 238–9
and language 238
and the media 240–1
and politics 241–2
and same-sex relationships 242–3
sentimental 243–4
hypothesis saving 66

'I', 'me', 'myself' 47–9
Iacoboni, Marco 9
ideas
   abandonment of 21–2
   and absolute truth 18
   and authority 2–3, 16, 87, 92
   and barriers 169–70
   and beliefs 177
   changing xvii–xx, 66, 111
   creating 262, 297
   extreme 183
   as guesses 329
   imposition of 307
   (mis)interpretation of 38, 303
   prevalence of 105, 110, 112
   and reality 203–4
   as reliable 130
   religious 108, 122–3, 174
   and sense of being 47, 48–9, 54,
      56, 69, 77–9, 135, 136
   supported by evidence 296
ideomotor model 10
illusion 31, 47
imitation 65–7
in denial
   as adaption strategy 233
   climate change 231–7
   familial 222–3
   Holocaust 226–31
   illness 222
   media error 221
   religion 225

stalking 224
war and conflict 220–1, 224–6
Incas 20–1
India 232
Inman, Phillip xvi
intercontinental ballistic missiles
   (ICBMs) 272–3
Intergovernmental Panel on Climate
   Change 231–2
internal object 210–11
introverts 134–8
intuition 39, 41–2
IRA 184–5, 225
Iraq 114, 170, 185, 220–1, 243,
   265, 271, 274, 285
Ireland 140–1
Irving, David 227
Isabella of Castile 177
Israel, Israelis 224–6, 271
Israeli Committee Against House
   Demolitions (ICAHD) 225

Jacobson, Howard 21, 174
Jacques, Martin, *When China Rules
   the World* 310–11
James, Bruce 287
James, Clive 229
James, Dan 23
James, William 62
Japan 282–3
Jenkin, Guy 255
Jews 87, 91, 106, 109, 158,
   162, 164–5, 200, 226, 229–31,
   251, 260–1, 262–3, 278–9,
   326
Johnson, Lyndon Baines 231, 283,
   284
Jollivet, Simone 163
Jones, Alan 287–9
Jones, Steve 255–6, 259, 297

Jones, Terry 181–2
journalism 26–8
J.P. Morgan 156, 172–3, 178, 196, 217, 218
Judt, Tony 200
Jung, C.G. 40

Kamitani, Yukiyasu 25
Karl Marx Psychiatric Clinic (Leipzig) 167–8
Kayishema, Clément 221
Kennedy, John F. 205–6, 244, 273, 283
Kertész, Imre 74–6
Khrushchev, Nikita 272, 283
Kidman, Nicole 229
Kim Il Jong 17
King, Martin Luther 244
King, Mary 211–16
King, Mervyn 314
Klamroth, Barbara 180, 181
Klamroth, Bernard 93, 180, 184
Klamroth, Else 91, 180, 181
Klamroth, Gertrud 94, 180
Klamroth, Hans Georg 90–1, 92, 93, 180
Klamroth, Kurt 90, 91, 92–3, 94
Klamroth, Ursula 184
Klein, Dr Fritz 113
Klein, Naomi 6, 317
Knox, John 131
Kobe 283
Kopelev, Lev 201
KPMG 246
Kraepelin, Emil 42, 111
Kristallnacht (1938) 91
Krugman, Paul 33
    The Return of Depression Economics 111

La Croix 93
Lanchester, John 248, 249
language 114–21, 213, 235–6, 238–9
Laval, Pierre 162
Laws, John 287–9
Lawson, Reverend Bill 244
Lay, Kenneth 244
Le Chagrin et la Pitié (film) 155, 169
Le Matin 154
Lebert, Norbert 260, 262
Lebert, Stephan 261, 262
    My Father's Keeper 260
Legge, Kate 139
Lehman Brothers 218, 323
Lehmann, Rosamond 214, 215
LeMay, General Curtis 282, 283
Lenin, V.I. 201
Lennon, John 153
lies, lying
    and changing the facts 66
    clear and plain 189
    as comforting 209–10
    consequences of xi–xii, xi–xvi, 86, 88–90, 219, 244, 249, 259–64, 277, 329–30
    definitions x, 1, 45
    denial and repression 149
    getting away with 188–9
    grading of 188
    identifying/recognizing 252–4
    and knowing the truth 169–70
    and language 213
    prerequisites of 69–70
    and re-definition of the situation 100–6
    reasons for x, 45–58, 168
    religious 193–4
    repetition of 208–19
    as self-justification 148
    successful 48, 209

to oneself x, xvii, 90, 198–207, 277, 298–9, 329–30
varieties of 188–207
see also familial lies; silent lies; superior lies; white lies
Lifton, Robert Jay 278, 279
Lightfoot, Elsei 166
linear causality 31–2, 112
London Metropolitan University (LMU) 308–9
London Olympics (2012) 242
loneliness of being 36–7
Lorenz, Ed 32–3
Louk, Dr Louis 113
The Love of Money (TV programme) 323
Lovelock, James 34–5
loyalty 89
Luce, Clare Boothe 267–8
luck 316–17
Luther, Martin 131

McGahern, John 259
McGreal, Chris 221
Macintosh, Jon 312
McKillop, Sir Tom 81–2
Maclean, Donald 270
McNamara, Robert 281–4, 285
  The Fog of War: Eleven Lessons from the Life of Robert S. McNamara (film) 281, 283
  In Retrospect: The Tragedy and Lessons of Vietnam 281
Madoff, Bernard 252–3
Mainwaring, Arthur 229
Malloth, Anton 262–3
Mandelson, Peter xii
Manning, Cardinal 256–7
Mantel, Hilary 299–300
  Giving Up the Ghost 195

Maratos, Olga 65
Mardell, Mark xviii
Marquez, Ramona 255
Marshall, George 231, 233, 234
Marx, Groucho 199
Marx, Karl 201
Maryville (Australia) 139
Marzel, Baruch 225
Mason, Paul xv
Matisse, Amélie 159–60
Matisse, Henri 159–60, 163
Matisse, Marguerite 159–60
Matisse, Pierre 160
Matviyenko, Valentina 203
Max Planck Institute for Cognitive and Brain Sciences 25
Mayo Clinic (Minnesota) 148
media 240–1, 251, 263, 311–12
Media Watch (TV programme) 288–9
Medvedev, President 203, 241
Meet the Press (TV programme) 170–1
Meltzoff, Andrew 65
Melville, Herman, *Moby Dick* 162
memory 40–1, 182–3, 194, 203, 209–11
men on the make 246–7
Mengele, Josef 278
mental illness 111–12, 124–5, 127, 182, 223, 249, 269, 276, 298
Menzies, Robert 154
Mesunov, Anatoly 203
metaphors 317–19
Meyers, Jeffrey 147, 148, 150
Meyers, Kevin, *Watching the Door* 183
MI5 269, 270
Michaela (code-name) xiii
Mollard-Desfour, Annie,

Dictionnaire des mots et expressions de couleur 13–14
Monbiot, George 234, 274
moral hazard 216–19
motor industry xiv–xv
Moulton, Jon 141
Movement for the Survival of the Ogoni People 240
Murray, Jenni 100–1, 193, 300
  Memoirs of a Not So Dutiful Daughter 83–6
Mutually Assured Destruction (MAD) 273
Myers, Kevin 114–15, 184–5
myths 178, 184–5, 264, 319, 320–2

Nagasaki 283
napalm 283
National Health Service (NHS) 303–4
National Socialism 97–8
Nazis 87–8, 91, 94, 98, 102, 105, 112, 156, 166, 200, 203, 260–1, 262, 277, 278, 278–9
neuropsychologists 9, 121
neuroscientists 24, 300
New Labour 196
New Orleans 328–9
New Scientist 14, 134, 175, 231
New York Federal Reserve 217
Newcastle (Australia) 227–8
News of the World 218
Newton, Paul 73–4
Newtonian mathematics 32
Nigeria 240, 328
Nighy, Bill 56
Noble, Denis 23
Noguères, Henri 155
Nora, Pierre 154

Northern Ireland 114–15, 183, 184–5, 225
Northwest Passage 19
nuclear weapons 272–3
Nuremberg trials 89

Obama, Barack xii, 113, 235, 257, 275, 303
obedience 92–5, 195, 255, 271, 300–2
On the Waterfront (film) 58
Ophüls, Marcel 155, 169
Orwell, George, *1984* 6, 76–9, 203, 291, 326
otherization 109, 118–19
Outnumbered (TV programme) 255
Ove Arup 241
Oxford University 209, 226

Palestine, Palestinians 21, 224–6, 251, 271
panic attacks 157
Papua New Guinea 254
paranoia ix, 224, 300
Parental Alienation Syndrome (PAS) 131
Paulson, Hank 217, 218
Pearce, Fred 242
perception
  individual 113
  ladle metaphor 107–8
  and time 30–1
personality traits 253
Pétain, Marshal 161
Petousis, Nikos 128, 129
Petroleum, Pollution and Poverty in the Niger Delta (Shell) 328
Philby, Kim 269–70
  My Silent War 270
phrenology 24

Piaget, Jean 65
Pisani, Elizabeth, *The Wisdom of Whores* xix, xx
Plimer, Ian 234, 235, 236–7
Plymouth Brethren 70–1
Poincaré, Jules Henri 32
points of view 17–18
politicians ix, xix, 41–2, 80, 114, 120, 189, 197, 198, 223, 236, 242, 250, 287–8, 294, 312, 313–16
Pope, Dr Roland 228
Positive Psychology 52–3, 106
primitive pride 54–6, 99, 297–8
Procter and Gamble Responsible Marketing and Innovation Award 239
psychiatrists 111–12, 124–5, 182, 223, 269
psychic numbing 280
psychoanalysts 104, 110, 121, 220
psychologists 50–1, 118–21, 198–9, 223
psychopaths 274
punishment *see* torture and punishment
Putin, Vladimir 241

Radio Vichy 162
Radiodiffusion Nationale 162
reality 108–10, 119–20, 294, 303, 322
Reddy, Michael 37
Reddy, Vasudevi 65, 66, 69, 73–4, 79
How Infants Know Minds 67
regret 74, 80–1, 280, 309
Reich, Robert 323, 325
relationships xiii–xv, 46, 56–7, 61, 157
religion

absolute truths concerning 176–8, 256
and anger of God 194
and being the Chosen People 55
and being frightened 256–9
belief in 122–3, 127–8, 133, 264
biblical myths 320–2
caring aspect 140–1
and Catholic Inquisition 129–30
and the Chain of Being 21–2
and children 133, 140–1, 151–2, 163, 167
Christians as similar to the Taliban 129
and comparison with science 108
and creationists 175, 206–7
and death to the Infidel 124
and differing points of view 17
and enforcing conformity 6
essence of 225
and faith as virtuous xvii, 177
fundamentalist 171, 257–8, 300
and God as critical 151–2
and God as the Great Insurer 217
and God as kind, loving and benevolent 127
and guilt 299–300
and hypocrisy 244
and ideas concerning Jesus 174
and interpretation of God's word 296
and legacy of the crusades 181–2
negative connotations 175
and omniescence of God 193–4, 196
prettifying belief in 175–6
rejection of 163
and rejection of science 175
respect for 173
stories concerning 21

and telling lies 255–6
and terrorism 301
threats to 22, 194, 297
and true believers 34
uncertainty and aloneness 295
remorse 280–92
Renouf, Sir Francis 229
Renouf, Lady Michèle Suzanne 227–31
Responsible Business Awards 239
retrospective diagnosis 66
risk-taking xv, 22, 25, 141, 145, 178, 179, 196, 217, 253
Roche, Daniel 255
Rome, Dr 148
Romme, Marius 182
Romper Room (TV programme) 115
Roper, Brian 309
Rose, David 113
Rose, Stephen 24, 109
Rotolo, Suze 49–50
Rowe, Dorothy
 Time on Our Side 306
 What Should I Believe? 55, 124
Royal Bank of Scotland xvi, 81, 141, 245–9
Royal Institution 318
rubbish 235–6
Rudd, Kevin 310–11, 316
Rugby School 95
Rumsfeld, Donald 220–1, 290
Russia *see* USSR
Rwanda 87, 88, 221

Said, Edward 109
Salinger, J.D., *Catcher in the Rye* 216
Sanghera, Sathnam 279
 The Boy with the Topknot: A Memoir of Love, Secrets and Lies 275–7
Santayana, George 312
Saro-Wiwa, Ken 240
Sartre, Jean-Paul 154–7, 158, 159, 161–4, 166, 168–70, 304
 Being and Nothingness 163
 Nausea 163
Saturday Live (radio programme) 290
scepticism 127–9, 146, 251–2, 302
Schwartz, Walter 154
science 108, 175, 255
scientific truth 128–9, 174
Sedacca, Bennet 117–18
self-confidence 80, 178–9, 234, 259, 268, 291, 297, 301
self-consciousness 20, 143, 145
self-help groups xviii–xix
self-justification 88, 148
Sellay, Richard 18
sense of being 322
 and babies 61–4, 65–9
 and becoming the person you are 57–60
 and being 'blanked' 67–8
 and bravado lies 73–6
 challenges to 124, 126
 and denial 236–7
 destruction of 75–9
 and emotions 51–3
 and errors of judgement 48–9
 and fantasy 153
 and fear of annihilation/disintegration xi, 49–51, 55, 68–9, 74, 85, 157, 253, 277, 291, 298, 322–5
 and humiliation 289–91
 internal/external realities 136–8
 and keeping clarity, order and

control 46, 47, 48
life story 280–1
and making guesses 48–9
and meanings 51–4
and primitive pride 54–6
and protection of self 69
and relationships 46, 48
strong/weak groups 53–4
threats to x–xi, 52–3, 55, 64, 68, 74, 81, 82, 204, 280, 291, 297, 322, 326
and torture 76
and the word 'ought' 56–7, 259, 299–300
sensory-motor model 10
Sereny, Gitta 88, 93, 326–7
Service d'Enquéte et de Contrôle (SEC) 164–5
sex 156–7, 208, 242–3, 294–5
sexual abuse 110–11, 263, 264
Seymour-Jones, Carole 167, 168, 169
A Dangerous Liaison 155
Shanghai World Expo 241
Shell Nigeria 240, 328
Shenzhen 6
Shlaim, Avi 225–6
Short, Clare 285
Sichuan province 241
silent lies 189–92, 196–9, 271, 275–7
Sinatra, Frank, 'My Way' 280
Skeptical Intelligencer 128
Skilling, Jeffrey 244
Skinner, Claire 255
Slater, David, *The Media We Deserve* 251
Smith of Clifton, Lord 120
Smith, Clive Stafford 113
Sobrinho, Archbishop José Cardoso 177–8

Solzhenitsyn, Alexander, *The Gulag Archipelago* 168
Soviet Union *see* USSR
Spectator 234
Speer, Albert 88, 93, 185–6, 279
Spender, Natasha 214
Spinney, Laura 14
Spock, Benjamin xx
Spooks (TV programme) 30
Spotts, Frederic 162–3, 166
The Shameful Peace 158
Spurling, Hilary 159
Sri Lanka 329
Stalin, Joseph 180, 201, 204, 272, 300
Stanford, Peter 209, 212
Stangl, Franz 88
Steiger, Rod 58
Stern magazine 261
Stewart, Ian 12
Stille Hilfe 262
story-telling 133, 144, 145–6, 147–8, 150, 164, 214, 280–1, 319, 322
Stothard, Peter 206–7
Stourton, Edward 292
Strachey, Lytton 95, 256
superior lies xvi–xvii, 27, 55, 64, 87, 90, 91, 102, 154, 225–6, 277, 278–9, 284, 287–9, 297
surveillance 6–7
survival instinct 22–3
swine flu 130, 233
systems biology 23

Taleb, Nassim Nicholas xv, 178
Taylor, Charles 220
Taylor, Kathleen 118
Cruelty: Human Evil and the Human Brain 109

terror *see* fear and terror
Terror in Mumbai (TV programme) 301
Tett, Gillian xiv, 116, 172–3, 178, 196, 198
   Fool's Gold 156
Thales 129
Thames Water 239
Thatcher, Margaret 136, 234–5, 309, 313, 314
Theodosius, Emperor 129
Theophilus, bishop 129
Theresienstadt concentration camp 262–3
Thöben, Frederick 227
threats
   and beliefs 140
   bombs and terrorism xii, 273
   childhood 5, 74, 79–80
   and fear of chaos 46
   and gender 43
   introverts and extraverts 136
   and punishment xvii, 102, 253
   and religion 22, 194, 297
   and sense of being x–xi, 52–3, 55, 64, 68, 74, 81, 82, 204, 280, 291, 297, 322, 326
time 28–31, 306–8
Times Literary Supplement 206
tipping point 34
Today (radio programme) 26
Tokyo 282
Tomasello, Michael 63
torture and punishment 74–80, 81, 84–5, 94–105, 115, 124, 275, 300
transcendental experience 279
trauma 69, 211, 243
Treblinka 87, 88, 326–7
Truman, Harry 272, 283

trust xiii, 93, 253
   abuse of 26
   child-parent 86, 216
   destruction of 250
   value placed on 254
truth 330
   absolute or relative 17–18, 35, 130, 296
   acknowledging 298–9
   alternative interpretations of 43–4
   belief in 2–3, 16–17
   and blame 327–30
   categories of 122–6
   and choice of words 114–21
   deciding what is 109–25
   definition 143
   denial of 101–6, 202–3
   doubts/uncertainty concerning 3–4, 5, 7
   hidden 299
   and introverts/extraverts 138
   and journalistic reporting of events 26–8
   knowledge of 1, 169–70
   and the media 251
   and myth 185
   perception of 138–42, 187
   and primitive pride 55
   as probability 44
   problems caused by 131–8
   and re-definition of the situation 100–6
   recognizing/discovering 261–2, 299–300
   respect for 160–1
   searching for 1–2
   as self-evident 207
   shared and individual 4, 5–6
   and sincerity 177
   and subversive ideas 16–18

and untruth 88
and vanity 27, 35
and wishes 173
Tsutsis 221
Tuchman, Barbara 284
  The March of Folly 205
Turack, Neil 29, 31
Twomey, Seamus 185, 187
Tyndall, John 318

uncertainty 322
  awareness of 295
  controlling 20–1
  coping with 259, 293–4
  facing 35
  fear of 5, 124, 179, 233, 234,
    236, 295
  as inherent 297–8
  and random events 112
  surviving 4, 49, 301
unconscious 39–40, 44, 99, 156,
  163, 298, 299, 304
Union of Physiological Sciences 23
University of California, Berkeley 25
University College, London 35
Urban II, Pope 181
USSR 6, 140, 158, 166–7, 180,
  181, 191, 200, 200–3, 204,
  272–3, 306, 328

vanity 297–8
Varikooty, Krishna 179
Vichy France 159, 165
Vidal, John 240–1
Vietnam 59, 173–4, 205–6, 281–2,
  283–5

war and conflict 87–8, 91–2, 95,

105, 114, 115, 155, 158–60,
  161–6, 183–7, 220–1, 271, 272,
  281–5
War on Terror 114, 217, 243, 317
Watson, Don 120
Weapons of Mass Destruction
  (WMDs) 133, 136, 275
Weber, Tim xi
Weimar Art Galleries xiii
Weinberger, Eliot 220
Weiner, Tim, *Legacy of Ashes: The
  History of the CIA* 265–6, 269,
  272, 274
Wheeler Avenue Baptist Church
  (Houston) 244
white lies ix–x, 45, 48
White Sea Canal 202–3
Wilde, Oscar, *The Ideal Husband*
  217
Williams, Rowan, Archbishop of
  Canterbury 107–8
Williamson, Bishop Richard 227
Wilson, Peter 229–31
Wittelsbach, Prince Heinrich von
  97
Wolff, Tobias 58–60, 173–4
  In Pharaoh's Army 59
Wollaston, Sam 301
Women's Movement 238
Work Foundation, The 141
World Economic Forum xi
World Wide Web xix, 204
writers, writing 304–5
www.hrono.info 203

Young, Marilyn 281

Zambia 231